To Barbara
For all the fun seasons

CALLING THE SHOTS

Calling the Shots

How to Win in Football and Life

David Dein

Foreword by Arsène Wenger

CONSTABLE

CONSTABLE

First published in Great Britain in 2022 by Constable

1 3 5 7 9 10 8 6 4 2

Section one pictures: p5 bottom Colorsport/Stuart MacFarlane; p6 bottom &
p8 top Stuart MacFarlane; p7 bottom left The Sun/News Licensing; p7 bottom
right CURLEYPAP/Alamy Stock Photo; p8 bottom Colorsport. Section
two pictures: p1 top, p1 bottom, p2 top & p3 top Colorsport; p1 middle ITV
Sport; p2 middle left Allstar Picture Library Ltd/Alamy Stock Photo; p2 middle
right Sky News; p2 bottom Stuart Macfarlane; p3 bottom Gerald Penny/Getty
Images; p4 bottom right & p5 middle PA Images/Alamy Stock Photo; p7 top
Stuart MacFarlane/Getty Images. All other pictures from author's collection.

A CIP catalogue record for this book
is available from the British Library.

ISBN: 978-1-40871-633-5 (hardback)
ISBN: 978-1-40871-661-8 (trade paperback)

Typeset in Bembo by Hewer Text UK Ltd, Edinburgh
Printed and bound in Great Britain by Clays Ltd, Elcograf, S.p.A.

Papers used by Constable are from well-managed
forests and other responsible sources.

Constable
An imprint of
Little, Brown Book Group
Carmelite House
50 Victoria Embankment
London EC4Y 0DZ

An Hachette UK Company

www.hachette.co.uk

www.littlebrown.co.uk

Contents

Foreword

Almost every night my doorbell would ring and there was David Dein. I soon realised why, when he had first persuaded me to join the club, he had encouraged me to move close to his own home. He found me a house along Totteridge Lane. It became like his bus stop on his route home, and our daily discussions were part of our lives. His wife Barbara always joked, 'I don't get jealous of any woman; I only get jealous when it comes to you!'

David and I became partners during a golden era for Arsenal. We shared the same priorities and we both put the interests of Arsenal above our own. But the secret of our chemistry was trust, the readiness to exchange information and opinions.

When I arrived in England, football was quite conservative, and what made our double act work was that we were both open-minded and forward-thinking. I would say David still is today. As he likes to say, he is not afraid to call the shots.

In life, you need some luck and ours was coincidence after coincidence for us to meet and eventually become close friends. I was a young manager. I wanted to discover the world and was keen to travel – anywhere. I went to a game in Ankara in Turkey and happened to pass through London on the way back to Nice. With some time to spare I asked Glenn Hoddle's agent, Dennis Roach, to find me a game to go to. There were four top division matches in London that day. I could have gone to QPR, Millwall or West Ham but as luck would have it he got me a ticket for Arsenal against Tottenham. It was my first time at Highbury and David invited me to go out with him and his wife Barbara that evening. We had dinner with some of their friends who were in the entertainment business, and they organised a game of charades. I didn't speak English so well – but I played and it was a funny night.

The next part of the coincidence is that David had a boat, *Take It Easy*, in Antibes. If he had not had a reason to come regularly to the south of France we would never have met again. Next time he came down, he called me, we had dinner together, and our friendship developed. Whenever he was in the area I invited him to watch our games in Monaco. He could see that we didn't play bad football.

I never imagined for a moment that I would manage Arsenal. Everything was going well in Monaco, where we won the league championship and then the Coupe de France. I was keen to experience the very different culture in Japan where I helped guide Nagoya Grampus Eight to the Emperor's Cup and the Japanese Super Cup. I thought that, if I did return to Europe, it would have to be for one of the twelve biggest clubs, but I was happy in Japan.

Throughout those years David and I stayed in contact. Even though Arsenal didn't quite have great global stature then – their history in the Champions League was virtually non-existent – they did have two advantages. One was David, who was very persuasive; and the other was that I could feel something there in that club. From that very first visit to Highbury I could see the club had values: attitude, tradition and class. I did have a sense that if one day I had the opportunity at Arsenal, I would take it.

David is tremendously tenacious. He wouldn't give up on the idea that I should be Arsenal manager, even though the board were not convinced about giving the job to a foreigner. His determination is one of his qualities that people don't know much about. You cannot believe his tenacity when he has something in his head. He needs a target. He needs a bone. When he has it, he doesn't give up. And when he does it, he does it like a perfectionist.

We had a similar philosophy on life. We connected. We had no disagreements. Well, maybe there was one area where we disagreed. His opinions on referees were much more generous than mine.

Overall, he respected my knowledge in my technical area and didn't want to interfere. And I admired the fact that when I said, 'David, come on, don't come back without the player,' I knew that he would come back with the player. When we negotiated together, we were always on the same wavelength. If we discussed how much a player was worth, or at what point we stopped, we always agreed. I must also say that 99 per cent of the time the numbers we chose were exactly the right amount to close a deal. It was uncanny.

I still marvel at how he was able to help to put together a team of the quality of the Invincibles for such a modest amount. The most expensive outlay was £9.5 million for Thierry Henry. It is amazing how that team didn't cost a lot of money. When you don't lose for thirty-eight games it is not just down to your quality, but to your moral values. I discovered something I never knew before – no fear or jealousy among the players. It is normal in a team sport that there is some internal competition and comparisons – is this or that player better? – but they just focused on getting better together. To see a whole team rise above their ego was an absolute delight. There was no complaining. Just growing together. I never thought I would discover that in my job, but the whole team enjoyed the process so much. I wish for every manager to experience that.

The players got in the spirit of 'Let's go play and see how good we can be'. But getting to the top meant less room for error. I sometimes told them, 'If we go to climb the mountain we have to know that if you make one mistake, you can be dead.' Refusing to make mistakes was the key, and the progress we made was even better than you imagined possible.

Of course we needed the best players, and this is where David did so much to call the shots. I don't think it would be too easy to sign Sol Campbell from Tottenham, or convince Juventus to let Thierry Henry go, or intercept Patrick Vieira when he was about to move to another club, or get Atlético Mineiro to release Gilberto when they absolutely were not interested, without David's commitment and connections. We got in all the right players and people to achieve something that still resonates today. He is one of the most connected and influential people in the game.

Another huge asset for the club was his personality. You could not find a better person than David when you wanted somebody to be looked after. The quality of the openness and hospitality was first class. I have spoken to so many people who were impressed by the way they were welcomed. You don't cheat people. They can feel there's something special there. That existed for a long time at the club and I was very proud of it.

I was shocked when David left Arsenal in 2007. There had been difficulties. There was a split in his friendship with Danny Fiszman and, after that, a battle for the club's shares. I was caught in the middle – although of course, I was on David's side. The unbelievable thing, when you look at it now, is that basically

David had to leave the club because he wanted to sell his shares to Stan Kroenke. Who is the owner of the club today? It's Stan Kroenke. So that was an ironic problem.

I remember we met at his house the night he left Arsenal. He asked me to stay at the club, to take care of the future. I wanted to be loyal to David. I knew it would be more difficult without him. I also knew, certainly subconsciously, that something had gone that would be difficult to repair. That fraternity and that warmth inside the club would be more difficult to preserve. Maintaining the spirit of the club would be a struggle. During that sensitive period, after moving stadium and having restricted finances, it would have been easier for sure if he was there. In fact the end of the season in 2007, I had a small burnout on holiday because I didn't feel comfortable staying at the club with David gone.

It was also a shock for David. He, like me, was sleeping in red and white and waking up in red and white. The whole schedule of his family was based on the games of Arsenal Football Club. I experienced it later when from one minute to the next there is nothing any more. You suddenly cannot go to the place you love, the place where you went for decades. What I admire in him is he continued to support Arsenal. He didn't go anywhere else. He could have gone almost anywhere in football and had many offers. I hoped at some stage, just to save him, that he would go to another club and spread his knowledge somewhere else. He always refused to do that. In fact, I thought that he would be the ideal person to take over at the top of FIFA, who were in a mess at the time.

Instead, he has put his energy into helping others, young people in schools and prisons, to try to make more of their lives. One of his biggest qualities is his caring and intelligent attitude about other people. The consistency of his positive approach to things is remarkable. You never see him thinking, oh, leave me alone. His helpful attitude, and the calm quality of his mood, is outstanding. There's no bitterness in him despite what he has gone through. One thing I like in David is that he lives as if dying did not exist. He thinks like a twenty-year-old boy.

He likes to make jokes – not all of them as funny as he thinks. But what really makes me laugh is his stubbornness. If he doesn't have the answer he wants straight away you can bet he will come back to it. Next time he rings, you know exactly what it will be about.

When you look at what David has done in football, it's amazing. He was the main architect of the creation of the Premier League, and when you see the stature it has today, you know that having the conviction to make it happen was a pivotal moment in football. He still has ideas to move football forward, and remains influential and respected at UEFA and FIFA. He never misses a tournament. He is always fighting to make football better and has been a pioneer of the women's game. He really has a deep love for the sport.

Our friendship has lasted over all these years and all these experiences. That will not change until the end of our lives. We have fundamental beliefs in common: we love Arsenal. We love football. We love to move things forward. We are not scared of new ideas. We trust each other.

I would never have come to Arsenal without David. For that, and much more, I am thankful to my friend.

Arsène Wenger
Totteridge, 2022

THE FINAL WHISTLE

The date and time haunt me to this day: 5 p.m., 18 April 2007. I was in my office in Highbury House and feeling distinctly uncomfortable. I called my lawyer, Oliver Barnes, and said, 'Peter Hill-Wood is coming to see me shortly. I think I'm going to be leaving the club.' He told me he was there if I needed him. I had kept him in the loop over the previous month.

Five o'clock arrives and my door bursts open. Peter, the club chairman, came through with director Chips Keswick and an employment lawyer from Slaughter and May, Arsenal's lawyers. Peter's delivery had clearly been well rehearsed. It was short and certainly not sweet. He told me the board unanimously decided that I should leave, and leave immediately. He presented me with a letter which was the board minutes, effectively signed by all the other members.

There was no explanation. To this day, not a word. The document described 'irreconcilable differences'. No discussion.

I asked Peter, 'Why?'

He said, 'The board are unanimous,' and that was it.

I was stunned and hurt.

I said to Peter, 'This is the worst day in my life since my mother and my brother died.'

I tried to keep mind and body together. I tried to talk, to reason, but to no effect. I explained that I was in the middle of dealing with players' contracts and negotiations. He said, 'Oh, don't worry, David Miles will handle that.'

He gave me a document with an offer of £250,000 as severance. It stipulated a signature to confirm I would not say anything negative or detrimental about the club. It was a gagging order. I read it and said, 'I'm not taking the club's money, the club needs it.' And that was it.

I felt that I was the target of a firing squad without any recourse. It was cold and clinical, delivered by a colleague with whom I had hitherto shared twenty-four happy years.

I remember having to pack my things, and that was not easy, turning my desk out. They left me to do that alone. I left without goodbyes. I walked away with tears in my eyes. It felt like being evicted from my own home. Twenty-four devoted years of my commitment to the club were over in a five-minute meeting without even a thank you. It was so brutal.

I went to switch on my mobile to find it had been cut off. I had to drive home from the stadium to Totteridge without being able to talk to any of my family. I thought, How low can they go? It was my own personal number from my previous business – but I was never able to get it back. It felt like a deliberate humiliation. It was putting the knife in and then turning it.

Arsenal released a public statement before I had even arrived home. My family found out via the media. When I got home, they were there to console me, and then Arsène came round. He'd heard about it because it was already on the news. The first thing he said was, 'David, I should leave. If you're not here, I don't want to be here.'

I thought about it and I said, 'Arsène, you have to stay. The club needs you, the club really needs you.'

The misery of that day will stay with me for ever. After everything I had delivered for the club during the past twenty-four years, my reign was over. Now others would have to captain the ship.

From time to time I still get a recurring nightmare of my office door bursting open and being presented with my death certificate.

I always regard myself as a team player, and maybe I had been focusing on the playing team rather than the board. How had I so badly misread the tea leaves? The fact that I hadn't seen it coming was what shook me most. No question, tensions had been developing. There were fundamental disagreements on the board, and I had even suffered slights from colleagues which I will come to in a moment. Even so, and even now, I still don't really understand the decision to eject me so abruptly and so ruthlessly. Perhaps it was jealousy and fear. Jealousy was because I had become too high profile – the names Arsenal and Dein had become entangled. And fear because I thought we needed outside investment for the club to progress and some board members didn't like that. Either way I should have seen it coming and it still bugs me that I didn't.

It took me several months to go back to the stadium as I was in a mental decline over the circumstances surrounding my departure. In fact, it was only on the persuasion of Karren Brady's father Terry who sent his driver to collect me and to be a guest in his box. It was an 'out of body' experience. When the Emirates was being built, each director had the opportunity to buy seats, and I had already bought ten regular season tickets and four club seats. Nowadays, I use my club seats and attend all home games.

As I say, the tension in the boardroom had been building for some time. The cracks began to appear shortly after the heights of the Invincible season. It was a tragedy because we had been a very happy family. Sometimes we would have different opinions, but decisions were taken for the greater good.

The beginning of the end revolved around the stadium move from Highbury to the Emirates. Until then we were all in everything together, but this project was so big that it made sense to allocate responsibilities to different members of the board. Danny Fiszman and Ken Friar took more of a lead on overseeing the new build, Keith Edelman focused on the finances, while I stayed with Arsène working on the football side. Naturally there was a lot of sharing of ideas, and sharing of decisions, but as the sheer scale of the new stadium took its toll on the team's resources, different groups were having different discussions, and we began to drift apart.

Arsène and I were very much at the heart of building a successful football club, developing the squad and maintaining a successful team. If you don't pay attention, someone else will eat your dinner! Others were deep into the construction planning, the finances and the legalities to drive the move to our new home.

It wasn't easy to run both a massive property development and a football club side by side. I needed to keep my eye on the ball, and my priority was the team, but for others the new stadium took precedence. The costs were huge, ending up around the £450 million mark, including the cost of the land, and all of a sudden we were taking out major loans to fund the new development. That meant what muscle we had in the transfer market and for wages was diminishing.

We needed to show the bank we had money. The only way we could generate any cash was either to sell players, or to take out equity in advance from commercial contracts. Arsène and I were firmly against selling members of our team, so that meant we had to negotiate upfront payments from Emirates and Nike, our two major sponsors. But even that threatened our football. In using our next seven years' money as collateral for the banks' loans it meant that for seven years we would be starved of sponsor income. We were robbing Peter to pay Paul. I feared that instead of the club acquiring a new stadium, the stadium was acquiring the club.

Even then it was touch and go. There were times when arrangements with the banks became precarious – they didn't think our collateral was good enough, or they didn't think our earning power was sufficient – and there was one particularly dramatic day when the financial backing collapsed. Eventually, through our lead bank, Rothschilds, we managed to get a consortium of lenders together, and the loans were finally agreed.

Historically, football clubs aren't great borrowers, and the banks wanted assurances that we could service the debt. They imposed a major condition – Arsène had to sign a new, five-year contract. They were right, of course. They thought that the club had more chance of being successful with Arsène than without him. But Arsène took some convincing. He'd already been at the club for seven years so that length of extra commitment was a big ask. We talked at length and, knowing he was critical to financing the stadium, he finally agreed.

Now we had bankers and financiers on our board. They

insisted that a chunk of money every year was garaged to repay interest. Arsène and I were worried that this would have an adverse effect on the team. In fact it was just this penny-pinching that led to us losing Ashley Cole – essentially over five thousand pounds later on.

This was during the period when Keith Edelman was managing director and had his hand on the purse strings. There was pressure there; if I was trying to promote something he would put another point of view to the board.

Keith did a decent job balancing the books for the new stadium and I take my hat off to him, and to Danny and Ken. The three of them worked really hard in getting the vast construction project from idea to completion. That left me to focus on my motto to Get-A-Winning-Team. But over time Keith began to take more of a day-to-day interest in the football side, which was not his forte, and it interfered with squad management. He became my nemesis and, to an extent, Arsène's.

We could see that, despite our warnings, football money was being redirected to the stadium development programme. Sometimes I would come out of the board meetings with Arsène and, as we were walking down the corridor, I would say despairingly, 'This is not right. We're in the business of winning matches, but we're fighting with our hands tied behind our back.'

Before long this simmering disagreement became really unpleasant. On away trips it became embarrassing and I found myself – and even Barbara too – increasingly being ostracised. We put on a united front when invited to functions by the opposition directors, but there was a serious and awkward undercurrent.

It came to the point where I felt that Keith had been deployed to man-mark me and watch my every move. I regarded myself as a free spirit with considerable experience and certainly did not need personal attention from somebody who was relatively new to the game.

Even my relationship with Danny Fiszman, an old friend, was deteriorating quickly. It felt as if he wanted to be in my airspace, which was awkward for me. We had had a social friendship with our families going back many years. I had invited him to the board in 1991, when I was struggling with having been defrauded in my sugar business. A lot of my personal funds were tied up in my Arsenal shares. Danny was an Arsenal fan, a wealthy guy, and we were friends. I said that if he wanted to buy some shares I would like to sell some, and perhaps, with the board's permission, a seat on the board and the ability to work together would be in the offing. He bought a block of my shares. With the benefit of hindsight, I regret that now as that gave him power.

The delicate situation over the stadium – his priority – got a bit personal and as a result we just drifted apart. These things happen sometimes – life gets awkward, and events change a relationship.

I realised how badly relationships were strained on a day that was supposed to be momentous. Arsenal said goodbye to Highbury on 7 May 2006. We played Wigan with big emotional and sporting stakes on the line that day. There was a place in the following season's Champions League up for grabs, with a direct contest between us and Tottenham for fourth place. Highbury had a wonderful send-off as Spurs lost 2–1 to West Ham, whilst Thierry Henry scored a hat-trick in our 4–2 win. There was a spectacle planned, with a parade of ex-players and greats associated with the club's history walking around the pitch as part of the farewell ceremony.

Unbelievably, Ken Friar and Danny Fiszman were invited, but I was not. It was vindictive. I was the vice-chairman, I had been there twenty-three years, I had helped Arsène to deliver the Invincibles in very recent memory and some of those players were carrying the club into the Champions League final that season. But I was shunned. I had to stay in the directors' box, looking down at the others, and I was pretty certain there was an agenda behind that decision. I remember saying to Phil Harris (a non-executive director) at the time – and I had a good relationship with Phil – that it was upsetting and petty. I was deeply, deeply hurt.

I was now seriously uncomfortable with the dynamics on the board. With so many of our assets tied up in funding the stadium I started thinking about other ways of raising money to improve the team. And there was an obvious lesson from not far away. It came from Chelsea, the club that had tried to pilfer Ashley Cole. Chelsea's finances had been transformed by the arrival of an owner who, as I described him to the press, had 'parked his tank on our lawn and it is firing fifty-pound notes!' Within a couple of months of becoming Chelsea's owner, Roman Abramovich had changed the landscape.

I came across him a few times. Nobody would even know if he spoke English at the time as he certainly didn't give me the impression he could. He would always answer through an interpreter or one of his colleagues. He seemed quiet and very respectful. But he started flashing the cash and he transformed the dynamics of transfers.

Having a billionaire on the board was a novelty in England, but as president of G–14, I could see what goes on in wealthy clubs. I was used to sitting with Barcelona, Real Madrid, Bayern Munich. I was looking around our own board and thinking, If we want to really challenge at the top of world football, we need a real heavyweight benefactor. Our board was lightweight by comparison – individually prosperous , but not at the top table. Somebody with plenty of zeros in his bank balance wouldn't do us any harm. The Premier League train was getting up to full speed and the fastest drivers were billionaires but we didn't have any.

Because I'm used to blazing my own trail, I started looking around privately, wondering who could be interested. But that opened up another area of friction with the board. When word got out that I was looking for other sources of funding, some thought I was going behind their backs. That had not been my intention but I can now see it looked that way. In the same way I got to know Arsène before suggesting him to the board, I was simply scouting around to see who was out there before approaching my fellow directors.

Which brings me to Stan Kroenke.

A chain reaction of conversations led to the introduction. It started with a man called Jeff Plush, who was managing director of Kroenke's US club Colorado Rapids. He was quite forward thinking and wanted to develop a working relationship with a European club. He kept calling the deputy commissioner of Major League Soccer (MLS), who he thought might have some contacts with Arsenal. That just happened to be a man called Ivan Gazidis. Ivan got in touch with Dick Law, whom I had employed as Arsenal's representative in South America and would eventually join me in transfer negotiations. Jeff was very determined and suggested to Dick that he would like his club's owner, Stan Kroenke, to meet me. In the summer of 2006, just as we were preparing to move into the new stadium, Dick called to say that billionaire Kroenke was in town. His wife, Anne Walton, is an heiress from the family that own Walmart.

We met on the third floor of Highbury House, having just moved across. There were boxes everywhere as offices were being set up and we found a corner by the window, before having to look around for some chairs. In attendance on their side were Stan, Jeff, and a Kroenke adviser who was a former basketball player. Dick and I were there from Arsenal. Stan explained he was interested in soccer and he turned out to be a good sportsman, with his network of franchises. I invited him on a tour of the new stadium and we crossed the bridge to take a look around as the final touches were being made ahead of our inaugural match. Stan's background was very much in the property business as he owned many shopping centres in the United States.

The Granada media company owned 9.9 per cent of Arsenal and Liverpool, and they had come to realise it didn't sit within their portfolio. I wanted the buyer of our shares to be a financially muscular, substantial and ambitious entity. My thinking was to have someone come in and be part of the team with that 9.9 per cent block, with the potential to do more and support my vision.

There were other possibilities besides Stan – we had a meeting with Tim Leiweke, president of the Anschutz Entertainment Group. Phil Anschutz was the co-founder of MLS. They had an interest in sport and were already involved in football. I also met Khaldoon Al Mubarak, who went on to buy Manchester City. In the end, it was Kroenke who purchased the Granada shares – which by then had been on the market for quite a while without a bidder. It was interesting that none of the board members wished to subscribe for those shares.

At an AGM, when challenged about Kroenke, Peter Hill-Wood summed up the board's reaction with a remark about not wanting that 'sort' of person or money involved in the club. 'Call me old-fashioned,' he said, 'but we don't need Kroenke's money and we don't want his sort.' Our objective, he went on, is to keep Arsenal English. I found that strange when the bulk of our successful players were from overseas. If Kroenke were to mount a hostile takeover for our club, 'we shall resist it with all our might'. He spoke as though the whole board was behind him: 'We are all being seduced by the idea that the Americans will ride into town with pots of cash for new players. It simply isn't the case. They only see an opportunity to make money. They know absolutely nothing about our football and we don't want these types involved.'

Peter, whom I liked and regarded as a friend until the bitter end, later sold out to Kroenke.

If I had any regret, it is that I began to put feelers out for potential investment privately, rather than going to the board and proposing it first. As I say, I had never intended to go behind their back, but by then the atmosphere at board level was already unpleasant. That's why I wanted to bring in somebody whom I could work with, who had the same ambitions for the club as me. And that, of course, is what other board members feared: that I would try to bring in someone who would undermine their power base.

I had a decent relationship with board member Lady Nina

Bracewell-Smith, a link with one of the great families that had been custodians for decades. I told her that the club had to go in another direction or we were going to lose ground to the opposition. That turned out to be a big mistake.

On Tuesday 17 April 2007, Arsenal beat Manchester City 3–1 at the Emirates in front of 59,913 people. The goal-scorers were Tomáš Rosický, Cesc Fàbregas and Júlio Baptista. The team were fourth in the table, which is where they would finish in their first season at the new stadium, to qualify for the Champions League for the tenth consecutive season. We'd been in the final the previous spring. Peter asked to see me urgently at 5 p.m. the following day. I had a nasty feeling then that it was not going to end well. And I was right . . .

A WHOLE NEW BALL GAME

I knew as I drove to Trevor and Jenni Hicks's house that football had to change. These wonderful, warm people lost their two beautiful daughters, Sarah and Victoria, in the Hillsborough disaster. Ninety-six, and eventually ninety-seven, Liverpool fans perished in the grim pens of the Leppings Lane end. As a parent, my heart broke for Trevor and Jenni. As a club official, my mind was made up that Hillsborough had to be a turning point, a watershed. Football fans were being treated like cattle, penned in behind fences. Human beings deserved better.

The day of Hillsborough, 15 April 1989, is seared into my memory. I was in London watching Arsenal play Newcastle United at Highbury when the news broke. Seeing as we didn't allow the TV on in the boardroom at half-time, we had to go into the cocktail lounge to see the pictures coming in from the Sheffield ground. Watching these fans fighting for their lives was horrifying.

'We must never forget this,' I said to myself.

The following day, my daughter Sasha, who was at Haberdashers' School in Hertfordshire, almost two hundred miles from Hillsborough, said, 'Dad, you know that two of the girls who died were at my school.'

The Hicks girls. The elder, Sarah, had just left for Liverpool University. Victoria was in her GCSE year.

'Do you think you can find a phone number? I'd like to speak to the parents,' I said.

Sasha managed to find a number, and I rang the Hickses.

Jenni Hicks answered.

'Mrs Hicks, I'm David Dein from the Football League Management Committee. I offer you my deepest condolences for your loss. I know it's a very sensitive time for you, but could I come and see you? I'd like to give my condolences in person. I don't wish to impose and wouldn't outstay my welcome.'

Jenni handed the phone to her husband, Trevor. We talked briefly and then I asked again whether I could come over to see them.

'Yes, I'd appreciate that,' said Trevor.

So that's how I found myself a couple of evenings later on the way to the Hicks's house in Hatch End. It turned out not to be the short visit we had all anticipated. I stayed with Trevor and Jenni all evening. They poured their hearts out and told me the graphic details of what happened. It was all so very raw, sickening and shocking. Trevor and Jenni were struggling to take in the circumstances of their devastating loss. They told me how they had been treated like criminals at Hillsborough. They told me how they had to look at a huge green board of Polaroid photos of over eighty of the dead in the gymnasium at the football ground, which was being used as a temporary mortuary, to try and identify Sarah and Vicki. They told me how Sarah and Vicki were wheeled to them on low trolleys in body bags. Jenni told me how she had got down on her knees on that dirty gymnasium floor to hug them both. How Vicki was cold, and Sarah was still warm. How they were questioned about alcohol. How statements were taken from them without a lawyer being present.

How not one of the police officers present had shown them an ounce of compassion. How they drove back to London that night with empty back seats in their car where only that morning their beautiful full-of-life daughters had sat.

As Trevor and Jenni continued talking they had tears in their eyes. (I had tears in mine.) I kept thinking that this was at a football match, that this just can't happen. People are losing their lives here. Children. Football is meant to be for entertainment, it cannot be associated with death.

I said, 'Trevor, Jenni, I don't know how I can console you, but I promise, from this moment, football will change. It has to.'

'Fans must never, ever again be penned in like animals,' Jenni said.

I drove away from Trevor and Jenni's thinking, I'm going to try my hardest to make football a better environment, a better place. It has to be much safer.

In August that year, I invited Trevor and Jenni to Wembley to watch Arsenal and Liverpool play Dinamo Kiev and Porto in the Makita International Tournament. Liverpool's chairman, Sir John Smith, escorted Trevor and Jenni to meet the Liverpool team in the dressing room.

I stayed in touch with the Hickses, and learned even more down the years about the scandal of Hillsborough, the cover-up, and the three high court judges quashing the original inquest verdict of accidental death. They ordered a new inquest which concluded in 2016 that all the victims, at the time ninety-six, were unlawfully killed.

I recently spoke to Jenni, for whom the loss of her children is still very raw.

'There were no official medics, no medical equipment, no

stewards and the police in the main just stood and watched,' she said. 'What you watched on TV from your cocktail lounge at Arsenal were Liverpool fans doing their best for their fellow fans, not emergency medics with proper equipment, not stewards, and very few police officers. Fans, some of whom just happened to be doctors, did what they could to help the dying and injured without any medical equipment whatsoever. The fans ripped down hoardings to make stretchers to carry the dying and injured fans to find the medical help they needed. The police wouldn't allow the paramedics and numerous ambulances outside the ground on to the pitch as they told them the fans were fighting and rioting. Numerous lives were lost, David, because of the police response. They called for dogs instead of emergency medical assistance. They felt the police they had previously trusted had let them down.'

Jenni made another point. 'One of the things I could clearly see was that the radial and particularly the pitch-side fences prevented the fans from escaping the life-threatening crush.' To this day when people talk about 'safe standing' at football grounds, I find it difficult to engage in the discussion; my mind goes straight to those horrific pictures of fans trapped behind the fences.'

The memory of that evening of April 1989 with Trevor and Jenni still makes me emotional now and my eyes well up at the thought of their experience.

It was most definitely a catalyst for change and a revolutionary idea was formulating in my mind.

English football began with supporters standing on the touchline, and as the game grew in popularity it simply herded fans into pens. We were stuck in Victorian times. It was so different in the USA, where I went often. Going to a stadium in the

USA was an event in itself. It was show business – cheerleaders, entertainment, sport, refreshments, giant screens. Come early, stay late, spend and enjoy. Instead of that, in England we had 3 p.m. to 4.40 p.m. and that was it. You arrive at 2.55 p.m., you leave at the end of the game, you couldn't get a pee.

I remembered seeing my first NFL game, Miami Dolphins, when Don Shula was coach. I'm trying to understand the rules – my late brother-in-law was sitting next to me, explaining, 'You get four opportunities to gain ten yards. It's a game of territory and the quarterback calls the shots' – but all around me I can hear, 'Hot dogs! Coca-Cola! Cold beer! Hot dogs, hot dogs, Coca-Cola, peanuts!' Everyone is seated, the crowd is friendly, and everyone's buying. So I'm trying to watch the game and I'm passing someone's dollar bill this way, a Coca-Cola that way, a hamburger this way, another beer that way. I said to the guy next to me, 'Don't they feed you at home?' But this was all a revelation to me. This was a family game, and more like going to the theatre than being locked in an enclosure.

You've got to understand just how Dickensian English football was in 1989, and how profoundly it resisted change. Three years previously, shortly after I joined the Football League Management Committee, I proposed there should be two substitutes instead of one.

One chairman put up his hand. 'You can't have that.'

'Why not?'

'It's an extra hotel room, an extra meal, an extra appearance fee.' Others nodded, the notion was rejected, and I came home and felt like putting my head in the microwave. 'How backward are we?' I said to myself.

What's more, in the 1980s football was in trouble – big trouble. We had hooliganism. There was fighting inside grounds, fighting outside grounds and attendances dropping like a stone. Highbury averaged between 23,000 and 35,000 in a stadium that could hold 45,000. I look at old pictures and there were hardly any women in the stands. The grounds were dilapidated, some fifty or even a hundred years old. As I say, the toilet facilities were abysmal.

The whole leadership of the game lacked vision. The old Football League had a chairman called Bill Fox from Blackburn, a tough Lancastrian, no-nonsense guy, I got on well with him, but he fought for the status quo.

'If football was a public company, what sector would we be in?' I'd say to Bill, explaining, 'We'd be in the entertainment sector or sports sector. You go there to be entertained.' But I really didn't think that Bill could appreciate the scale of the problems facing us. Nor the opportunities. At Highbury in 1989, the average fans' spend was £1.50 per head. On moving to the Emirates in 2006, it was £12.25 because we made sure there were plenty of food outlets and merchandising points, and the stadium was a place where you were happy to stay.

Football was in a difficult place in the 1980s. I met publisher Robert Maxwell a few times. He owned Oxford United and was a handful. In November 1987, Maxwell did a £2 million deal with Elton John to buy Watford. Robert owned Odhams Press, based in Watford. Before anybody could buy a football club, the deal required the blessing of the Management Committee on which I sat. We looked at Robert's track record and it was complicated. He and his family had stakes in Oxford United, Derby County, Reading and Manchester United. Robert wanted to merge Oxford and Reading to make Thames

Valley Royals in 1983, which understandably enraged fans of both clubs and unsurprisingly failed. Robert had grandiose ideas; he was larger than life. More than once, I went into his offices at the Mirror building and was invariably kept waiting. Hanging around was made easier by waiters in white gloves serving smoked salmon sandwiches. It all felt a bit of a show. I could hear Maxwell in his office, jumping from one phone to another, changing languages. One minute, Maxwell was talking in Czech, then French, then German, then English. Incredible guy in many respects.

Anyway, he now wanted to buy Watford. When the Management Committee had a meeting, I said, 'He can't do it. He's got to divest himself of one of his other clubs first. He's getting too powerful.'

We all agreed on that.

Then somebody said, 'Does anybody know this Maxwell character?'

'Well, yes, sure, I've met him a few times,' I said.

'Well, David, you go. We deputise you to tell Maxwell he can't do it.'

'Well, thank you very much! That's a hospital pass!'

So, I rang Maxwell.

'Robert, David Dein here. I'm sitting on the Management Committee, and we have your contract with Elton for Watford. I'm afraid we've got a problem. I need to talk to you about it.'

'Oh, yes, OK. Where do you live?'

'Totteridge.'

'I'm going into Odhams Press on Saturday morning, I'll drop in. Where can I land my helicopter?'

'The farm next door.'

'Get me the coordinates.'

Saturday morning, 9.30 a.m., the helicopter whizzes in. Maxwell, in a baseball hat, marches towards the house. My wife Barbara and I are there to greet him at the door.

'How do you do? I'm Maxwell,' he said to me. To Barbara he said, 'I'll have a cup of tea, dearie.' That did not go down well with her. Barbara's a dab hand at Scrabble, and she certainly had some choice words for Maxwell.

We sat down in the lounge, and I said, 'Look, Robert, we love the fact that you love football and that you're involved in it, you're doing a great job, but Watford's a bridge too far. You currently own Oxford, your sons own Derby, you've got 25 per cent of Reading and you've got 5 per cent of Manchester United. Now, you want to buy Watford . . . '

'Well!? What's the problem?'

'What's the problem, Robert? You only need to buy another eighty-seven clubs and you're bound to win the league!'

'What do you mean?'

'We don't have multi-ownership. It can contaminate the sport. It's about the integrity of the competition, Robert. You're going to have to understand that we really can't allow it.'

'What do you want me to do?'

'Well, if you divest yourself of one of the two main clubs, Oxford or Derby, we'll let you buy Watford.'

'No,' Maxwell replied. 'Derby are in financial difficulties. Oxford is where I live. It's my home team. They're both suffering financially.'

'Well, that may be, but nevertheless, the Management Committee can't allow it.'

Maxwell drained his tea, climbed back into his helicopter, and that was it. No deal. He was a controversial character, and you never really knew what was going on in the background, but I have to say that Maxwell genuinely liked football. I honestly don't think he expected to get any money out of it, he just really enjoyed the joust of owning a football club.

When I first came to Arsenal, we had a little shop run by a famous old goalkeeper, Jack Kelsey. I was in there one day and this kid asks, 'I'd like to buy a football.' The assistant simply sneered at him, 'You don't want it blown up as well, do you?' That was the mentality.

I had to change all that. I want to see theatre, I want to attract more people, I want to give value for money, and I want to make it entertaining.

I remember at one Management Committee meeting, I proposed that we should put names on the backs of the shirts, as they did in America. This was not just to make it easier for fans in the stadium to follow the game but also for a global TV audience, where commentators invariably talk only about the player in possession and not the other players in the picture.

One owner of a big club said, 'I'll vote against that.'

'Why?'

'We don't have a big enough laundry room.'

That's what I had to contend with. Obviously, with names on shirts, each shirt is specific to a player rather than 1–11 which anyone can wear. 'It's all about identity,' I replied. I tried to reason with them. It took about three meetings to get that through. Finally, in 1993, when I produced a Manchester United shirt with 'GIGGS', number 11, Blackburn Rovers with

'SHEARER', number 9 and Arsenal with 'ADAMS', number 6, it finally went through. But, significantly, that was only after we had formed the Premier League.

At Football League meetings, I used to have terrible rows with Ken Bates, the Chelsea chairman. People asked me whether Ken and I argued frequently, and I would reply, 'We only ever had one argument. It just lasted fifteen years!' Even then, we'd still have a drink together afterwards because Ken did have the interests of the game at heart.

Ken had an acerbic sense of humour. He was very sharp, very quick-witted, good company but difficult to deal with. I'd just joined the Arsenal board in 1983 and had never met Ken, but he invited me for lunch. I knew that was unusual. At Arsenal, we invited everybody from the visiting club to eat with us. But Ken was picky about who came into the Chelsea boardroom for lunch. The first thing he said to me was, 'Mazel tov.'

'What for?' I asked.

'Isn't that what your people say?' Ken said.

'No,' I replied. 'My people say, "good morning", "good afternoon", "good evening", depending on the time of day. What do your people say?' Ken was trying to be funny, but his first remark had missed the target.

It was an unusual relationship between Ken and me, but I enjoyed the frequent jousts with him which were often amusing. At one stage he actually campaigned for me to represent the Premier League at the FA. I guess we had a mutual respect. But we were very often polar opposites. I remember us having a terrible argument about electrified fences which Ken was trying to put up at Stamford Bridge in 1985.

'What are you trying to do to the fans?' I asked. 'Fry them?'

Ken said he was trying to control the rowdiness that now plagued the game.

Hooliganism was nothing new. In 1885 'howling roughs' had rioted at a friendly match between Preston North End and Aston Villa, and the word hooliganism itself came from the 1890s. But it had been a growing problem in the 1970s, and by the mid-1980s it was seen as a national scandal. Police were even lobbying to suspend domestic football for a season. Finally, in 1985, following a riot by thugs in Millwall colours at Luton Town, the prime minister, Maggie Thatcher, waded in and summoned FA officials to Downing Street.

'You have to do something about your hooligans,' Maggie said.

'They're not our hooligans, Prime Minister,' the FA secretary Ted Croker told her. 'They're your hooligans, Prime Minister.'

It was easy to agree with Ted that the problem lay in society, that hooligans were out there anyway and had simply latched on to football. Of course on reflection that wasn't true. Edward II had banned football in 1314 because it attracted violence. There had never been these sorts of brawls, let alone ritual riots, at cricket, or rugby or any other sporting events – or anywhere else. Nor did this army of hooligans reform and converge on any other target after the problems were tackled in football. At very least, football had to share some of the blame. Many clubs tolerated or even encouraged tribalism. Sexism and especially racism were rampant. Fans were corralled like wild animals. The clubs were not fined or relegated for bad behaviour by their supporters. By pinning the blame on society, or anyone but themselves, the clubs were passing the buck.

In any case, whatever the cause, we had a responsibility to help sort things out ourselves.

One of Maggie Thatcher's MPs, David Evans, wanted fans to carry identity cards.

'They won't work unless each one is checked,' I told him at Downing Street. 'They'd simply get swapped around.'

Eventually a whole range of solutions was found. Banning orders helped – troublemakers could be stopped from using public transport or match venues – but many other answers lay within football itself: encouraging more tolerance, modernising the grounds, all-seater stadia, better control of alcohol, and, importantly, attracting more families to the game.

Again and again it was clear to me that football had to change.

At another vote, I proposed a fifteen-minute half-time, instead of ten minutes. 'What do you want that for?' someone moaned.

'What's the manager going to say for that amount of time?' one committee member said. I looked at him.

'What's the manager . . .?! We've got to think of the fans! This is an event we're holding here. With fifteen minutes people have a pee and a drink at half-time.'

The room looked blank, so I thought I'd liven up things with a joke.

'Look, I'm at a game, at half-time, and I'm standing in the queue and there's a guy in front of me hopping from one foot to the other. He turns to me and says, "I've got to have a pee, I'm bursting, I'm bursting." So I say, "Why don't you pee in the bloke in front's pocket?" He says, "Pee in his pocket? Won't he know?" So I reply, "Well I'm peeing in your pocket and you don't know."'

Some of the committee laughed. It was a gag but it was also very close to the bone. That was football in 1989. Broken.

I reflected on my meeting at the Hicks's house. I knew from experience how slow-moving the Management Committee were, how stuck in their old ways. What's more, the voting structure was all wrong. The Football League gave First Division clubs 1.5 votes each, Second Division clubs a vote each and the Third and Fourth Divisions eight votes between them. The intention was that the lower divisions could protect themselves against the big boys. They had a veto. But the big clubs generated the bulk of the income. Come on! This was pushing to the lowest denominator rather than encouraging the highest factor. The voting structure was one of the reasons we had to break away.

The biggest issue was broadcasting. All the clubs shared the income from TV coverage, but there was little money to begin with. The two-year TV deal negotiated by the Football League in 1986 was worth only £6.3 million and the big clubs, the real draws, were getting chicken feed.

The turning point came in 1988, and the breakthrough was inspired by the commercial broadcaster, ITV, trying to get one over on the BBC.

Back then football and television were uneasy bedfellows. BBC and ITV were the only broadcasters. Their negotiators were Jonathan Martin from the BBC and John 'Brommers' Bromley and Trevor East from ITV. Nice guys, but there was a clear cartel which, today, would be illegal. Brommers and Jonathan would arrive for meetings in the same taxi, and thought they were doing us a favour by offering coverage at all. They reasoned they were giving us publicity, and we should be lucky that we could sell sponsorship on the back of the publicity they gave us. They offered us next to nothing.

But that year ITV tried to outsmart the BBC.

ITV's man Trevor, who became a good mate, said, 'David, I want you to meet a friend of mine. He's a programme controller for London Weekend Television.' Accordingly I had lunch with Greg Dyke – I remember it vividly – at a Japanese restaurant called the Suntory on St James's in London. I immediately took to Greg. He's a man after my own heart. He doesn't knock on doors, he kicks them down. He's a doer, a visionary – opinionated, passionate, and he loves the game. I think the world of Greg and we became instant friends.

'You know, you're not getting the best out of television,' Greg said.

'We're getting nothing,' I said.

'We have to change that, David. I'd like to propose ITV buys the rights to show the Big Five.' Wow, I thought, this would be game-changing for us, along with Spurs, United, Liverpool and Everton.

(It's funny, very few people get Everton when I ask them to name the Big Five now. People think, Well, Chelsea or Manchester City . . . But Chelsea and Man City were nowhere to be seen in those days. Everton have a big history. Their chair, Sir Philip Carter, and I were good friends as were Noel White of Liverpool, Martin Edwards of Manchester United and Irving Scholar of Spurs.)

Arsenal's closest allies at Football League meetings back then were always Spurs, no matter what people may say or think. I was very close to Irving, followed by Alan Sugar when he took over in 1991, and subsequently Daniel Levy in 2001. Why? Because they're our neighbours. We used to share gate men, we shared caterers, we shared police. Because we're so close the fans have an intense rivalry, but at board level we all had the same objective.

The five of us were really important in our fight against the old school at the League. 'How do we drive the game forward?' While other members were worried that I had my foot on the accelerator, they had theirs on the brake.

Greg wanted to show only the Big Five.

'It's not going to be easy,' I told him. 'You can't just do it with five clubs, we have to take others with us. And that's going to be a bit of a challenge.'

'Well, I'll leave that with you, you'll have to be the team leader,' Greg said.

I spoke to Martin, Philip, Irving and Noel and explained Greg's plan. We met Greg.

'What are you going to offer us?' Philip quickly asked Greg.

'£750,000 each.'

£750,000! That was huge at the time. We paused. There was silence.

Eventually, Greg said, 'We'll give you one million pounds each.'

To put that in context, Arsenal's entire annual turnover was £1.5 million back then. On the face of things Greg seemed the perfect ally. But was this as straightforward as it seemed? 'Do you think there's been a cartel between the BBC and ITV?' Irving asked him.

'Yes, it looks that way to me,' Greg said with surprising candour. Now we really knew what we were up against. This was the clubs versus the broadcasters, and we knew at this stage that we had to bring in the whole of the league.

Greg eventually bid twenty million pounds for exclusive rights to the whole of the Football League on top of the million pounds for each of the Big Five. However, another player now entered the market – BSB (British Satellite Broadcasting, eventually to become part of the Rupert Murdoch empire), and they bid forty-seven million pounds.

Naturally the League wanted us to sign with them. The Big Five didn't – we had the promise of one million pounds each from Greg and we liked his vision. What's more, BSB's satellite service was pie in the sky. It was an entirely new technology, no one knew if it would be successful – and in BSB's case it wasn't (which is why it was folded into Rupert Murdoch's rival station eight months after going on the air). Ultimately, after some heavy negotiations, the League accepted an offer of forty-four million pounds over four years from ITV. Greg still got a lot of flak within ITV because they thought he'd paid too much. Of course he got a bargain. Nowadays the Premier League clubs are getting four *billion* pounds over three years in domestic rights alone!

When the Football League found out about the Big Five's private talks with Greg, and the proposed offer of a million pounds each a year, the situation got messy and embarrassing. At our next general meeting, the mood was tense, and the other clubs wanted revenge. Philip Carter and I were ousted from the Management Committee. 'That's just vindictive,' I said to Philip. That was also the biggest mistake the Football League could have made. The battle lines were truly drawn between the Big Five and the League, and we were even more determined to break away. We bided our time.

On 26 May 1989, Arsenal's last game of the season was

famously at Anfield. This was the first year of our television contract: Greg had broken the mould, he deserved this trip up to Anfield with the board. What an unbelievable end to the season and all televised exclusively live by ITV Sport! I turned around to Greg and said, 'You've got it cheaply!'

'What?! I spent a lot of ITV's money!'

Greg laughed even more when he saw the record viewing figures – twelve million! I was pleased for him because he was very brave in what he did. He stuck his neck out. That's one of the many reasons I liked him.

As we flew back to Luton, I realised even more that football and television were a match made in heaven.

'We're a country of fifty-five million, you can only get 41,000 into Anfield and everybody wants to see it, Greg,' I said.

After the Hillsborough disaster, we got hit with the Lord Justice Taylor report. It was a hugely significant piece of work, vitally important and a wake-up call for football. His interim findings came out on 1 August 1989, when the fences were already coming down. The judge highlighted 'the failure of police control' and described the Leppings Lane end as 'unsatisfactory and ill-suited' for the numbers of fans expected. Taylor published his final report on 18 January 1990 with his main recommendation being the introduction of all-seater stadiums. It made sobering reading. He depicted a sport in decay. He wrote of nearing a stadium and encountering 'the prevailing stench of stewed onions' and finding 'lamentable' facilities. I nodded as I read. 'At some grounds the lavatories are primitive in design, poorly maintained and inadequate in number,' he wrote. 'This not only denies the spectator an essential facility he is entitled to expect. It directly lowers standards of conduct.'

The report was spot on. I immediately called our architects into Highbury to ascertain what needed to be done to make the stadium more compliant and welcoming.

I knew Taylor was right. He demanded change to save the game we all loved. I felt exactly the same, yet I knew his call for seats was going to cost and, frankly, we didn't have the money. The Football Foundation came in with a chunk of cash, the FA put in money but we still needed more help. We saw TV as our rescuers.

Greg gave me a call shortly after the Taylor report was published.

'Can I invite you guys to a dinner? Can you get the other four to come?'

I rounded up Martin, Irving, Noel and Philip, and swore them to secrecy. We daren't risk the Football League finding out about the meeting. The news would have caused uproar.

Friday 16 November 1990 was the night that changed football for ever. I made my way discreetly to London Weekend Television on the South Bank, took the lift to the twelfth floor, walked into a dining room and looked around the table.

There was Noel, who was a very nice, sensible, level-headed football-loving individual. He started at Altrincham, became a director and the chair of Liverpool and was on the FA's International Committee. Sir Philip Carter, the chair of Everton Football Club was an absolute gentleman. The first time I met him, he was director of Littlewoods who ran the football pools, Spot the Ball. He took me to the Littlewoods factory in Liverpool where women in hairnets counted the coupons and guys checked the competition in a massive warehouse. It was all manual. Nothing was automated.

'If Liverpool and Everton lose at the same weekend, our efficiency drops 50 per cent,' Philip told me. 'They're all miserable, they don't want to work. If we win – whether Liverpool win or not – I can tell who is working well because of their different spirits.'

And there was Irving, chair of Spurs. He and I got on famously. He has a great football brain and wonderful knowledge of football statistics. A good guy to have on your team for a football quiz! We thought similarly. Similar upbringing.

Martin, chair of Manchester United, who was very sound and analytical, was passionate about United, great fun and very entertaining company. Yes, Martin got into a few scrapes in his private life which were always amusing stories, and was always very supportive in our Big Five meetings. There was great camaraderie between us.

I glanced around the table again at LWT and thought, What a civilised gathering. Then Greg spoke. He had a warning.

'You won't get as much money next time around,' Greg said.

In fact, for some time, the five of us had been discussing the nuclear option and I seized the moment. It was time for the breakaway!

'Greg, we're proposing a new league,' I said. 'What we have to do is try and take the whole First Division with us, all twenty-two clubs.'

Greg questioned whether we had the nerve to do it.

'Yes,' I replied. 'If we set up a new league would you buy the rights?'

'Of course I bloody would!' Greg said.

'The time is right,' I said to the other four. 'Let's do it now.'

The whole idea had been simmering ever since Philip Carter

and I had been ejected from the Football League's Management Committee; why should we be held back by people who couldn't see the future? Why don't we break away? But I don't think Irving, Martin, Noel and Philip expected it to happen that quickly. We went around the table asking who was in favour. I glanced at Noel. I was worried about Liverpool. Historically, Liverpool were a very conservative club, tending to lead from the back. And now this dastardly plot was being laid to break away from the old Football League and form a revolutionary Premier League. There was a moment's silence. Then Noel said, in his calm and soothing voice, 'Let's do it!'

Everyone understood we had to act fast, not least because of the Taylor report. I had this image of seeing us starting afresh with a whole new league, new structure, different voting, and reinventing ourselves. None of us was aware we were making history. No doubt Neil Armstrong knew that he was when he landed on the moon, but for us, forming the Premier League was more about natural survival.

'We have to make football appealing to the public again,' I said. 'It's the people's game. We have to break away.'

Everyone around the table nodded.

'Let's call it the Phoenix League,' somebody said.

'No, we want to be the best,' I said. We discussed it and decided on 'Premier League'. 'We can't do it without the FA's blessing,' I said. 'We need to get them onside.'

Every league must be registered with the FA on an annual basis. For this I turned to Noel, a senior councillor for the FA. They used to call the council chamber 'death row' because, as you get older, you get nearer the front! Noel knew how the FA worked. He and I were deputed to go and see Graham Kelly, the

FA's chief executive and chairman Sir Bert Millichip on 6 December. Why us? Noel had impeccable connections and pedigree with the FA and I had the balls!

'I'm not sure how they will welcome us,' I said to Noel as we walked up the steps into Lancaster Gate, the FA's ancient offices.

'Have we got the guts and determination to fight the fight?' Noel said. We both agreed we had. As we stepped inside, I thought of Neil Armstrong. One small step for man, a giant leap for football.

Noel and I were stepping into a civil war between the FA and the Football League. At the time, Graham Kelly was writing the FA's *Blueprint for the Future of Football*, a riposte to the Football League's *One Game, One Team, One Voice*, which called for power-sharing and, as you'd imagine, massive tension resulted. Then there was the Swindon Town affair . . .

Swindon had been promoted from the Second Division in 1990 and were punished for financial irregularities. The Football League disciplinary commission relegated them to the Third Division. But Swindon appealed to the FA who adjudicated they should be left where they were in the first place! Incidents like these typified the boys' own self-indulgence of the system, and helped accelerate our exit towards the Premier League.

The animosity between the FA and the League was huge. The old secretary of the Football League, Alan Hardaker, who passed away in 1980, had moved the League offices to Lytham St Annes, near Blackpool, Lancashire, a move his daughter Lesley always said was 'to be as far away as he could from the FA' in London. The gulf between the Fylde coast and Lancaster Gate was as wide as it was geographically. Graham Kelly himself had just made the journey, moving from the Football League to the FA, and I knew he didn't have much empathy with his old colleagues.

'Look, Graham, we need to change football,' I began as we sat in Kelly's office. 'We'd like to form a new league.'

We explained our vision about the Premier League, how it should consist of eighteen clubs resulting in fewer games, helping the England national team (the FA's pride and joy), and allowing for a mid-season break to help the players.

'Good idea,' Graham said. Noel and I were amazed.

'Yes, you know what? The time is right, you go ahead. We have started writing this blueprint, and this could really work. This could easily slot into place.'

Well! I was kicking down an open door! I'd not anticipated one held open so willingly by the FA's chief executive. Graham was a good administrator, quiet and introverted. A sound guy with a good sense of humour. But he delivered here, big time.

Noel and I spoke to Sir Bert, too. Bert was nice, old school, cared passionately about the game.

'Sir Bert, we have to accept football is in decline. We have to do something really dramatic to turn it around,' I said. 'The Premier League will save the game.'

Bert nodded. His focus was solely on helping the game he loved. Ordinarily, the FA would never have backed the idea of the Premier League, but they'd been looking at ways of shaking up the Football League and the time was right. 'I can't be seen to be too involved,' Graham went on. 'You need to hire somebody to put the plan together. I'd recommend Rick Parry at Ernst & Young who's working on some projects for us as an independent consultant.'

Parry was an accountant from Chester who had run the

Manchester Olympic bid which had just failed that September. Rick knew Graham as the FA's representative involved with the British Olympic Association. Rick was still in Manchester, no doubt wondering what he could do that would be half as exciting as bidding for the Olympics.

Graham rang him, and the wheels of the Premier League started turning.

'I've got a project that might be interesting, Rick,' Graham said.

'I'll come down to London,' Rick said.

'No, I'll drive up,' Graham said. 'This needs to be kept secret.'

They met in the lobby of the Midland hotel at 1 p.m. on Thursday 6 December at precisely the same moment the entire Football League Management Committee walked into the hotel foyer for their Christmas lunch! Rick and Graham made themselves scarce. It was a miracle that we kept the Premier League project quiet for so long. I remember thinking at one meeting of the Big Five at the Excelsior Hotel, Manchester that we were going to get busted. Rick was told to ask for 'Mr Smith' at reception.

'Ah! You're here for the Manchester United meeting.'

And when we came out, Neil Kinnock was in the lobby having a bloody press conference. The whole place was full of cameras.

We were so impressed with Rick. Immediately, we realised he was a sound operator. Although we had the idea, we needed capable people to put the nuts and bolts together. We were building a Ferrari and Rick was an excellent engineer. His strength was administration. He was extraordinarily logical – often regarded as a dangerous thing in football – sensible and understood the issues.

Our next clandestine meeting was at Whites Hotel, Lancaster Gate. But unbelievably, this coincided with Graham Taylor holding an England press conference at the same location. Irving left through the kitchen window. When you're planning something as seismic as this you just couldn't get caught.

'You only have five clubs,' Rick said at one meeting. 'You can't break away with five. You need at least ten.'

That made sense, I realised immediately. If we had ten, we could almost operate like Scotland. We could play each other four times if we had to. If we had ten, I knew the other twelve First Division clubs would pack their tents and follow us. 'It's critical we get five more,' I said. 'We all need to choose a dancing partner, the club we know best, and get them on the floor.' I went with West Ham. The others took Aston Villa, Newcastle United, Nottingham Forest and Sheffield Wednesday. They needed little persuading. The moment they heard what we were planning, they were in. They saw our vision.

We still kept it all quiet, all sworn to secrecy. A leak would have killed us. Football's such a gossipy world – and yet from September 1990 to April 1991, not a word got out.

Some of the other five got cold feet from time to time, asking did we really have the courage to break away? Liverpool were always very cautious and I was worried that Irving would get distracted as he was considering selling Spurs to Alan Sugar, yet he remained gung-ho. Meanwhile Martin was involved with the Manchester United flotation. I was persistent. I called Rick at 11 p.m. every evening, then at 8 a.m. the following day.

'What's happened, Rick?'

'Not much since we last spoke, David!'

Now we had ten of the most glamorous clubs and it was a formality that the other twelve would follow.

Yet momentum was incredibly important. If we stopped or even paused the Football League would find out and fight back. I had to keep pushing it along. All credit to Graham Kelly: the FA had never moved as quickly.

But just as we got a green light, we hit a massive hurdle. Under Football League rules, a club has to give three years' notice of resignation. We had to find a way to get round this. So the five clubs hired two smart barristers, Michael Crystal QC and his junior, Mark Phillips. Mark and Rick worked closely together, and went through the Football League and FA rulebooks with a fine tooth comb. They spotted a section in the FA rulebook that clearly contradicted the three-year requirement in the Football League's rules. It said 'no league' can require its members to give more than six months' notice of their intention to leave. To this day they both remember with a smile what they realised was that 'Eureka!' moment.

'No league? That must surely apply to the Football League!' Mark opined. 'The League's stipulation for three years is in direct contravention of the FA rulebook.' Yes! I don't usually get carried away but I knew how key this was. It's simple, Mark said. 'You have to resign under the FA rules, not under Football League rules.'

We went back to Lancaster Gate, explained our plan to resign under FA rules and, to Graham's credit, he said, 'Yes. We'll agree to that.' It was so reassuring of the FA. I insisted on calling our new organisation the FA Premier League. They had a golden share and they provided the mechanism to get out of the Football League's three-year notice rule.

On 8 April 1991, the FA held a council meeting, announcing the intention to form the FA Premier League and said it was dismissing the Football League's three-year rule. The doors were well and truly kicked off the hinges.

With the news out, the twenty-two clubs met on 8 May. Bert and Graham spoke and gave the plan the FA's blessing with one stipulation – the new league had to be made up of eighteen clubs.

'We have to go to eighteen for the benefit of English football,' I told the clubs. 'English players are exhausted when it comes to World Cup and Euros in the summer. England suffer. We need a smaller league.' We could have a mid-season break, which would reduce the amount of stress injuries and it would have been beneficial for the Football League. Arsenal fans could have gone to see Leyton Orient or Barnet during the break.

Although Arsenal were at the forefront of pushing for eighteen clubs, the others ultimately agreed.

When Graham mentioned having eighteen clubs, Peter Swales of Manchester City launched in with the first question, 'Is there any scope for negotiation?'

Before Graham could say anything, Bert Millichip replied, 'It's your league, you decide.' Wow!

Rick whispered to me, 'Isn't that pretty fundamental?'

I whispered back, 'Not only has Bert just retracted on the eighteen clubs, but missed a great opportunity.' Most of the clubs would have accepted it but the FA effectively ceded control to the Premier League.

We couldn't have formed the Premier League without FA support and they didn't ask for anything in return. (Even now I still campaign for an eighteen-club league – the French league are going down to eighteen next year).

Bert was even so kind as to let the clubs use a conference room at Lancaster Gate to work out the shape of the new league. For a meeting that changed football for ever, it was very quick and simple. It took only two hours to produce the Founder Members' Agreement: one club, one vote, two-thirds required for a decision. Fifty per cent of the domestic broadcast money would be equally distributed between the clubs, twenty-five per cent would go by the position each club achieved in the league, and twenty-five per cent was based on appearances. The overseas broadcasting revenue was shared equally as at first there was virtually no take-up. Today it outstrips domestic revenue! Had we known then what we know now, we might have thought differently. Rick still has the copy of the Founder Members' Agreement on his phone. He occasionally shows it to me. It's headed 'Premier League' in Rick's writing. Graham added 'FA'.

We showed the agreement to Greg, and he kept a copy on his desk in his house for weeks. It didn't serve just as a memento. We were insistent on getting all the clubs onside, but some of them were still wary, so having that scrap of paper to hand was wise.

'Is this a trick? Can we trust you?' they asked. 'Aren't you glamour clubs going to try and run away with the money?'

'You can trust us,' I replied. 'Look at the Founder Members' Agreement.' They could plainly see what they were guaranteed. It was there in black and white that they would be treated fairly and, above all, that the TV money would be shared equitably, though not equally.

'If we go down the Spanish route – where Barcelona, Real Madrid and Atletico Madrid get the bulk of the money – you don't get a very competitive league,' I told the other clubs. It was important to get that agreed before the TV money came in because otherwise there would have been a fight.

'It's not just the TV rights,' said Sam Hammam of Wimbledon. 'We have to be like the NFL, we have to share everything equally.'

'That's never going to happen, Sam. We have to have some compromise. Fifty: twenty-five: twenty-five is simple and fair.' It meant the smaller clubs generated enough to buy decent players so we could have a competitive league.

The idea of parachute payments to soften relegation from the Premier League came from the Crystal Palace chairman, Ron Noades. The reasoning was that twenty-two clubs had the courage to give notice to the Football League but not all of them would remain in the old First Division. (Three of them, Luton Town, Notts County and West Ham United ended up being relegated.) It seemed fair, since they were all handing in their notice, that they would all get a share of the revenue even if they had to drop out. Parachute payments were £750,000 in the first year and it wasn't thought of as controversial at the time. Now they're forty-five million pounds, and I agree with those who say it distorts the division below.

We eventually went four down and two up to give us twenty clubs. In a later meeting, I again raised the possibility of eighteen. 'No, we want the money,' Ken Bates said. 'We want the income from as many matches as we can get. We don't want to lose two home games.'

'It's crazy,' I replied. 'When the TV money goes up, there'll be eighteen clubs sharing it instead of twenty.' Ken didn't realise that it was going to be four billion pounds instead of £400 million; but in fairness nobody knew at the time.

The Football League were still trying to stop us. 'Betrayal!' they screamed. On 10 May, two days after the FA's agreement, the League's chief executive Arthur Sandford wrote to the FA saying how 'dismayed' they were by the FA's attitude. But instead of calling us together to say, 'How can we sort this out? What can we do to make you stay?' they just ran off to court. 'We'll block this,' the League shouted. 'See you in court.' It was inept and it was naïve.

One day I was talking to Ken, who until then had been fairly neutral about the formation of the Premier League. 'I'm a Football League man,' Ken said, 'but no one from the Football League has ever phoned and asked me to stay. So, fuck them, I'm off.'

Understandably, league clubs outside the top division were feeling bruised and nervous. What mattered to them was the prospect of promotion – three clubs going up and three down – to keep the dream alive. We never even thought of taking that away. They kept contacting me. 'I passionately believe in the pyramid,' I told them. 'We're renaming the First Division the FA Premier League and still keeping promotion and relegation. It's good for everyone.'

Now we were out in the open and heading to court for an almighty bun fight of a legal case. FOOTBALL AT WAR, read the headlines and the papers were right. It was a civil war, never seen before, and it raged at the high court in London. I read the court papers. It was 'R v. the Football Association Ltd., ex parte the Football League Ltd. (Queen's Bench division)'. Serious stuff. It all came down to whose rules were superior. The FA spent

£1.5 million in the high court fighting the Football League. Our lawyers, Mark Phillips and Michael Crystal played a blinder, and Rick did a great job working alongside them. And, on 30 July, because the FA are the governing body, Lord Justice Dyson ruled in the FA's favour. I punched the air. We could now resign from the League.

Once we had our freedom, Rick had to drive up to Lytham to hand over the twenty-two clubs' notices of resignation to the Football League.

'I'll get lynched when I knock on the front door,' Rick told me.

But this being England, the new secretary of the League, David Dent, opened the door and said, 'Why don't you come in and have a cup of tea?' Rick told us later he felt almost embarrassed handing the letters over. 'Why are they doing this? What are they unhappy about?' Dent asked.

'Well, that's quite a long story, David,' Rick replied.

Chair Bill Fox was apoplectic. You can imagine why: we're breaking away, we're leaving them with what they thought was the rump of football. But we said, 'Football's going to be healthier through the pyramid as a result. There's going to be more money now, trickling down.' They simply couldn't see that at the time.

Rick then had another meeting with the FA. 'Thanks for fighting off the Football League and winning the case but we actually don't want to be in the FA,' Rick told Graham and Sir Bert. 'We want to be a separate company.' Which made a lot of sense. 'How can we enter into TV contracts if we're just a committee of the FA?' Rick said.

Again, the FA went, 'OK!' They couldn't have made it easier for us.

By now, the Football League were panicking and called an emergency meeting for 10 a.m. on 23 September in the Connaught Rooms, London. The twenty-two First Division clubs were kept in an anteroom, while the seventy clubs from the Second, Third and Fourth Divisions were in the main hall. Our plan was for Graham Kelly, the FA's chief executive, to address the main hall and to give the clubs guarantees that none of them would be worse off. We needed him to encourage them to vote for the Premier League. At 9.50, no sign of Graham. Unfortunately he couldn't make it at the last minute. I turned to Pat Smith, the FA's administration manager.

'You'll have to do it, Pat,' we told her. This had to come from the FA, not from someone like me who plainly had a vested interest. 'You'll have to stand up in front of the ninety-two clubs and give all the assurances.'

Pat was only five foot four. She had to stand on a chair so they could all see her. She initially addressed the First Division and dealt with questions from Ken Bates and Ron Noades. That was straightforward, as all the clubs in the division were committed to the formation of the FA Premier League. My concern was the other three divisions. This could be awkward. They were lined up in rows, facing a top table as if they were in an exam hall. Everyone in the room knew Pat embodied the heart and soul of football. She is a remarkable, redoubtable woman who was the backbone of the FA. She'd been there for years having joined directly from convent school. Everybody respected Pat – and she did brilliantly.

She climbed on a chair, looked at everybody and said, 'As you're all aware, we have had a proposal to start a new league, which is going to be called the FA Premier League. The idea is to have twenty-two clubs. I wish to announce on behalf of the FA that we approve of this new league.' Pat spoke from the heart for fifteen minutes, talking about why the FA was behind the Premier League. 'It'll be under the umbrella of the FA and will be good for the game. It will be good for England.' Pat had a background in amateur dramatics and I believe that helped her present to the whole room. She knew how to project her voice.

After she finished speaking, one question was fired in from the floor. 'Is the FA selling out the League?'

'No,' Pat replied firmly. Silence. This was the FA, this was Pat Smith speaking and it was truly a Churchillian moment. 'You can trust the FA,' Pat said. 'We will support you.'

Her words helped win the vote fifty-one to nine. Game, set and match. I sent Pat a giant bouquet of flowers the next day. 'Well done, Pat.' And that was it. The FA Premier League was formed.

The TV negotiations really began to accelerate and the trading and charm offensive intensified. Sam Chisholm was Rupert Murdoch's right-hand man at his satellite venture BSkyB. BSkyB was then a wildly speculative start-up, the first successful attempt in the world at direct satellite-to-home broadcasting (by then they had swallowed their only would-be satellite rival), and they badly needed viewers. A sure way to get people to subscribe was to show live football.

Sam Chisholm invited Greg Dyke to lunch – and I know what was said.

'I want you to know that the only person who knows I'm here is Mr Murdoch,' Chisholm began. 'The question we want to put to you is, what are we going to do together to fuck these football clubs?'

Greg left and never considered the deal offered by Chisholm.

Greg was a football fan himself, so Sam's pitch was wildly misplaced. But in any case Greg was confident ITV would get the FA Premier League contract.

Sam then took me out for lunch. He was lobbying the clubs and trying to win over the Big Five. 'David, I'm going to teach your granny how to watch footy on telly,' he said.

'Sam, that's a bloody clever trick; she's been dead for twenty years!'

He was a showman, good old Sam. He wanted the rights and if he couldn't bamboozle the clubs to get them, he was going to pay whatever it took. He had to get Murdoch's satellite operation off the ground.

Rick Parry set a deadline for TV bids of 17 May 1992. Our big broadcast meeting took place the following day at the Royal Lancaster Hotel, London. Trevor East arrived early and handed us an envelope which contained ITV's bid of £262 million over five years for thirty live games a season. ITV had done their sums, regarded themselves as the incumbent, and remained confident that would swing the deal.

How would BSkyB respond? Parry contacted Chisholm with the news, and Chisholm woke Murdoch up in New York. BSkyB had to get the rights. We knew they had debts of more than two billion pounds. They needed to sell subscriptions and they weren't going to do that with documentaries or with news, or even movies. We knew football was their rescue plan. And Murdoch knew it too. The Premier League would be the driver.

Alan Sugar had become part-owner of Spurs the previous year and, during a break in the meeting, he rang Chisholm. I really like Sugar, but in today's world he would not have been allowed to vote. He had a conflict of interest. He was Amstrad. He made satellite dishes. While he declared as such, obviously, he was going to be favouring BSkyB. 'Get your fucking arse round here and blow them out of the water,' Sugar shouted down the phone. People heard. You couldn't really not hear.

'Who are you speaking to?' Trevor East asked.

'I'm talking to my girlfriend!' Alan replied.

Rick was listening and told me what went on. 'Sam was saying to him, "Get off the bloody phone, I'm trying to get this thing sorted!"'

At the last minute, BSkyB trumped ITV. Murdoch authorised a new bid of £304 million over five years and owes a huge debt to Alan Sugar for winning the bid. BSkyB also played another ace: they got the BBC on board. At these stratospheric sums for TV rights the corporation had long dropped out of negotiations. But Marmaduke Hussey, then chairman of the BBC, had worked for Murdoch at *The Times*, and Murdoch called him to try and get him on board. In fact, BSkyB had a problem on their hands. They rightly feared it would cause an outcry if a subscription-only service was seen to have commandeered exclusive access to the nation's most popular sport. The upstart broadcaster needed an alliance with the BBC to disguise or dilute its near-monopoly.

Perhaps wiser people at the BBC would have refused the bait, and some at the time argued that they should. Why, they asked, are we helping a potential rival, when we could kill it by saying no? But in those days the BBC was fixated on competition with ITV. It does not seem to have occurred to most of the bosses that they were feeding a dragon whose revenues would soon equal, then double and almost triple their own. So the BBC said yes, adding a very clear snub to ITV. They would pay ten million pounds for *Match of the Day* rights, but they wouldn't buy them if ITV won the main contract.

Arsenal, Liverpool, Everton and Man U felt we owed Greg a huge debt. As I put it, 'ITV held our hand, broke the cartel and helped us establish the Premier League. And now we are not going to stay loyal to them?'

The twenty-two clubs voted on the two bids. But football was strange back then with little infrastructure in most clubs. QPR sent along the office junior.

The final vote was 14–6 in favour of BSkyB. Arsenal, Manchester United, Liverpool, Everton, Aston Villa and Nottingham Forest voted for ITV, but Spurs and the others chose Sky. Two clubs abstained on the vote, and I still have no idea who they were – or why! The biggest vote in the history of English football and they abstained! Crazy. I like people who've got opinions. (One of my good friends, businessman Tom Toumazis, gives talks in which he says that the two words he dislikes most in the English language are 'if' and 'maybe'. I agree. We both lecture for Speakers for Schools and I always tell students at my talks to be decisive – even if you get it wrong, I don't mind. But, gosh, when people abstain from such an important a vote, that's cowardice. Take a position.)

Personally, I believed the national broadcaster should really have tried to rustle up more money to show the national game. But there was a logic to those who voted for BSkyB. All these clubs thought they'd been screwed over the past four years by ITV for giving that million-pound guarantee to each of the Big Five. For some, like Chelsea and Palace, this vote was out-and-out revenge. On top of that the switch by Tottenham to favour BSkyB shifted the vote. And then there was Murdoch's brilliant intrigue of getting the BBC onside. That gave them credibility and strongly influenced the vote.

We needed terrestrial exposure to keep the fans onside. We couldn't just go to a channel that didn't have any subscribers at the time. 'If the BBC had said, "Sorry, we're not going to show *Match of the Day* if the live games are on Sky," we wouldn't have done the deal with Sky,' Rick told me. We had to have *Match of the Day* at the very least to promote the new league. In fact the Premier League would almost have paid to keep *Match of the Day* on BBC.

I felt really sorry for Greg because he did all the hard work. He won the battle but lost the war. He was upset, naturally. But we couldn't have done more. Money spoke loudest again. Greg was always gracious. 'David Dein was the most revolutionary bloke I've met in football,' he told the *Financial Times*. 'David Dein created the Premier League, it was his idea.' Which, given that the Premier League had now abandoned him, was generous.

I've spoken to Greg many times about that meeting at the Royal Lancaster. He was sanguine. He always knew what he was up against. He understood that football rights were always going to go to pay TV at some stage. It was simple maths. Murdoch had deeper pockets than terrestrial.

The race was now on for the winning team to get up and running and establish all the production in three months in time for the start of the new season. It was still tough watching their first live broadcast, Nottingham Forest versus Liverpool on 16 August. I had divided loyalties because I felt for my friend Greg.

Many in the TV old guard assumed that the vulgar newcomers at BSkyB would be amateurs and technically inept. But I have to admit the presentation was exceptional. It was more than a match, it was an event.

For all those initial reservations, who can say Sky have not done a brilliant job for football? Their money bought the football, the football brought the viewers, and the viewers bought subscriptions. They've given it what the terrestrial broadcasters could not; they had that magical ingredient in their favour – time. On terrestrial, football would be squeezed between *Coronation Street* and *News at Ten*. Sky actually needed it to fill its airtime, and so devoted two hours before and an hour afterwards. It was their treasure and they gave it tender loving care.

And it gave us money. In 1988, ITV paid eleven million pounds a year for all ninety-two clubs. Now broadcasters pay that per game. Amazon is now the new kid on the block and have successfully bid for some of the live matches, so who knows where it will go next? But Greg gave us the courage, he opened our eyes to the relationship between TV and football.

For a long time in broadcasting the big money from pay TV got lavished on football. That's changed in the past five years; Sky (as they now call themselves) realised they might not have football for ever, so they've invested in original drama, blockbuster films and so on. I'll admit that I didn't foresee just how quickly satellite broadcasting would grow, and how big it would become. For me I feared going with Murdoch would limit the number of people who could watch. 'Well, you've got *Match of the Day*,' I was told. But that's not quite the same as screening the matches live. I was all for trying to carve out some games for terrestrial as well. I wanted football to go to a mass audience.

On the best day, Sky may get two to three million viewers. Meanwhile there's sixty million out there who can't see it and can't subscribe. But in the end, the money buys the beer and that's what happened here.

Since its launch in 1992, the Premier League has become the most respected, most successful, most entertaining league in the world. And the most watched. We've gone from being televised in a few countries to 189 territories with 1.7 billion viewers around the world. When we were forming the Premier League, the overseas rights were sold by CSI, the company founded by Mike Watt. I was on the TV committee and English football was sixth in the world ranking, after Italy, Germany, Spain, France and Holland – and we got precious little for the overseas rights. Today English football is number one by a country mile in overseas rights, even passing domestic rights in the 2022/23 season (by £5.3 billion to £5.1 billion for the following three years). Everyone wants to watch the Premier League and it's easy to understand why.

'The best foreign players want to play in the Premier League,' Arsène told me. Every foreign player loves playing here. And the money from TV raised wages so it was easier to attract the best of the overseas players. They've helped the game here and improved their English colleagues. It's made the players multi-millionaires.

I have to mention how vital Rick Parry's contribution was as CEO in setting up the Premier League and dealing with all of the mechanics including of course skilfully negotiating the television deals. He was eventually succeeded by Richard Scudamore who became chief executive in November 1999 and later executive chairman and took the league to yet another level. Those regulators who still hankered over breaking up the Premier League model were sent packing by Richard. Now when I fly long haul on a plane I can watch Premier League games live as an example of its popularity. We owe Rick and Richard a huge debt. So do the players. And so, for good or ill, does the gambling industry. The global betting market is worth around one trillion dollars and 80 per cent of that is football. The Premier League attracts about one billion dollars-worth of bets per match.

All the time, we had other leagues asking, 'How did you do it? Can we have the blueprint?' The other European leagues were jealous. They fell behind, still are to this day, and that would go on to be a sub-plot of the 2021 ill-conceived attempt to set up the European Super League. I'm not being unkind to them, but I know how much they'd love to slow down our train. When Richard left the Premier League in 2018, I wrote in his farewell book, 'To the driver of the fastest train on the track'. Richard was a good leader of people and brilliant at negotiating the TV rights, working with the talented Paul Molnar who has done a spectacular job in masterminding the TV sales. All the clubs should be very grateful.

Nobody back in 1992 could have envisaged what's happened with the Premier League. I know people say English football is not English football: it is owned by foreigners, managed by foreigners and played by foreigners by and large. But this is the proof of its success. The Premier League is an English institution, it plays in England, its greatest fans are English, it draws viewers around the world to England, it brings huge amounts of money to England and to the Revenue by way of players' income tax. Its stadia are now the best in the world, and its training grounds and academies are revitalised and nurturing talent in England. Look at the genius and flair coming out of English clubs, like Jack Grealish, Phil Foden, Bukayo Saka. That's hope for the future.

When I joined the board of Arsenal in 1983, I was a local businessman putting money into the club that I love. Then it became millionaires investing, then it became billionaires, then it changed again and now sovereign states are investing. Manchester City are owned by an investment fund of the Abu Dhabi government and, more recently, Newcastle United have been bought by a consortium connected to the Saudi government.

It wouldn't be fun if the wealthiest just threw money at players – denying talent to all of the others – so the Premier League introduced financial fair play. Every club has to have audited accounts and is not allowed losses of more than £105 million over three years. If they overspend they could get punished. It helps keep the Premier League competitive.

The dynamics of the fans have changed: 24 per cent of Premier League crowds are women and that's very impressive; 12 per cent from black, Asian and other minority ethnic groups and 12 per cent of season-ticket holders are under sixteen. It always worried me that the 18–24 age group, often the most passionate, were being priced out. At the end of each season's board meeting at Arsenal, pricing was always on the agenda and I was always arguing to keep at least some of the tickets as cheap as possible. But with salaries always going up, we were chasing our tail.

The coaches from overseas – like Arsène Wenger, Pep Guardiola, Josè Mourinho, Jürgen Klopp – have raised standards. 'The quality of football in England has been improved beyond recognition by the Premier League,' Arsène told me. Italy and Spain were the elite leagues when the Premier League started. Not now. We launched a revolution. But what was once seen as insurrection has become the accepted way of English football. Fifty clubs have already featured in the Premier League.

The Premier League now is England's largest sporting export. It grosses over ten billion pounds over three years from television alone and is head and shoulders above any other league in the world. I remember being interviewed for its twentieth anniversary and, when asked about the formation, I said, 'We knew we had an aeroplane on the runway, we just didn't know how high it was going to fly!'

We have come a long way from the darkest day at Hillsborough. It's a whole new ball game. And that meeting with Trevor and Jenni Hicks was the starting point.

ARSÈNE FOR ARSENAL

It turned out to be a fateful day when I met Arsène at half-time during a north London derby at Highbury in 1989. It was a 'sliding doors' moment. Many things that day could have gone differently but the stars aligned. Arsène was passing through London. He was manager of Monaco at the time and had been scouting a player in Istanbul and was on his way back to the principality. With a day to spend in transit, the only thing he wished to do was watch a football game. He got in touch with Dennis Roach, the agent of one of his players, Glenn Hoddle, and asked if he could find him a ticket to a match in London. That ticket happened to be at Arsenal.

There was a room next to the boardroom at Highbury called the cocktail lounge which hosted female guests (in those days women were not allowed in the boardroom) as well as any officials from other clubs, scouts or VIPs. The centrepiece was a Grecian statue, his modesty almost covered by a laurel wreath, on an art deco plinth. At half-time all guests watching from the directors' box were invited to make their way either to the boardroom or the cocktail lounge for some refreshments.

Arsène was a smoker. He was standing in the corner of the cocktail lounge wearing a beige trenchcoat and rimless glasses, looking tall and elegant. My wife Barbara and her friend Penny

Grade, who was also a smoker, went over for a light. This turned out to be perhaps the most serendipitous smoke he ever had. Barbara was impressed by this suave, continental man of football and sent a message to me in the boardroom; there was someone here she thought I would want to meet – the manager of Monaco. I made my way to the lounge to meet him. He didn't look at all like a football manager. He didn't speak like a football manager. He didn't seem to think like a football manager. He was urbane and interesting.

I hijacked him.

I asked him how long he was in town for and he said, 'Tonight.' Had he plans? He didn't. Would he like to join us that evening, as we were going to dinner at a friend's house and he was welcome. The answer was about to change all of our lives: 'Sure.'

Barbara offered Arsène a lift back. She had a small car at the time and stuffed him into the back seat with his long legs folded up to his chest. They proceeded to head back to Totteridge. He had no idea that it was nowhere near the centre of town where he was staying!

We went to eat at the home of our friends Alan and Louise Whitehead in Elstree. Alan was the drummer in the pop group Marmalade. Louise was an actress and very effervescent.

After a lovely dinner, Alan and Louise, being natural entertainers, suggested a game of charades. When Arsène joined in it just underlined what an interesting guy he was. At a spontaneous evening with people he had never met, not speaking his mother tongue, playing an unfamiliar party game, he demonstrated the combination of intellect and personality necessary to take part in miming the titles of books and films. Within a few minutes he was acting out *A Midsummer Night's Dream*. 'Arsène for Arsenal'.

It flashed into my head like a premonition. I am not spiritual but it did feel like destiny. An accidental meeting, an instant impression. I had a feeling there and then that one day he would be our manager. First impressions mean a lot to me and on that first day there was chemistry. It is a similar feeling to that of a relationship in which, from the first date, you can sense something there, an instant bond. There is an old saying – you only get one chance to make a good first impression. The moment I met Arsène he did exactly that.

Over the years Arsène and I kept in touch. I was often in the south of France, so we would meet up and I attended quite a few Monaco matches. I noticed how he handled the players, the public, the press and the directors and it only reinforced my impression that he was special. He would hit the bullseye with the first arrow. He was very quick to read situations, he made his point succinctly. Little did he know that he was auditioning for the job at Arsenal.

The people I knew around Monaco said that he fashioned a good footballing team. Players of the calibre of George Weah went from an unknown to a world beater, Glenn Hoddle and Jürgen Klinsmann played for him. He developed Lilian Thuram.

The more I got to know him it was more apparent he was a cut above the average that I have seen in a football manager. Quite apart from his intelligence and his command of languages – English isn't even his second language – is his demeanour. His global knowledge of the game was striking. In those days, when information on foreign players in overseas leagues tended to come through notes or from a VHS video, recommendations coming in via a phone call or a fax message, he built up an encyclopaedic knowledge in his memory bank. He didn't need others to tell him about a footballer because he generally already knew and he had this knack of assessing qualities very quickly. All in all, he was strikingly impressive.

One night in the winter of 1994, when the financial scandal around George Graham was flaring up (more of which later), Arsène was over for a game and was staying at our home in Totteridge. I told him we were having a bit of a problem at Arsenal and asked him if he would like me to promote him as a potential candidate if George had to go. He said that it would be an honour.

Peter Hill-Wood and I had a good working relationship and he was quite relaxed that I would take the lead on many subjects. After I mentioned Arsène's name at the next board meeting, Peter agreed to meet him at his favourite restaurant in Chelsea. However, Peter had made his mind up about staying with a tried and trusted British manager. I'm afraid my proposal on this occasion got resoundingly rejected by the board. The view was that we needed someone like George who would understand the lower divisions and local clubs where we had been so successful in our recruitment with the likes of Lee Dixon, Steve Bould, Alan Smith and so on. They did not think someone from overseas would work. The decision was taken to go for Bruce Rioch who had managed Middlesbrough, Millwall and Bolton.

It was frustrating. I saw qualities in Arsène that I had not seen in any British manager. I felt certain he would bring elements to the job and the club that could be transformative. The fact was he wasn't your average ex-player becoming a manager – even though he had been a decent player in the French league. He had been to university and had a degree in economics which gave him an appreciation of the business side of football and he had studied medicine, so he had such an understanding of the physiology of a human being in the case of injuries. He was worldly and interesting.

Unfortunately, I had to tell him that the board decided not to go for him which I was embarrassed about. He then took the decision to take himself off to Japan. Nagoya Grampus Eight had approached him and he was intrigued. He wanted to test himself and see how good he was in an environment that was away from the mainstream. I thought that was unusual, a risky move, but we kept in touch throughout his time there. I always used to send him videos of our games on Philips VHS tapes that were rather like bricks. He didn't realise, but he was my personal pundit, offering pearls of wisdom on the team and on players. He would pick out things I had never thought of. We often communicated by fax in those days and it made me chuckle that the faxes used to whir through the machine with the name 'Lineker' at the top. Arsène lived in the property in Nagoya that Gary Lineker had previously stayed in when he played for the club.

By the time we realised that Bruce Rioch wasn't working out as George's replacement, Arsène was under contract and on the other side of the world. I decided to bat for him again, but more strongly this time. I called Glenn Hoddle to get the players' view and asked his opinion. His words to me were very simple: 'Just take him.' That gave me an extra resource for the board – a reference that came from someone they respected within English football. I also asked my good friend Gérard Houllier, who had taken his coaching licence with Arsène at Clairefontaine and who warmly recommended him. At the next board meeting I made my case once again, but went in harder this time. Peter Hill-Wood had the chair at the end of the oval table, I was to his left, we all sat round.

'We made a mistake,' I told the board. 'We could have had Arsène the first time round and he went to the J-League while we tried Bruce. I happen to know he has a break in his season in November. If we really want him, I think we can get him. Let's not make the same mistake again. This guy is special. I will stake my reputation on it.' This time the board approved, everybody agreed. Leadership is being brave enough to make a decision even though it may not be popular, being able to convince other people and making it right but a bold step has to be collegiate. You have to get everyone to believe in it strongly enough to stand with you.

After the meeting, I called Arsène. I told him we were serious this time and everyone really wanted him. It wasn't a fait accompli, though. He was happy in Japan, he didn't like to break contracts and felt a certain loyalty to the team that had responded to him so well. They were bottom of the league when he arrived and were flying high and had won the Emperor's Cup. But deep down we both knew that to miss this opportunity twice would be stupid.

During the summer, Peter Hill-Wood, Danny Fiszman and I flew to Japan to negotiate a settlement with Grampus Eight. Arsenal finished the season in early May, and a few days later we made our way to Asia. Arsène had an away match on the day we hoped to see him at Shimizu S-Pulse. No problem, we said. We will come to you. It happened to be a journey of roughly five hundred miles, taking five hours, from Nagoya. We took the Shinkansen (bullet) train which was magnificent, to meet him at the hotel before the game.

We arrived knowing we had to get Arsène to formally agree but as I had teed everything up it wasn't a difficult meeting. After that, it was on to part two of our tour, back to Nagoya to meet the Grampus Eight hierarchy at their enormous Toyota office. It was so big you could get a cab from one end of it to the other. They were very respectful and amicable. We had to convince the president to release Arsène, who had done some of the groundwork and had already stressed he would not leave before the natural break in their season. We agreed the compensation.

We did have to keep Arsène's appointment a secret, though, because he promised to stay until they lined up a replacement, which didn't happen until October. Stewart Houston and Pat Rice took the reins as caretakers. The board took quite a lot of criticism during that period. Since the media and public didn't know that we had to wait for our man there were questions about the timing of Bruce's termination, just a few days before the start of the season, apparently without someone notable lined up. These are the situations in which the directors have to have the courage of their convictions and ride it out.

At our AGM in late August, Peter Hill-Wood was asked who was going to be our next manager by a shareholder. Peter said that he couldn't answer the question as he was under an NDA. The shareholder was persistent and asked Peter who the NDA was with. He replied 'Arsène Wenger'! That was awkward.

When Patrick Vieira and Rémi Garde were signed it was a clear indication that things were moving behind the scenes and we were indeed preparing for Arsène's arrival. Bruce knew nothing about the talks over these players and, in hindsight, it felt underhand to have been arranging transfers without his involvement: but we had to do what was right for the club. It was only a question of timing when Bruce would be leaving and Arsène arriving.

Arsène was effectively managing by remote control from Japan. He wanted Patrick and identified Rémi as a solid player to help the club and specifically to help Patrick, who had the potential to be an extraordinary talent. I did the negotiations. Patrick had two guys as his agents, Jean-François Larios, an ex-player, and Marc Roger, and they were sharp. Larios had built a good relationship over the years with Arsène. They were a force for good rather than evil for us in delivering Patrick. A couple of days after Bruce was relieved of his duties, Patrick and Rémi were parachuted in.

I will always remember going to see how Patrick was getting on and we had a chat in French. I asked him how he was settling in and he said he was fine. I asked how his English was going and that wasn't so fine. I said in my best schoolboy French, 'Patrick, *est-ce que tu peux dire quelque chose en Anglais?*' ('Can you say something in English?')

He replied, '*Oui, Monsieur* Dein: Tottenhaaaam are *sheeeet.*'

I said to him, '*Qui t'as dit ça?*' ('Who told you that?')

He replied, 'Ray Parlour.' Ray had been giving him English 'lessons'. It just goes to show what the priorities are when settling into a new culture.

Arsène's imminent appointment was difficult to keep under wraps as we were not allowed to say anything official until a time that was respectful to Grampus Eight. However, we managed it. On the day he was announced the headline in London's *Evening Standard* read ARSÈNE WHO?, which captured the typically insular mood of English football at the time. I always felt that was a bit of an English malaise. I could see it as a global game, while a lot of people were entrenched in the view that the England team manager should be English and that British managers and players should be more trusted in our clubs. There was some resistance in certain areas. Well, I always think you go for the best person, no matter their nationality.

That was the message I had for the players when I went to the training ground at London Colney to inform them of our new manager. It was very rare that I would go there and have an audience with the squad. I told them the announcement was soon to be made official and that Arsène Wenger was joining us. Quick as a flash Ray Parlour said, 'Who the fuck is that?!'

Once the laughter subsided, I tried to give the players the lowdown. I told them, 'I have been following this guy for years. He is a winner, he is different and he is a wonderful human being. I want you to give him a chance.'

Appointing a manager is the single biggest decision a board has to make. If you choose the right one life is easy. If you choose the wrong one you've got headaches. Across the ninety-two professional clubs in England the average manager stays in post for twelve months. Who would have imagined this marriage would last twenty-two years?

By the end of September, Arsène was in situ and was due to start work on 1 October. There was a lot of attention on how we would fare because there was so much curiosity about his appointment. We won our first game, 2–0 away at Blackburn Rovers and the new era was off and running.

Almost immediately, there was a very peculiar and unpleasant episode which threatened to derail the entire situation. We were playing a reserve game at Highbury in the afternoon but, when I arrived at the stadium that morning, the mood was unsettled and unsettling. There were rumours, and they were rife, that something unsavoury about Arsène's private life was going to come out in the press. He was driving from the training ground to the stadium. I called him and said, 'Arsène, when you come in, there's going to be a lot of press around. Come straight to your office through the car park entrance and I'll come and see you.' I didn't tell him what it was about. When he arrived, I said, 'Arsène, there's press downstairs in the Marble Halls and there's been a very, very ugly story circulating today on the wires about your private life.'

He said, 'What do you mean, David? You've known me long enough. You know my private life. What is it – about a girlfriend?'

I said, 'No, no, it's worse than that.'

He said, 'What do you mean – something to do with my sexuality?'

I said, 'No, it's actually worse than that.' And I'm not sure we ever got to explaining what it was.

He stood up and said, 'Who are these people?' He started walking down to the entrance of the Marble Halls and eyeballed about half a dozen of the press. They were there with their cameras, and he said, 'I understand you want to talk to me. Feel free to. I've got nothing to hide in my private life. Ask me any question you like.' They all put their heads down. Nobody said a word. I was standing behind him in the hallway watching. The way he handled these scurrilous rumours was very brave and very clever. He challenged the press to say what they had on him, and nobody dared to speak. I remember when the press didn't look up at him, he said, 'You'll have to excuse me. I've got a game of football to see.'

It was a horrible episode. Arsène and I had discussed the press many times before he actually signed the contract, so he was aware that he was going to be under scrutiny. He was used to being scrutinised on the pitch. But this was personal and vicious. It was a low blow. I thought it was ugly, it was unseemly, it was unedifying, it was embarrassing. But we had to move on.

In those early weeks I saw it as my business to support Arsène in every way I could. The first thing I did was to help him find a house near me in Totteridge. We found him a place which he liked and the location was ideal. Virtually every night, after training, I would pop in and we would chat and often ended up sitting down to dinner together. I think that that was wonderful for the club, but I'm not sure it did much for his marriage!

We spoke about every minute detail that might impact the club. Arsène walked into a team that was still coming to terms with Tony Adams's recent admission of alcoholism. Socially and culturally, within the group, there was a lot going on. In the 1980s and 1990s there was a drinking culture at every club (in France, it was a smoking culture). An overseas player coming in couldn't understand how much drinking went on and the English players were bemused by the foreign players smoking. Of course I had alerted Arsène to it before he arrived and he recognised it was part of English football. Arsenal had an established drinking club even though George tried to curb it. But from what I knew of Arsène I imagined that he would want to educate the players into a new way of looking after themselves. I think he always felt that his intelligence, leadership and inspiration would challenge the drinking culture. He was confident in his own ability on that front.

He was quite evangelical about things like nutrition, drinking water, stretching and living by the idea that if you look after your body your career will thank you. Tony's announcement made it the right time to change the environment with Arsène's revolutionary ideas about training and nutrition. One day I hitched a lift back from an Aston Villa game on the team coach. After the players had had their meal, they broke into a chant 'We want our Mars Bars back!' from the back of the bus. Arsène just turned around, smiled politely and waved a finger. Arsène listened, he watched, he made suggestions, without ramming ideas down anyone's throat. He didn't turn up with an ego – he still doesn't have one.

When, over our dinners, we discussed everything going on at the club in those early days, he took it all in his stride. Nothing fazed him. He took to English football like a duck to water. It was a gradual revolution. The way he handled it was very, very intelligent. He did it stage by stage, winning the players over, getting their confidence, getting them fitter mentally and physically. And winning their hearts and minds. The fact he ended up not only modernising the club, but also having an impact on English football generally, epitomised the way the game in our country was ready for a radical reform. Still, it is one thing talking about it and another actually achieving it.

The contrast in style compared to his predecessors at Arsenal was striking. George was a very good organiser and a disciplinarian. Bruce was regimented and too inflexible. All of a sudden, under Arsène, the regime became one of intelligence, cooperation and it used a collegiate approach, a much softer environment. I could see the players buying into Arsène's philosophy: how he wanted the team to play. I got a great impression from the players and staff when we chatted in passing. After the initial scepticism there were a lot of positive vibes and a good feeling of camaraderie around the place.

Arsène was also a great organiser and did so much research. People have no idea about the amount of preparation that provides the foundation to any performance. People just think, 'Well, we've played well,' or 'We haven't played well.' Arsène would be on the training ground for days in advance, planning, studying the opposition carefully. He is a deep thinker.

In his first season the signs were that Arsenal were moving in a bold new direction. We made a cluster of signings: on 1 July, a sunny day at Highbury, we unveiled our two major incoming players, Marc Overmars and Emmanuel Petit. Overmars was world-class but had suffered a serious injury. We were assisted by Rob Jansen, Dennis Bergkamp's agent and, once the medical reports convinced us to sanction the deal, we knew we had an exciting talent who would have an instant chemistry with Dennis. Petit was down to Arsène, who had managed Emmanuel at Monaco. He had the idea of re-inventing a strong but stylish left back into a perfect midfield foil for Patrick Vieira.

We were unfortunately late to the party with Petit. Once Arsène mentioned him, we found that he was at Spurs, being interviewed by Alan Sugar. I made it my business to try to intercept the transfer. I managed to get hold of his agent. I actually buzzed him while he was in the meeting at Tottenham and said, 'Please don't do anything. We want to see you. Please come straight to Arsène's house from the meeting. We'll be waiting for you.'

Larios, who was also the agent who organised the Vieira deal, announced, 'We need a taxi.' Alan Sugar not only arranged but paid for the taxi that took Emmanuel Petit to Arsène's house. Every time I see Alan, I always put my hand in my pocket and say, 'What do I owe you for that cab, by the way?' To his great credit, Alan takes it in good spirit.

Naturally the French market was one Arsène knew well and he had an advantage with his contacts and reputation in a football nation that was producing outstanding talent. Petit joined Vieira and Nicolas Anelka, who had arrived a few months earlier. That deal was quite a controversial one in France, where they had a big national debate about young players moving abroad before they had played much first team football in their own country. Arsène told Nicolas he would be in our first team squad immediately, at a time at Paris Saint-Germain when he felt underused – he had such confidence in his ability even though he was only seventeen. The rules in France made it more difficult for clubs to offer teenagers professional contracts. That wasn't a problem in England.

He was a prodigious local talent so it was a tough deal. We paid around £500,000 as compensation but that was a bargain. Larios helped out again. He was responsible for some good transfers. I did the deal with PSG and it helped that I knew the people at the other end. I had good relations with Jean-François Domergue, their sporting director, who had coincidentally played with Graham Rix at Caen.

The jigsaw was coming together. With any purchase you can never be certain how it will turn out, even though obviously everyone hopes for a happy marriage, but with Overmars, Petit and Anelka, Arsène struck gold. They had a transformative impact on the team. Amongst the other signings were some promising youngsters – Luís Boa Morte, Matthew Upson and

Alex Manninger, and a couple of useful squad signings in Gilles Grimandi and Christopher Wreh to bolster the options. Most of the arrivals were in their early to mid-twenties, addressing a gap in the age of the squad.

Adding the new components of the team to the best qualities that were already in house, what happened next was extraordinary. In his first full campaign, Arsène guided Arsenal to the double. It took a while for the campaign to get going, and the crowd and team were emotional and a bit restless when we lost 3–1 at home to Blackburn in December. There were a few home truths spoken in the dressing room afterwards. The reaction was sensational. Arsenal didn't lose again in the league until the Premiership trophy was hoisted by Tony Adams. A sequence of ten consecutive victories in the title run-in was a joy. Arsenal felt unstoppable. The wind was in our sails. We enjoyed a statement win at Old Trafford where Marc Overmars scored and was a wizard on the day. Considering Man U were the dominant team at the time, having won the league four times in the previous five seasons, that game left a big impression.

We celebrated the title win with a 4–0 win against Everton in the sunshine at Highbury. Tony scored a sublime goal from a Bergkamp-esque pass from Steve Bould and that was so symbolic of the renaissance Arsène encouraged, with even hardened defenders encouraged to express themselves. Arsène ended up immortalised. Watching these scenes unfold from the directors' box was pure happiness. The first person to congratulate me was Bill Kenwright, the chairman of Everton, who gave me a bear hug and said, 'I am so happy for you, D. D. I only wish that happens to me one day.' That was a resonant thought. We are buddies and go back a long way.

The football family is always gracious to each other in moments like that. It's very rare that polite sportsmanship gets lost even in the most heated of battles. We are all competitors but nevertheless we have a duty to make sure the game is healthy. Of course it hurts when you lose but you've still got to put on a brave face and congratulate the opposition – whether it's the Wimbledon final, the Ryder Cup, or a Sunday morning game in the park – you must try to show sportsmanship.

A couple of weeks later it was FA Cup final day. There was Arsène leading the team out as was tradition. It was a colossal achievement for him – someone who, as a boy, would watch English football's showpiece on a black-and-white television that would be wheeled into the school in his village in Alsace – to make that walk onto the turf. His players did not disappoint. Two of the hotshots of the season made the difference again with acceleration that was too much for Newcastle's defence. Overmars and Anelka scored to crown a wonderful season.

To see Arsenal win the double as part of the club, when I had witnessed it as a fan, from the stands, in 1971, was poignant. I was at White Hart Lane that famous night. I could hardly see the game. I was stuck right at the top of the stand, sitting with my late brother Arnold, and when Ray Kennedy scored it was bedlam. It meant so much to Arsenal and there were fans on the pitch at the end. Five days later Arsenal had the FA Cup final against Liverpool on a boiling day at Wembley. We managed to get two tickets. My nephew, Alan, was nine years old at the time and my brother said, 'Wouldn't it be wonderful if we could get him in?'

I said, 'Yes, don't worry, we'll manage, we'll buy a ticket

outside.' I was confident – if necessary, we'd buy a ticket on the black market. There are always touts up for a fast buck but when we got to Wembley, it was mobbed and there were no tickets anywhere. You normally get people saying, 'Do you want to buy a ticket? Do you want to sell a ticket?' Nothing. We couldn't buy one. By the time it got to 2.45 p.m., close to kick-off, I said to Arnold, 'Look, you and Alan go in. Don't be late for the game. I'm sure I'll get sorted out.' I listened to the roars and the start of the game from outside. Nothing. A little after three o'clock I was walking down Wembley Way, away from the stadium, with tears in my eyes. I watched it on television at home. We beat Liverpool in extra time with the classic Charlie George goal and iconic celebration where he lies on his back on the grass with his arms outstretched.

The '98 double laid down a marker for a different way of doing things. People had been very sceptical that it was possible for an overseas coach to be successful. There was a powerful sense of vindication because we had been criticised for going for an unknown quantity in Arsène. Football is about judgement and on this wonderful occasion it was very satisfying to have made the right call and see it work out so beautifully.

I remember once somebody asked me, 'How did you know that he was the right man for the job?'

I said sarcastically, 'When he won the double in his first full season that was a pretty good clue.' You just have to have faith in people and let them get on with it.

We celebrated as the Arsenal family. At the time we were using Sopwell House, a hotel in St Albans, as a base for the play-ers. We knew the owner, Abraham Bejerano, very well. He was a big Arsenal fan and he put on a magnificent party for us – and at very short notice. You cannot pre-plan victory parties in case the result doesn't go the way you want. But he was standing by with all his staff, with the food and drink, ready to party. At full time we called him to say that if he was willing we would be on our way. He produced a banquet for five hundred people. The players, coaches, staff at Highbury, directors, and everybody's families. It was phenomenal. Ian Wright as usual was the life and soul, proudly wearing his medals round his neck. For the young players who had not long been at the club, like Vieira and Petit, it cemented that relationship and sense of belonging to the club.

May 1998 was unforgettable. At the end of the month, the Champions League final took place in Amsterdam between Real Madrid and Juventus. I arrived with Arsène and, as you can imagine, he was mobbed by autograph hunters in the lobby of the hotel. I said, 'Don't worry, Arsène, I'll check in for you.' I filled in the form, 'Name – Arsène Wenger. Address – Arsenal Football Club, Avenell Road, London. Occupation – miracle worker'. The receptionist, being a football fan, smiled, nodded and gave me Arsène's room key.

Vieira and Petit, on a high already, went on that summer to reach another summit as they won the World Cup with France. What an extraordinary few weeks. As an Arsenal man I was extremely proud to be there in Paris and watch Patrick pass to Manu in the last moments of the final for France's crowning goal as they beat Brazil 3–0.

Patrick went on to be adored by everyone but I was also very fond of Manu. He's talented and a very cerebral, deep-thinking boy, not easy to get to know. I was fortunate I got to connect with the real person. He was a true pro, and he had this routine that every game he would go to the corner of the penalty area and pick up a bit of grass and throw it up to the sky to honour his brother who had died of a heart attack on the pitch. Every week I used to watch that moment. And he just gave everything.

I was in the VIP box at the Stade de France as France celebrated victory in the World Cup, just a few weeks after we won the double. Fortunately, I was on an aisle seat in the area the players pass as they come up to get their medals. As they were coming up, I deliberately got out of my seat and stood in the aisle so Manu couldn't miss me. We met eye to eye. We gave each other a great big bear hug. It was hard to find the right words for such a monumental, once in a lifetime experience. With a broad smile I just said to him 'Quelle saison.' What a season. To this day, we greet each other with those words in recognition of a special moment for a special guy. He has a big place in my heart.

What a season, indeed.

HERE WE GROW

Every night before I fell asleep in my early teens, I sat up in bed at our home in Alyth Gardens, Golders Green, north London, and recorded the events of the day in my diary. I still keep one year, written when I was fourteen, on the coffee table at my home. Occasionally I pick it up and look at the neat handwriting, the schoolboy indignation over 'Bus Strike (Sixth Week)', the growing pains ('had boil on nose burst by doctor – ouch'), and always the love of sport, especially football. And there it is, the entry for 19 May 1958, in the locked caps I reserved for the biggest events: 'ARSENAL MANAGER JACK CRAYSTON HANDED IN HIS RESIGNATION. ARSENAL NOW MANAGERLESS.'

I wasn't surprised; results at the club were poor. But I'd boarded the Arsenal rollercoaster and for me every match was thrilling, even when we lost. My uncle Issy used to take me. We would stand in the North Bank, and I still smile when I read my excited diary entry dated 1 February 1958. 'Uncle and I had lunch and went to the Arsenal, greatest game I have ever seen. All the Arsenal team played well except for Kelsey.' (Jack Kelsey, the keeper, rarely escaped my critical schoolboy gaze.) It's a match I still remember, and the diary entry still stirs my emotions. I was privileged to be amongst the 63,578 at Highbury for a game of high drama which ended Arsenal 4, Manchester United

5. I recorded the result excitedly, '4–5!' We scored a lot of goals in those days. 'We are now middle of the league,' I added with slight disappointment.

The really serious stuff I wrote in red ink. Five days later, I recorded, 'MANCHESTER UNITED IN AIR DISASTER WHEN ON WAY BACK FROM EUROPEAN GAME'. I couldn't believe it. The whole country was shocked, but for me, young as I was, it seemed especially personal. I felt a special attachment to that United side not least because I'd just watched them play my team. I listed all the players who died, those critically injured, and Matt Busby being on the danger list. 'IT'S SHOCKING. JUST TERRIBLE. THE WORST I'VE EVER KNOWN IN SOCCER.'

Over the coming days, I willed Matt Busby and Duncan Edwards to survive. Everyone across the country did. When Arsenal's next game with Leeds was postponed because of snow on 8 February 1958, I went to support our reserves against Southend United. I didn't note down any details of the game in my diary, just, 'Observed 2 mins silences for Man United players who died'. For me, that show of respect was the most important part of the day.

I filled my diary with words of grief when Duncan Edwards passed away and then an outpouring of relief as Busby pulled through. Manchester United weren't my team, of course, but they were special. Arsenal were my team, and had been before I even saw a game, because my brother Arnold, who was eight years older than me, was a passionate fan. I'd heard his stories of going to Highbury and couldn't wait to go with him and Uncle Issy. My big brother was simply wonderful. Whatever I wanted to do, I felt he was behind me. There was no rivalry at all, no jealousy, just support – and, of course, he fired my passion for football.

My background was working class, very loving and humble, a very close-knit family. I'm proud of my roots and how all of the family have worked hard to try to succeed. My ancestors were Jewish immigrants who arrived from eastern Europe around the turn of the century with only the clothes on their back. They settled in Forest Gate, east London, where my dad Isidore supported Leyton Orient – although he was old school, big on history, and usually referred to them as Clapton Orient.

By the time I arrived in this world on 7 September 1943, my father was managing a tobacconist shop opposite Leicester Square station and didn't come home until 9 p.m. because that was West End life. So I didn't see a lot of him. But every morning, I did have a family duty to perform for him before hurrying off to school. Dad was a diabetic and he wasn't crazy on injecting insulin, so I volunteered to do it for him. Every morning, I prepared the needle with insulin and then injected it into Dad's stomach or leg. Another morning ritual was going down for breakfast and finding a freshly baked crusty roll with an initial 'D' on it. My grandfather, who was an immigrant from Poland, was a master baker who worked through the night and made sure that I had a delicious sample of his work to start my morning. (To this day, every time I go to a restaurant or hotel, I will judge it by the quality of its bread.)

I'd have an hour at night with Dad before I went to bed and, really, that hour was so special. We'd kick a ball about, or he'd tell me stories. Often when Dad came in from work he'd ring up his bookmaker. They had this blower system so he could catch the commentary, and I'd listen in, fascinated, as he had a punt on the greyhounds. 'I'll have two-twos and a two on Number 6 at Hackney Wick,' he'd say. Then sometimes I'd hear, 'Fuck it' as he slammed the phone down.

Because my dad was always late home, my uncle Issy on my mother's side was virtually responsible for bringing me up. He lived in the next road and was a bachelor, so was often round at our house. My mother used to cook for him. He was self-educated, taught himself how to play the piano, was very well-read, but most importantly, of course, he took me to Arsenal.

My dad never had a lot of money but he was generous with what he had. He would give me my two shillings pocket money for the week, then sometimes whispered, 'Do you need any more?' We used to go by bus everywhere. But when we had a day out, Dad sometimes said, 'Come on, David, let's take a taxi.' A London black cab was such a treat. Opening the big door, choosing a seat – the tip-up or the one the size of a sofa – and then instructing the driver where to go. And they always knew! By magic, they steered us directly to our destination. They had The Knowledge, and we had the privilege. I always take black cabs now in London, never Uber or one of the other fleets of hire cars.

My father's shop was on Cranbourn Street opposite the Hippodrome. I remember the venue becoming the Talk of the Town and greats like Frank Sinatra, Ella Fitzgerald and Judy Garland performed there. I felt dazzled being so close to such glitz and glamour. All the theatre managers, producers and actors came into Dad's store for cigarettes and cigars and would often give him complimentary tickets. 'What do you want to see this week, David?' Dad would say. This was my first introduction to theatre, and I began to love shows.

I'd stand outside Dad's shop and soak up all the theatreland buzz. I'd see people rushing to shows, full of excitement. I was beside myself with joy and anticipation when Dad managed to get me a ticket to a dress rehearsal of *My Fair Lady* at the Theatre Royal Drury Lane. 'Marvellous show, best I've ever seen,' was my breathless diary entry. I sat and wondered at Rex Harrison as Professor Higgins, Julie Andrews as Eliza Doolittle and Stanley Holloway as Alfred Doolittle. I even marvelled at the costumes designed by Cecil Beaton. It ran for 2,281 performances – and I got to see it before the premiere!

The curtain also went up on my passion for theatre at Orange Hill grammar school in Edgware, now Mill Hill County high school. I always volunteered to be in the Orange Hill play. If there was a good part going, I wanted it. I performed in *Julius Caesar* – as Caesar – and getting stabbed in the back was good preparation for some of my football experiences, I can tell you! I honestly believe that drama gave me courage. If I had my life again, I'd want to be a stand-up comic or an actor. I just like making people laugh. I'm not needy for attention, I've never gone out of my way to seek recognition, and I know a lot of comedians are insecure, but I just love the humour. And I owe so much to my father for feeding my passion for theatre and performance.

My mother Sybil was the main breadwinner in the family, and a huge influence on my subsequent career. She ran a small grocery shop which specialised in serving the Afro-Caribbean community in Shepherd's Bush market in west London, QPR country. My mother had developed it into a self-service super-market in the 1950s to cater for the influx of the Windrush generation. She was very adventurous for that era. Mum thought nothing of travelling to Africa and the Caribbean to source yams, sweet potatoes, okra, plantains, bread fruit, or other products rarely available in England.

She was entrepreneurial and one year she somehow managed to acquire the rights from Austrian manufacturers to sell Pez sweets in west London. Pez were a craze. Almost everyone loved them. They were these little, brick-shaped candies that popped out of a dispenser with tops in the shape of Tom and Jerry heads, or Mickey Mouse, Donald Duck, Goofy and Bugs Bunny – all the Disney A-team. Mum and my brother Arnold, who worked with her, used to come home with buckets of Pez sweets. I scooped them up, crammed them in my pocket and set off for Orange Hill.

'The Pez man's arrived!' they shouted in the playground as I swaggered in, weighed down with sweets. Everyone wanted to see the Pez dealer. I was only twelve, hardly Pablo Escobar, but I went from selling a dozen Pez a day to twenty, thirty and fifty and I now had a business going here. My mother knew, of course. She liked me having a business mind and I was doing very nicely, thank you. My diary read like a ledger at times. 'Took 18 shillings and 6 pence in the canteen'. 'Took 15 shillings at canteen'. One day I put all my money in my raincoat, as I couldn't take it into the classroom and left it there on my peg. Where else could I put it? I was hardly going to go down Mill Hill Broadway and stash it in a bank. But I learned a costly lesson at school that day: look after your money. When school finished, I went to my raincoat and there was nothing there, all the coins taken, a whole day's take. I felt as empty as my pockets. Not thinking straight, I reported the crime to the headmaster. I had busted myself for trading. Red card.

'You can't do that inside the school,' shouted the head.

My Pez racket was over.

I was an average student at Orange Hill, but English, French and maths I loved. French especially because the teacher, M. Franoux, was funny and eccentric. You've got to make lessons fun and M. Franoux did just that. He gave me a foundation for my motivational talks later in life in schools and prisons.

'Before you sit down, boys, just watch me,' he'd go. 'In this country, you don't have the "OU" sound. So repeat after me. Ur sule mur mur sur le mur. OO.' So we were all standing up, giggling, making this strange sound. 'OO!' we'd shout.

'Very good,' M. Franoux would say. 'Now in this country, you don't have the "RRRRRR" sound. Now repeat, "*Henri rit sur le souris.*"' ('Henry laughs on the mouse.') M. Franoux contorted his face to make the guttural French R sound and we loved it and learned. Whether you're a teacher, a football manager or any other sort of leader, one of the greatest skills in life is to transfer your knowledge successfully to others. A lot of footballers can be very successful players but don't make good managers because they can't convert their knowledge and experience. But look at Arsène Wenger. He managed to get his message across very easily. Maybe his academic background has something to do with it.

When I speak in schools nowadays I often think of Orange Hill. I wish I'd paid more attention in class and been more diligent. I always tell pupils, 'Your teachers are there to help you; take advantage. This is your moment in time to accumulate as much knowledge as you can which will be the launching pad for your careers. Don't lose this moment in time. It's so precious.' My mother drove me to try and do better at school. She went to educational bookshops and made sure I had next year's textbooks in advance, and with her support I passed my O- and A-levels.

My closest friend at primary school was Tony Reiff, who, fortunately for me, had a voracious appetite. I used to slip him my greens at lunch when the teachers weren't looking. I hated spinach, cabbage and broccoli and, if you didn't finish your meal, you couldn't go out to play football. I didn't like beetroot either, horrible stuff, but one day Tony was absent and I still had beetroot on my plate. I was so desperate to get outside to play football that I stuck the beetroot in my pocket. As I walked out, the teacher on lunch duty barked, 'Dein? Are you bleeding, boy?' The beetroot juice had dribbled down my leg. I was caught red-handed – or red-legged.

I once got the cane from the physics master. I dropped a bottle of sulphuric acid in the lab and it was pretty spectacular, as you can imagine, fizzing away and making very enjoyable sounds which delighted the class. Unfortunately, it also triggered a reaction in my physics master. Orange Hill was big on discipline. Teachers grabbed me by the earlobe and lifted me up at any sign of disobedience. Funnily enough, I did focus more. What really concentrated my young mind was the thought of being gated from playing sport.

I played football for Orange Hill school on a Saturday, often as captain, and for the Golders Green synagogue team in Dunstan Road, in the Association of Jewish Youth (AJY) League, on a Sunday. I was fortunate that one of my classmates, David Morris, was a very fast runner who played centre-forward. We developed a wonderful partnership: I would chip the ball forward to him and his speed would do the rest. David became my wingman socially as well. I was decent enough to play several dozen games for Hendon Boys as an enthusiastic right half, a No. 4. I even played trial matches when scouts watched. Of course, I'd have loved to have been a professional footballer because I'm obsessed with the sport and the camaraderie, but I realised when I was sixteen or seventeen that I simply wasn't good enough.

I loved watching football on 'tele', as I called it. I noted in my diary the excitement of the 1958 World Cup on the day of England's opener, against the USSR – the Soviet Union – on 8 June at the Ullevi Stadium in Gothenburg. I had a cricket fixture for Finchley against Edgware, but I got home in plenty of time to watch England because the cricket match was called off for lack of players. ('ONLY 6 OF OUR TEAM TURNED UP', I fumed to my diary. 'Shocking!')

I loved cricket – albeit not as much as football – and whenever there was a Test on I recorded the scores in my diary, even the state of the pitch. That summer of 1958, England played New Zealand, and I dreamed I could bat like Peter May or Colin Cowdrey.

In fact all sports appealed to me. On 27 May that same year, I went to the Empire Pool, Wembley to watch basketball legends the Harlem Globetrotters take apart the United States Stars 57–30. 'They were marvellous,' was my considered verdict in the diary.

A week later, Dad and Arnold were at White City to watch Brian London knock out Joe Erskine in the eighth round for the British heavyweight title. I was too young to go so I listened on the radio. I could just imagine the scene as Erskine had his eye split, and I couldn't wait to grill my father and brother about the night and the fight, and then report it in my diary.

To keep ourselves amused, every so often I'd go with my best friend Tony Reiff to Cricklewood station, which was a bus ride away, buy a one-penny platform ticket, stand on the platform all day with my *I Spy* book, and note down the trains as they flew past. Ch-ch-ch-ch, ch-ch-ch-ch, they'd go, as the wheels clattered over the joints in the tracks. (I rather miss that sound now that the rails are welded together.)

Cricklewood served St Pancras and the Midlands so these famous trains flashed through: 'Oh, that's *Mary, Queen of Scots*!' You had to be very quick, ch-ch-ch, de-de-de-de-de, as the train rattled past, to find it in the *I Spy* book. That was our day's entertainment. I've always loved trains. So much so that a few years ago my wife tried to cure me; as a surprise birthday trip, she arranged for me to drive an old steam train on the Swanage railway. Not only did I drive the train one way but coming back I had to stoke the fire and make sure there was enough steam. I still love trains almost as much as I did when a boy.

I wouldn't say I was religious. I'm proud to be Jewish but we weren't particularly observant as a family, and I'm not now. I know friends who had religion thrust on them by their Orthodox Jewish parents and they went totally the other way. We flirted with religion. I had my bar mitzvah at thirteen and that coming-of-age ritual was an important day of my life. I went to synagogue once or twice a year, but I never really became attracted to the rituals.

My brother Arnold went to Regent Street Polytechnic to study business and then helped our mother out in Shepherd's Bush. I couldn't wait to join in and, by fifteen, I was standing outside Dein's food store selling damaged tins of Christmas pudding or dented tins of beans, anything to generate a profit. My experience selling Pez had given me a taste for trading. I was ready to start climbing up the ladder.

Arnold and I decided that the business could be expanded,

and we formed 'Dein Bros. Food Importers Ltd.', rented a warehouse, and employed a few staff. Within a few years, we became the largest importers of West African and Caribbean food for distribution around the country. Whilst developing the business, we used the services of a very talented shipping agent, Roger Drew, who handled all our documentation for the produce to ensure that it arrived on time. We travelled the world together on our numerous successful adventures. Roger and I are still very close friends to this day. When eventually we sold the business, Arnold stayed on under contract for several years, while I decided to blaze my own trail in the sugar business through contacts I had made in Africa.

I've never really believed in love at first sight, but when I met Barbara Einhorn of Miami Beach, Florida, I came close.

Back in 1972, Barbara lived on Eton Terrace, working as a publicist in London, and we got fixed up by a mutual friend for a blind date. I picked her up at her flat and she got in my car and told me about her life, Miami Beach high school, Boston University, the move to London. I drove and listened and almost lost my way because all I could think about was this amazing woman next to me. She was beautiful, confident and fun. I'd been living with my previous girlfriend so it was a bit awkward because I'd had a decent relationship with her, but I felt Barbara was the one, immediately. No question.

We drove to the Empire, Leicester Square, to see the George C. Scott film *The Hospital*. As we arrived, I saw the queue wrapped all the way around the corner. I didn't have advance tickets, I thought we could just rock up. 'Hang on,' I said. I went to the person fifth in the queue with his date: 'If you buy four tickets, I'll pay.' He agreed. I think Barbara was impressed by my quick thinking. Our romantic life started at *The Hospital*!

Our next date was an Arsenal game; she had never seen a football match. 'That guy in the green jersey?' Barbara asked.

'You mean the goalkeeper? Bob Wilson. Club legend.'

'Yes, him, what does he get paid a week?'

'I don't know, a hundred pounds, if he's lucky.'

'For stopping the ball going in the net?!'

'Yes!'

'Wouldn't it be cheaper if they just boarded it up?'

I laughed because it was funny and because I was already deeply in love.

I believe in serendipity. She's special. She was special in 1972, and she still is as I write this in 2022. The fact that we've suffered each other for half a century, and are still in love, shows how intrinsically right our relationship is. We had only nine incredible dates over three months before Barbara returned briefly to the US. She didn't even know how to spell my name. I was David 'Dean' in her diary.

'Call me when you get back?' I asked. And she did, and I almost couldn't speak I was so relieved, excited and just totally, madly, deeply in love with her. 'Oh, great,' I said eventually. 'I have tickets for *Cabaret*, the movie.'

'Oh, I've just seen it in Miami,' she said. 'I don't really want to see it again, but I'll tell you what, I'll meet you afterwards for dinner.'

'Either you come for the whole evening or you don't come at all,' I insisted.

'OK, I won't come.'

'OK!' I was surprised.

'We'll go out another night.' My heart rose. And we did.

Cut to the chase, I planned the quintessential English summer day for an American. Tickets for Wimbledon, champagne and centre court, strawberries and cream, when rain stopped play. Well, I had planned the quintessential English summer day, I suppose. At least, I'd brought a present. My mother knew I was going out with someone from Miami, so she brought me a mango to give to Barbara.

'Wherever man-go, woman go!' I said to her. I wasn't sure how Barbara would take to my humour. I'm still not! I then gambled. 'Come away with me for the weekend.'

'I can't possibly come away with you. I hardly know you.' Barbara was right. We'd held hands, that was it.

'I'll take you to Sardinia. It's really beautiful weather there. I'll get you your own room, I promise. It'll be just the same as if we were going out in London. Just with better weather.'

Long pause. Then, music to my ears, 'OK!'

We flew to Costa Smeralda. I was true to my word, Barbara had her own room (sea view, not me view) and I whisked her out for dinner. Well, I was on a mission. 'Marry me!' I said. I was twenty-nine, this was the biggest decision of my life, but I knew it was right; the chemistry was right, Barbara was so right.

'And marry me now.'

There was a pause. Barbara had been engaged twice before. Third time lucky? Fortunately, the pause was brief. 'OK. But where?'

'Here.'

First thing in the morning, I contacted the British Consulate on Sardinia. A rather serious voice explained, 'Sir, you have to be resident for three months to get married in Italy.' Well, that wasn't in the plot.

'But at sea?'

I sensed the serious voice soften. 'Well, if you can find a captain who will conduct the ceremony at sea, then I suppose . . .'

'Perfect, thank you.' I rang off. 'If the boat's at sea, the captain's granted a licence to marry us. Our boat's about to come in. Well, go out, actually.'

We hired a motor-cruiser and headed out to the rather grander vessels moored off Costa Smeralda. I was in a blue, open-necked shirt and orange trousers. Barbara wore a white T-shirt mini dress and looked spectacular. Even so, I must admit we didn't exactly look like a couple about to get married.

We drew up alongside Jackie Onassis's huge yacht *Christina O*, and I had the chutzpah to ask, 'Can we come aboard and get married, please?'

Jackie was absolutely charming but she knew her sea rules. 'I'm afraid you have to stay on board for two months and be thirty miles offshore for the marriage to be valid,' came the reply.

We tried a few other boats but with no luck. Everyone wished us well. Everyone liked the idea of what I called a shotgun-boat marriage.

One captain said, 'Get married? Why don't you just live in sin?' No, I had to marry Barbara.

Some forty years later a friend was staying at the same hotel in Sardinia and noticed a photo in a book on fashion which looked remarkably like Barbara and me. Amazingly that's what it was. The two of us dancing in the hotel nightclub a few hours before I had proposed to her. He sent me a copy, and it now hangs proudly in our home.

Having failed at sea we decided to try our luck on land. Barbara called up her dad in Miami and announced, 'I've got the best news. I'm engaged. Can we get married in the back-yard of the house?' I imagined what we call a backyard in England, full of dustbins and rubbish, but Barbara explained it was the dock of a house in Pine Tree Drive with a view over Indian Creek waterway.

'Yes!'

Quite what went through her father's mind I don't know. He had never met me, or even heard of me. Given she had broken off two earlier engagements maybe he was just relieved she was finally resolved. Nor to this day do I know how her dad got through airport security when we landed in Miami. Almost as soon as Barbara had put down the phone we had packed and flown from Sardinia to London, and then straight on to Florida. There, right at the top of the steps when the aircraft door was opened, was Barbara's dad. That was quite an introduction.

We got married on 4 August 1972 in a marquee sitting on the dock of the bay. It was perfect. We wore the clothes we had had on the boat. Barbara walked down the aisle in that white T-shirt mini dress and I sported my blue, open-necked shirt and what I thought were fetching orange trousers. Even at short notice, more than a hundred people turned up, including twenty-eight from London.

It was the perfect wedding and, well, I'm so lucky, it has been the perfect marriage. I'm a great believer in the old adage of never go to bed on an argument. Stay up all night and fight! We talk and work things out.

Barbara's been phenomenally supportive and it hasn't always been easy because I was an absentee husband for quite a bit of the time. I was still working my way up the business ladder, travelling to Africa virtually every other week for three to four days. I'd always come back on the Friday night on Ghana Airways or Nigerian Airways at least to be around for the weekend. Barbara's a very understanding wife. But make no mistake, she's opinionated and a powerful character in her own right. I trust her judgement and I love her independent streak. I applaud her spending twenty years as a senior marriage counsellor, working as a Justice of the Peace and being promoted to chairing her court. She could send people to prison: Lordship Lane magistrates court was in Spurs territory . . .

Barbara's also very sporty, and despite her original bewilderment about the strange game she called soccer, she soon came with me to all of Arsenal's home games when I was on the board, and to many of the away games too. I had almost made a condition before our marriage that she had to learn all the words of 'Good Old Arsenal'; but she needed little persuasion. Barbara made sure she was by my side especially during the rough times.

After our wedding, Barbara and I returned to London and began looking for a home. A good friend of mine lived in Totteridge and recommended the place. I had a bachelor pad in St John's Wood which we quite liked but it was too small. We wanted to start a family. An estate agent showed us The Long Pond House. The seller was in and introduced himself, 'Hiya, I'm Michael Morley Joel.'

'Not the Morley Joel from Magnet Advertising?' I asked.

'Yes!'

'My late uncle used to work for you! Israel Waintraub.'

'He was my best salesman! Come in!'

Well, talk about a serendipitous moment! I got shivers. I immediately thought, I'm going to buy this house because it belongs to my uncle's boss.

But I needed help.

'I can't afford it,' I confided in my close friend and neighbour in Avenue Road, Geoffrey Kaye. He owned Pricerite supermarkets at the time.

'I'll lend it to you and you pay me back when you can,' Geoffrey said. Wow! I was able to get properly on the housing ladder. And Long Pond is where we raised our family.

CATCH HIM IF YOU CAN

And now we come to a chapter which is very painful. I have not said a word to anybody about it before. But now I am going to open my heart, which I hope will be cathartic. I've kept this wound covered up for nearly forty years.

In 1984, I was swindled out of fifteen million pounds – which is equivalent to more than a hundred million pounds today. The more I look back on that terrible time, the more it hurts. I'm angry with the conman, Rajendra Singh Sethia, who defrauded me and put my family's future at risk. I'm angry with those irresponsible banks who were actually his accomplices. And more than that, I'm angry with myself that I was too trusting. But that's life, I realise. You get reversals and it's always the same – how do you recover from a loss? Truthfully, I still bear the scars from what Sethia did. He made dealing with football agents a walk in the park.

I've always been into business, I enjoy the joust. I took inspiration from my amazing mother who set up her own business. One of Mum's sayings was, 'Shoot for the moon. Even if you miss, you'll land amongst the stars' and that's what I tried to do all my life, shoot for the moon. I was going to go to Leeds University to study French and economics but dropped out at eighteen to go into business full time with my brother, Arnold.

I owe my late brother a lot. Arnold was very devoted, very conscientious with a great sense of humour and the successful food-importing and distribution business we built up gave me the opportunity to go to Africa. When I had to go to sign Kolo Touré in Abidjan, Ivory Coast, I'd already been there! I could speak conversational French. We started small, working out of a shed in Shepherd's Bush market not far from QPR, and expanded quickly, eventually moving to a 30,000-square-foot warehouse in St Albans which Barbara decorated. The business flourished. After we sold the company I felt the time was right to do something else. Since I used to travel around the Caribbean and Africa to buy produce, I naturally made friends and contacts there. One day, when I was on a visit to Accra, I happened to know the guy running the Ghana National Trading Corporation.

'By the way, David, do you know where I can buy sugar? I need to buy ten thousand tons,' he said.

It was a challenge I couldn't resist. I sensed a chance of a contract and a new venture. On my return to London I literally looked through Yellow Pages. Everyone I spoke to was wary of any deal involving an emerging market they didn't know well.

'Let me see the colour of your money,' they said, 'let me see a letter of credit.'

So, I managed to get a letter of credit. But it was from the Ghana National Bank in London, and nobody wanted to touch it, they were scared. Except for one company, Rionda de Pass, in the City. 'We will take it on from you,' Rionda told me. 'We want a dollar a ton commission, so it will be ten thousand dollars for ten thousand tons.' They arranged all the shipping for me, we got paid, and they got their commission. From that day onwards, we worked together; Rionda were my procurement agent, I guess. I did the deals and they executed the business for me. It was an amazingly simple arrangement.

That was my entry into the sugar market. I formed my own company called London & Overseas (Sugar) Co. Limited on 13 July 1976. I built the business up, calling on all my contacts and, within a few years, I was selling half a million tons of sugar into West Africa. I took over the market. At the time, West Africa didn't have any refineries, so we sent refined sugar to Africa – for their breweries, for their sweet manufacturers, everything else. They were major consumers, particularly Nigeria: it was the biggest single market in the region. So, you can imagine, later on, when I signed Kanu in 1999 for Arsenal, I knew all about his home town, Owerri.

I was getting a name, a good reputation and people were coming to me. I had very smart offices in Pall Mall. Then one day I met Sethia, a meeting I wish had never happened. Sethia was in the commodity business, had a business in Nigeria and wanted to buy sugar. Quickly, Sethia became my best customer. He would contract for one cargo a week, of around ten thousand tons valued at the time at between seven and eight million pounds per cargo. I got on very well with him; he was an interesting guy, had studied at the London School of Economics and was certainly a flamboyant businessman. He had a beautiful house in Hendon, three Rolls-Royces and a Boeing 707. Sethia seemed a symbol of success. He had a hotel in mid-Manhattan, and a tea business in India. We socialised and I even invited Sethia to be my guest at Arsenal games. That's how close we were.

Sethia was a hard negotiator, of course. That's business. His company was called Esal Commodities and he paid on time until, all of a sudden, there was a drop in the market. I remember distinctly where I was when I got news that Sethia was not what he claimed to be: Lagos, late 1983, staying at the house of a friend who was head of Lagos Port complex. He was a wonderful guy with a magnificent house and I much preferred to stay with him when I was on business. My relaxed evening was wrecked when I received a call to say that a ship called the *Sea King* – full of sugar that I had sold to Sethia – was waiting in the harbour at Dunkirk in France. Indian banks realised they had similar bills of lading for the same cargo on the *Sea King* as well as other ships.

A bill of lading is a document of title saying you are the rightful owners of a cargo – for example, stating that you have ten thousand tons of sugar. Basically, what Sethia did with bills of lading was criminal. When my ship arrived, Sethia would use my bill of lading to go and collect it, and was also taking the bill of lading to the Punjab National Bank, getting finance for it, then taking the same bill of lading to the Central Bank of India, then doing the same with the Union Bank of India. Now the alarm bells were starting to ring. One of the banks, realising the fraud, foreclosed on him. I didn't know he was in debt and was shocked to hear he had liabilities of £170 million. He was drowning in debt brought about by fraud. It was outrageous, really, and the banks were certainly culpable. Sethia had his own ships and also used some of the bills of lading with them. It was all a scam and it was revealed when the market crashed. Sethia couldn't meet his obligations. When the banks took a close look at the *Sea King*, the house of cards collapsed and Sethia was in deep trouble.

It hurt because I always believe in being honourable. In the sugar business, you make money by taking a position. Sugar's like any other commodity, you trade it on the futures market. Because I knew I had buyers coming up for my cargoes, if I thought the market was going to go up, I'd go long. If I thought it would go down, I'd go short. I took calculated risks on cargoes because that was the commodity market. I believed everyone else involved was playing by the rules. Sethia wasn't. I didn't know that. At the time, I'd bought four cargoes, anticipating I was going to sell them. Then the banks got twitchy about the *Sea King* when Sethia's bill bounced.

I rang him from Lagos.

'What's going on?'

'Oh, I've got a little problem with the banks,' Sethia said. 'But don't worry, it'll be fine.'

And then he couldn't afford his second payment, the next cargo. I was now long in the market and Sethia was not paying for cargo he'd bought in advance. I was exposed. I'd to meet my obligations to the market.

So, 1984 was a blur of pain. I was the single largest creditor, apart from the Inland Revenue, and once they weigh in, it's tough. The taxman gets looked after first and they came piling in. I made sure I was the leading voice on the creditors' committee. The banks, the Punjab National Bank, Central Bank of India and Union Bank of India, lost fortunes over Sethia. I was furious with the bank boards, too, for not doing due diligence. Everyone I spoke to, and every article I read, suggested fraud was going on.

We served notice on Sethia. I went to Scotland Yard and they called in the fraud squad. DCI Cooper, a trusted, determined copper, was set to work. But Sethia had already fled England. He knew he was going to be made bankrupt by me. My life became a whirl of lawyers, court dates and anguish about my own liabilities and business reputation. I retained the services of the City solicitors Norton Rose to hold my hand in the proceedings. Val

Davies, one of their senior partners, led the case for me. I now knew Sethia not as a friend but as 'the respondent/judgement debtor' while I became the 'plaintiff decree/holder'.

On 3 August, we petitioned the High Court of Justice in Bankruptcy in London to take action. The court passed a receiving order in November against 'the respondent/judgment debtor'. The court noted we had 'lodged a claim in the sum of £22,666,919.69 in personal bankruptcy of the judgment debtor' with an accountancy firm and experts in bankruptcy, Stoy Hayward. On 7 November, we got Esal wound up with debts of $350 million. The net was closing in, or so I thought – but Sethia was on the run and the bankruptcy notice had to be served personally. I talked to Norton Rose, the lawyers, who dispatched a very nice guy, Dermot Hanna – quite a stocky guy – on the chase. Dermot was the process server.

'I've had word that Sethia's at the Lew Hoad tennis club in Mijas, near Marbella,' I told Dermot. 'What you've got to do is get the papers, you've got to meet him and you've got to serve it on him.' OK, Dermot knew his job, but I was by now obsessed with catching Sethia and bringing him to justice. Dermot flew to Marbella and three days later, I get a call.

'David, job done.'

'What happened?'

'Sethia was having a game of tennis with the coach and I said to him, "Would you mind having a knock-up with me?" So, he started knocking up with me and I called him to the net. As he came to the net, I pulled out the papers and I said, "Here's a service you won't be able to return!"' What a delivery from Dermot! Game, set and match! I had to laugh.

That document officially made Sethia bankrupt and he

landed up in the *Guinness Book of Records* as the single largest bankrupt in the world at the time. He always wanted to be number one for something.

Sethia never came back to the UK. He had a nice wife, kids and I felt for them, as any human would, because Sethia was just leading a fantasy life. It was like the film *Catch Me If You Can*. I never spoke to Sethia again. What could I have said to him? Shout at him? Scream at him? That's not me. Anyway, it wouldn't have made any difference, it wouldn't have brought the money back.

Sethia owned a plane, property, cars, racehorses and businesses, including Esal Bookmakers (appropriately, he was a heavy gambler). The plane and a few other items were repossessed, but most of the money had gone on Sethia's lavish lifestyle. In the end, I regained 2p in the pound, nothing really, even though we spent a lot of time chasing, chasing, chasing.

Sethia himself, meanwhile, was still on the run, living in Dubai for quite a while. Then he got picked up in India, for having a false passport, of all things. Not for fraud! Once they had him, the Indian authorities wanted him kept under police remand to force him to reveal who had benefited from his money. They believed there was fraud going on within some of the banks. Sethia tried to defend himself in court. He claimed he'd travelled to India to gather the money to repay the loans. He even had the nerve to blame London & Overseas Sugar for an alleged rescue package from Indian banks falling through. He was a fantasist. Back in the real world, Sethia damaged me terribly.

During insolvency proceedings against him in London, I said, 'As long as there is any breath in my body I shall follow Sethia.'

The chase obsessed me for a while. It was more the principle than the money.

I spent an inordinate amount of time going to creditors' meetings and Scotland Yard. They told me, 'Sethia's a fugitive from justice.' I knew that. I wanted him back in London to face the music. The fraud squad had contacted India's Central Bureau of Investigation (CBI) in New Delhi to request Sethia's extradition. I was frustrated the Indians didn't send him back to England. They had him. We wanted him. The crime was committed here, not India. Sethia remained in India, where he was grilled by the CBI. They wanted information on possible collusion and corruption in Indian banks. This was a huge scandal in the Indian financial community and there were some sudden retirements of senior figures within the banks. The CBI suspected that a dozen employees of the three banks had loaned Sethia money on the fake bills of lading.

I lost patience and went to the Bank of England. Fortunately, I happened to know a director, Mervyn King – later the governor – who I used to see in the boardroom of Aston Villa, as he was a fan of the club. Mervyn kindly put me in touch with the right people. I told them, 'You gave these banks licences but they're not fit to trade in England. They're clearly not reputable.' Of course, the horse had bolted, the damage was done, but I was full of anger over what had happened to me and felt it was a matter of principle, really, that action should be taken. Some of the people in the Punjab National Bank were in Sethia's pay, according to the press in India. They gave him credit lines which he didn't merit. Whether or not that was true, I didn't know.

The Bank of England agreed that the three Indian banks

should explain the actions of their London branches. The Reserve Bank of India became involved, too, and they and the Bank of England ordered the Punjab National Bank, the Central Bank of India and the Union Bank of India to close their London branches. It felt a massive triumph although it didn't get me my money back!

Sethia got slammed into prison, and not a particularly pleasant one. Tihar jail in Delhi was hardly the Ritz. Charles Sobhraj, the international serial killer known as the Serpent, was in Tihar at the same time. He was surrounded by gangsters, terrorists and rapists and was in there a long time. When Sethia got out, he tried to paint himself as a victim. He talked of his personal losses – he had lost his first two wives to divorce and his third wife to a car crash. Look, anyone would have sympathy for somebody's personal issues but this was purely professional. There should be a film about it and there will be at some stage; somebody will pick it up, it deserves to be, but every cinema-goer will assume it's fiction. It's not. It's real.

Sethia owed me about fifteen million pounds. I had some money of my own that I'd accumulated but even so, having been a comparatively wealthy guy, my debts stood at eleven million pounds. But I had to get on with life. I was the bread-winner for the family. I had to make sure that, whatever happened, we were successful.

I wasn't being paid by Arsenal, so I kept on trading in sugar for several years. I made a compromise deal with all my credi-tors. Fortunately, they trusted me, which was important. I will always be grateful for the sympathy and support of the industry. They realised I'd opened up a market almost single-handedly and knew I was the biggest exporter of sugar to Nigeria. They wanted to help and it suited them that I kept supplying that market.

'Look, I'm going to trade out of this somehow,' I told them. 'Bear with me.' I did trade my way back. But I had to work doubly hard to make sure that they were repaid. That was a point of principle for me. I was determined that nobody else would suffer. I paid them all back, everybody. They were my trading partners and I always pride myself on my loyalty to people. One of the companies we were doing business with in Antwerp – one of the refineries, very nice people, Sucre Export, now known as Group Sopex – bought London & Overseas out for several million. That gave me a bit of breathing space.

I still needed cash and between 1995–6 I sold eight thousand Arsenal shares to an old friend, the diamond dealer and fan Danny Fiszman. That saddened me as I felt I was cutting away part of the club I loved. I wanted to make a mark but I had this heavy weight on me, really pulling me down. I didn't go to work for Arsenal full time until 1989, although I was spending more and more time there, but the Sethia saga continued to take its toll on me. At least when I was able to commit myself fully to Arsenal it was just in time for us to win the title in glorious style at Anfield. I managed to focus on Arsenal which was such a delight and camouflaged the dark period in my business.

Mentally, Sethia's fraud left a scar, but I had to show strength to the outside world, which I did, I think. I always see good in people rather than bad. I just felt badly let down by somebody I trusted implicitly.

With a heavy heart, I kept pursuing the case. I remember

listening to Lord Justice Peter Gibson on 19 November 1993, in the court of appeal in London, outlining the case we were trying to bring against Punjab National Bank, who were Esal's principal bankers from 1980. The court heard that Punjab National Bank was 'knowingly a party to the carrying on of the business of Esal . . . with intent to defraud creditors and for other fraudulent purposes'. We desperately wanted to show how badly we felt Punjab National Bank's London branch had acted. We were trying to make the bank liable for Esal's debts.

It was serious legalese but made clear sense. The court then heard, 'The liquidators therein alleged that Esal had traded fraudulently since 31 March 1981, that the bank participated in that fraudulent trading and that in consequence Esal was enabled to continue trading and to incur ever-increasing credit from and liabilities to its creditors.'

I felt the judge said it all when he mentioned that 'a remarkable amount of litigation against the bank has been spawned in consequence of the bank's involvement with Esal'. It felt chilling to hear the judge read out the sums we claimed Esal owed us, including 'a proof for £5,764,392 lodged by L&O and one for £7,447,052 lodged by Mr Dein'. I knew how bad it was, but to hear those figures in court shocked me again.

It was a really dark period in my life. I was a high flyer and now here I was, hitting rock bottom. This shook me. I'm quite a proud person. Am I bitter deep down? I'm hurt, I'm wounded because of it. I try not to think about what happened because it simply re-opens the wounds. That festers. I want the sun to shine, I don't need darkness in my life and despite what happened, I have not lost my trust in people.

Anybody who's successful, they've all had a reversal; maybe it's God's way of saying 'It's time to appreciate what you have in life.'

After that I *had* to be successful.

Now that I have told the story, I promise myself it will never see the light of day again in my mind. I only want positivity.

CATS AND DOGS

'I'd like you to meet a friend of mine – he's an up-and-coming theatrical producer.' So said the dancer I was dating in 1969. She was in The Young Generation, the BBC troupe who did TV specials with Val Doonican, Lulu and Shirley Bassey. They were wildly popular at the time. I had the good fortune to be dating Linda, who knew loads of people in show business, and she was very keen I meet this producer friend of hers.

'You love theatre, David, you'd enjoy meeting him.'

Well, I'll admit I was a bit surprised by her friend, who had holes in his trousers and his shirt was hanging out; not really my idea of a West End musical impresario. Anyway, I listened to him. He was twenty-three and full of energy.

'I love musicals and I want to do a revival of *Anything Goes*,' he said. 'We'll do a short tour and then West End. But I need money. Linda said you may be interested in backing me.'

This was a Cole Porter classic, packed with great songs: 'You're the Top', 'I Get a Kick Out of You' and, of course 'Anything Goes' itself. I found myself almost singing them as I thought about the proposition.

'OK, what do you need?'

'Twenty thousand pounds.'

'OK, I'll help.' And so I became an 'angel'. It was an investment and I'd recoup my outlay if the musical did well, plus a share of the profits. It was more than that, though. I loved going to shows as a kid with the comps that producers gave Dad. I loved being in shows at school. Now I could be involved.

The producer cast Marion Montgomery as Reno Sweeney, the nightclub singer. I knew Marion as an accomplished jazz singer, a fixture at Ronnie Scott's club and regular on Michael Parkinson's celebrated chat show. Good signing, I thought. *Anything Goes* went on all over the country. It was quite exciting. I felt it was building up steam before taking London by storm. Then the producer came back.

'David, we're a bit short of money. Salaries. I'm going to need another twenty thousand pounds and I'm prepared to give you a bigger share.'

'OK, let me see what I can do.'

Look, it was a new world but I believed him – and I was in love with the idea.

'Thanks, David. I'll tell you what I'll do, I'll make you co-producer.'

'Thank you very much!'

From being a little investor I was co-producing and taking off in the West End. I was an angel with wings. *Anything Goes* opened in London on 18 November 1969 at the Saville Theatre on Shaftsbury Avenue. I stood outside and looked at the venue. The Beatles had performed here, so did Chuck Berry and Jimi Hendrix. The Rolling Stones were booked in for a couple of gigs. But now it was ours. *Anything Goes* was up in lights. I looked at the bill. My name was there: 'In association with David Dein'! I'd invited all my friends and was bursting with pride.

It was a decent production and the audience seemed to enjoy it. But I learned you're at the mercy of the reviewers. One of the headlines in the *Evening Standard* was 'ANYTHING GOES THE SOONER THE BETTER'. So I knew we were in trouble. The show was largely set on a boat – we were sinking fast.

'We're in big trouble here, David,' the producer said. 'The advance bookings are not good, do you want to put in some more money . . .'

I interrupted him. 'No thanks, I've put my money in. That's it.'

'Well, we'll have to pull it off next week. You're the business-man here, do you mind telling the cast?'

What?! 'Me? Tell the cast?!'

'Yes, you can do it.' He pushed me forward. I went to Marion Montgomery's dressing room at the Saville. I mean, this was a new challenge, informing a star that the final curtain was about to fall.

'Marion, I've bad news,' I told her. 'I'm afraid the advance bookings are just not good enough and we're going to have to pull the show next week.'

A flower vase whizzed past my head. I ducked but I under-stood. This was Marion's career, her life, her passion. Marion was a star. But the reviews killed us. *Anything Goes* ran for fifteen more performances. Then Anything Went. The money went, too, but I had enjoyed the journey. It was exciting. It was an introduction to show business at a high level. I was working my way up in life and this was a fun sideline.

On the last night, the producer, Linda's friend, came up to me and said, 'I'll make it up to you. I'm going to be a success. You wait and see.'

Almost a decade later, I received another call from the producer.

'I've a new idea,' he said. 'You must come and see me because you were so good to me early on. I've got an office above the Fortune Theatre in Covent Garden.' Barbara and I were out for dinner in town so we popped in to see him. The room was tiny. The producer could scarcely squeeze the three of us in. 'Listen to this song,' he said. There was no melody. It was just one guy singing. I listened to the chorus. 'And we all say, Oh! Well, I never! Was there ever a cat so clever as magical Mr Mistoffelees.'

He rose from his desk and began leaping around the room. 'Look, it's about the alley cat and then, all of a sudden, you got the street cat and then you got the cat in the back garden.' Yes, the producer was none other than Cameron Mackintosh.

'Hold on, Cameron. What is this all about?'

'Cats! It's all about cats! Look, David, for £75,000, you can have 20 per cent. And the overseas rights. We will sort it out because I owe you something.'

I then uttered the words that will haunt me for the rest of my life, words of which my family are very fond of reminding me. 'Cameron,' I said, grandly, 'we are a nation of dog lovers.'

And I turned down *Cats*.

The West End production of *Cats* opened at the New London Theatre on Drury Lane on 11 May 1981 and ran for twenty-one years and 8,950 performances. And, yes, I know it's since been revived in the West End twice. *Cats* has more than nine lives, I've learned! So every time I see Cameron in a restaurant once or twice a year, I walk past his table and say, 'You know we're a nation of dog lovers!' You have to laugh, don't you?

I love theatre because it's live and the actors go out there and there's no safety net. Like football I guess. You have to deliver live. And I often refer to football as live theatre. If Barbara was busy playing Scrabble, I would regularly come out of Highbury after a hard day in the office and head off on my own to a local theatre like the Hen and Chickens, Almeida, King's Head or the Park Theatre behind Finsbury Park tube. It was escapism and for a fiver or so, you'd go in and often see very good theatre that would ultimately go into the West End or on a national tour. One of the best plays I saw at the Park in 2015 was *Dead Sheep* by Jonny Maitland, a big Charlton Athletic supporter, about Margaret Thatcher's downfall. I remember watching that thinking, This should be on in the West End. *Dead Sheep* did go on tour after breaking the box-office record at the Park.

I can relax in the theatre. There's so much less pressure being an angel than a football director. I could never relax at a match. My children, as I see the players, are playing out there, so I'm emotionally engaged, there's so much at stake. If they struggle, I get upset because you're paying good salaries. And I always felt responsible for the tens of millions of Arsenal fans around the world. I'm carrying their weight on my shoulders. It's different in the theatre, it's seven nights a week, it's well-rehearsed, it's easier, it's another performance just like the last.

I even managed the impossible in the West End. I got Arsène Wenger to come to a musical. Arsène very rarely went out. He is a very private man who didn't much like to venture far from Totteridge. One day, shortly after he finished at Arsenal in 2018, I said, 'Come on, Arsène, you have to come and see this West End show. I know you'll like it.'

It was *Tina: the Tina Turner Musical*, which opened at the Aldwych Theatre on 17 April 2018. I knew Arsène loved her songs. The Arsenal players told me he would play 'Simply the Best' on the coach heading to games. As we stood outside, I said, 'Look up, Arsène. It's a theatre, not a football stadium! This must be your debut.' By the end of the show, Arsène was up out of his seat, punching the air to 'Nutbush City Limits'. He loved it.

I was even given the privilege of being named chairman of a group that gave young producers and performers a helping hand, the Theatre Investment Fund, which morphed into a charity called Stage One. Suddenly, I was mixing with council members such as Dames Thelma Holt, Judi Dench and Maggie Smith, Lord Attenborough and Cameron Mackintosh were patrons. I was catapulted into a world of people who ran theatres or performed in them, encouraging the next generation as I'd done with Liam Brady's amazing youth team at Arsenal. The fund handed out bursaries up to fifteen thousand pounds and organised apprenticeships so they could work with the National Theatre or Andrew Lloyd Webber's Really Useful Group.

I only had to attend a meeting every two months so I didn't take my eye off the ball at Arsenal. The charity provided a diversion from the pressure of match day, as did spending time with Bill Kenwright, the Everton chairman and West End producer. I met him through his then girlfriend, Koo Stark, who was living over the road from us in Totteridge at the home of Robert Windsor, a colourful character who used to throw showbiz parties. Koo and I arranged a dinner at Langan's Bistro in Marylebone, after an Arsenal reserve game.

'How did you do?' Bill asked. 'How did Rixy do?' Graham Rix was coming back from injury. We bonded immediately. We've become close buddies. Barbara and I always attend Bill's first nights. Even now, I ring him up and ask, 'Bill, what's good coming up in the West End?'

When Bill was negotiating to buy out Peter Johnson to take control of Everton in 1999, he rang me. I was in hospital having just had a hernia operation and was still doubled up and, frankly, bloated. Bill asked me how I was and then almost immediately said, 'I don't know whether I can do the deal, David.' He explained a few of the figures and how he was a bit short of what Johnson wanted. Bill was almost in as much agony as I was. I found the doctor and told him I had to discharge myself. It was important to be there for Bill, he's a mate. I sat in Bill's garden in Maida Vale, and listened to him prevaricating. I stopped him.

'Bill, you've got to buy the club. It's your dream.'

'Well, I haven't got all the money.'

'Let's work it out.' We juggled the figures and Bill was eventually able to buy out Johnson.

I've been lucky to make many friends in show business. One of my closest mates was the TV presenter Jeremy Beadle, a Gooner. Jeremy was a very misunderstood and underestimated guy. Yes, he was a prankster who was expelled from school and people thought he was just a joker. Jeremy was actually widely read: I went to his home in Hadley Wood and saw the size of his library, literally thousands of books, all of which he'd read and written notes in. I once visited his grave in Highgate cemetery, north London, which appropriately has four books carved into the headstone.

Jeremy was self-taught but had such a quick mind that he wrote many books himself and starred in quiz shows. But people just associate him with *Beadle's About*, where he played practical jokes on passers-by. He had that mischievous side to him, of course. In restaurants, Jeremy would pull out a little John Bull printing set and stamp 'Lucky winner, free meal' on the napkin.

'Excuse me,' Jeremy would ask the waitress or waiter at the end of the meal. 'What does this mean? "Lucky winner"? Clearly, I've won a prize here, what do I get?!' Jeremy would only spin it out for a bit.

I did a reverse scam on Jeremy one day. He was coming by car to Highbury, it was raining heavily and I said to the stadium manager, John Beattie, 'Look, when Jeremy comes, I want you to put up a board saying "Game postponed".'

When Jeremy tried to drive in, we filmed as the gate steward said, 'I'm sorry, Mr Beadle. As the sign says, the game's off. I'm afraid you can't come in, you'll have to go back home. The pitch is waterlogged.'

Jeremy was furious. 'What are you talking about? There are other people coming in.' They eventually let him in – when we'd got the footage we wanted. I enjoyed showing it to Jeremy. We wanted to give him some of his own medicine! Watch out, Dein's about.

Although my theatre investment was not a resounding success for me, most unexpectedly I managed to ride another horse which proved to be a winner.

In the early 1980s one of my closest friends, Geoffrey Kaye, invited me to share an investment with him in a horse racing stable in Newmarket, run by Paul Kelleway. Although I knew nothing about horse racing, I thought it might be fun.

Within five years, we were regulars in the Winner's Enclosure at Royal Ascot, standing next to the Queen, often with horses ridden by Lester Piggott. Indeed we won the Prix de Diane at Longchamps with a horse called Madam Gay ridden by Pat Eddery. I live by the saying: 'You'll never win the raffle if you don't buy the ticket'. We had a remarkable few years but the game changed when yearlings were traded for huge money by overseas investors. This was perhaps a signal for what was about to happen in the world of football.

SERVING MY APPRENTICESHIP

It was Uncle Issy who took me to my first match. Arsenal of course: it was in my family's blood. Issy was very influential in my life and introduced me to concerts and theatre. But it was football that thrilled me most.

Uncle Issy would write to the box office for tickets, which would come back with a compliments slip that I used to collect for the Arsenal cannon logo. Eventually, we managed to get season tickets, first in the lower East Stand and then the upper East Stand – we were graduating within the club. By the late 1970s I was fortunate enough to own one share. That was a major turning point. It gave me a certificate, which I put proudly on my wall, but it also gave me access to the accounts. Every year, I would get the financial records and study how the club was doing.

On one occasion, I noticed, fortuitously, that 15 per cent of the club's capital equity had not actually been issued. For some unknown reason the club was still sitting on a sizeable chunk of unissued shares. In the summer of 1983 I made my first move towards having a meaningful involvement with the club, as more than a supporter. I was not well known to the hierarchy. I didn't know the board. I had met vice-chair Clive Carr socially once, but I didn't have any real connections. I wrote a handwritten letter to the chairman, Peter Hill-Wood. I outlined a bit about myself and my intentions: I've been an Arsenal fan all my life. I'm a current season-ticket holder and had some success in the sugar business and feel that I've got something to contribute because of my commercial acumen. It's a club that I love dearly. I'd like to contribute in some way and be more deeply involved. I am interested in buying the 15 per cent shares.

This was during the era when football was not a glamorous sport. Totally the opposite. Hooliganism was a terrible blight on the game, most stadia were unwelcoming and old, and we were heading for the Heysel and Hillsborough tragedies. The total turnover of Arsenal Football Club was about £1.5 million. Today, a single player in the Championship would get that in wages.

I've always lived by my own motto, the motto of the turtle – you don't get anywhere unless you stick your neck out! I had the temerity to really stick my neck out. I enclosed a blank cheque with my letter. I thought, What have I got to lose? They are not going to run off with my money. With an open-ended offer, at least they'll take me seriously.

I was waiting for a letter to come back. Instead, I got a call from general secretary Ken Friar. He invited me to lunch. I was getting somewhere, and Ken must have been deputed by the board to sound me out. He took me to a little Spanish restaurant near the club just off Avenell Road and discreetly – as only Ken can – checked my intentions, undressed me financially, and formed a view of whether or not I was worthy to be involved with the club.

I could understand that. The club clearly needed to make sure I would be suitable. There is a wonderful line from Leonard

Cohen's song 'Anthem', 'There is a crack in everything. That's how the light gets in.' I sensed the light coming in.

Next, came an invitation to meet the entire board in the renowned oak-panelled boardroom. Here was my chance to impress them with my vision. I arrived at the Marble Halls and, for the first time in my life, entered the inner sanctum, past the statue of Herbert Chapman, up the elegant staircase and through the imposing, solid door into the boardroom. To me, it epitomised the aura that inspired the nickname the 'Bank of England club'. I felt as if I could have been going into the Bank of England itself. It had that feel of quiet, stately, English power. The board included three knights of the realm. There was so much history and I almost pinched myself, thinking, I'm the boy from Temple Fortune who used to stand in the North Bank. What am I doing here? I just liked seeing Derek Tapscott score a goal.

Peter Hill-Wood chaired the meeting. His brother-in-law Tony Wood was on the board along with Sir Roger Gibbs, a financier and an old Etonian schoolfriend of Peter's. There was Sir Robert Bellinger, a former mayor of London, Sir Stuart McIntyre who was in insurance, and the two Carr brothers. Ken Friar was there as general secretary, with David Miles his number two.

I recall Bellinger and McIntyre did not get on. One wanted a television on in the boardroom and the other didn't. Anyway, they were all polite and dignified, and I thought it went well enough. Afterwards I met Peter Hill-Wood privately and felt it was time to try to agree a deal. I said, 'Look, I've got no idea what the shares are worth. You tell me. Let's agree a figure.' And that was it. We agreed a number there and then. Something in the region of £275,000.

Did I ever think that I'd get a return on my investment? It never crossed my mind. In fact, at the following AGM, Peter Hill-Wood came straight out saying, 'It's dead money. I don't know why he's doing it.' Frankly, I also thought it was dead money. I wanted to invest because I loved Arsenal and wanted to be involved and be a part of the decision-making process.

I remember Peter saying on my first day, 'Don't get too excited when we win, and don't get too depressed when we lose, because you get plenty of both.' It was memorable and one of the best pieces of advice I ever had. I always tell it to anybody else who buys into a football club.

I got on famously with Peter and loved his understated sense of humour. To his great credit, he gave me extraordinary latitude. He could see I was keen and he allowed me to run with the ball. Although nominally chairman he seemed happy to take a back seat. In fact, soon after I joined the club he offered me the chair. I declined on the basis that I felt that we were known as the Bank of England club and he epitomised that air of quiet authority. Perhaps I made a mistake. In any case, he effectively allowed me to take charge. If he was happy with that so was I. I'm not a good backseat driver.

The club for which I took virtual responsibility was struggling. It was 1983 and the season before had not been particularly inspiring. In an attempt to solve Arsenal's shortcomings in front of goal they had recruited two forwards for half a million pounds each, Lee Chapman and Tony Woodcock. But that was not enough to push Arsenal any higher than a tenth-placed finish and they were dumped out of both domestic cups by Manchester United. That season Arsenal played Spartak Moscow in the UEFA Cup and were thumped 8–4 on aggregate. The

A talented midfielder who didn't quite make it to the top!

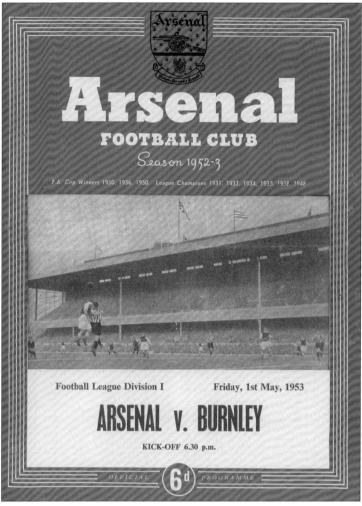

Arsenal v. Burnley, May 1953. Where the love affair started – aged nine.

Captain of the U12s at Orange Hill Grammar School. A good team but the keeper was vulnerable to high crosses!

Mum and Dad, 1950.

On holiday with my Dad and older brother Arnold.

My diary entry, February 1958. Written in red are my reflections on the Manchester United air disaster in Munich.

Learning to trade in Lagos Market, 1965.

Imitating James Bond.

A few hours before proposing to Barbara. Despite my dance moves, she surprisingly said yes!

Brother Arnold wishing me luck.

The beginning of another love affair – wedding August 1972.

The Mural, 1992. The game against Norwich was so bad, fifteen people in the mural walked out.

1992–93: the 'Double-Cup' season. Holding the League Cup with George Graham and Ian Wright. The parade had been organised before we won the FA Cup replay against Sheffield Wednesday 2–1.

Starting as we mean to go on. Arsène's double in his first full season, 1998.

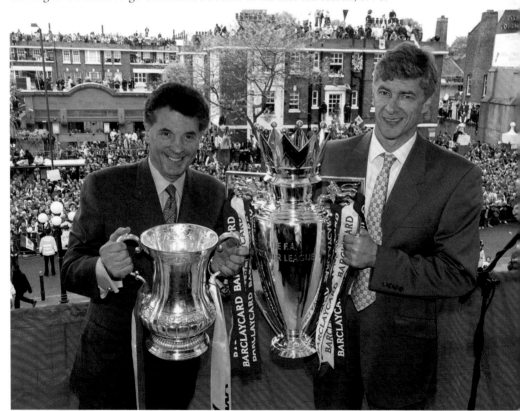

Continuing what we started, 2002.

The 'Five Conspirators' who founded the Premier League.

| Martin Edwards (Manchester United) | Irving Scholar (Tottenham Hotspur) | DD (Arsenal) | Noel White (Liverpool) | Sir Philip Carter (Everton) |

David is Goliath behind Arsenal double

FORGET Arsene Wenger – David Dein is the architect of Arsenal's storming League and Cup double.

No disrespect to the French genius, who has crafted one of the most exciting teams ever to have played football. But without Dein there would have been no Wenger at Highbury.

Dein is the business brain behind the Gunners and the man who has steered Arsenal to a position where they can seriously rival the previously invincible Manchester United.

Dein was the man who persuaded Wenger to give up coaching in Japan for the high-octane pressures of a job in the Premiership.

He was instrumental in negotiating the signings of top players such as Dutch mastermind Dennis Bergkamp.

And, critically for Gunners fans who cannot get tickets to watch their team in Arsenal's cramped Highbury home, he has masterminded plans for a huge new stadium at Ashburton Grove.

Dealing

Dein gets little credit for his work but prefers it that way.

He is a private, almost shy man who comes from a hard-working Jewish background.

His family were poor immigrants from eastern Europe who arrived in London's East End in the early 1900s.

Dein's father, Isidore, forged a career in tobacco – allowing young David to grow up in relatively prosperous Golders Green.

As a child, he was a regular at Arsenal games but – as a part time market trader – was also showing a flair for wheeling and dealing.

His friends were not surprised when he dropped out of university to build up the family food trading business launched by his mother Sybil of importing special foods from the Caribbean for newly arrived immigrants who were homesick.

The business made David a multi-millionaire after it diversified into sugar and commodities trading, espe-

cially with Nigeria. It was this wealth which allowed David to buy into Arsenal in August, 1983 – paying £290,250 for a sixth of the club.

In those days football was still a game watched by supporters crammed on rain-swept terraces in dilapidated stadia and run on the whole, by small-time local businessmen with little ambition other than ruling the roost in oak-panelled boardrooms.

Arsenal was run by Peter Hill Wood, an old Etonian banker whose family had owned the club since the 1920s.

Hill-Wood chortled that the investment was "dead money." Never was he more wrong – even though Dein has sold off most of his £6.4 per cent stake to his friend, Danny Fiszman, he still retains a holding worth many times what he originally paid.

When he joined Arsenal's board the club's annual turnover was just £2mil-lion – but Dein soon changed that.

He created a commercial department, giving up his other business interests to become a full time paid director of the club allowing Arsenal to generate more cash for the first time from commercial activities than

from gate receipts. He made enemies too. Former Gunners manager Terry Neill claimed he had been undermined by Dein's close friendship with key players such as Kenny Sansom and Graham Rix.

Neill's successor Don Howe also blamed Dein for his eventual departure, which came amid claims Dein had offered his job to Terry Venables.

Dein also spent the fans by launching a controversial bond scheme to raise money towards stadium improvements while also rattling cages in the football establishment.

Suspicions

He was booted off the league's management committee in 1988 after holding talks with ITV over a new telly deal – raising suspicions he had tried to stitch up other clubs in favour of the so-called 'Big Five' of Liverpool, Everton, Manchester United, Arsenal and Tottenham.

It was these talks which ultimately led to the creation of the Premier League in 1992.

And, although Dein has been credited for his role in the creation of the

Premiership, critics point out he mis-takenly tried to sell TV rights to ITV instead of satellite broadcasters BSkyB which is 36 per cent owned by The Sun's owner, News Corporation.

Had ITV won those rights, it is doubtful English football would have received the millions which allowed it to attract the world's top footballers.

There have been other crises for Dein to face down, with 1990 an especially bad year. Not only was there the George Graham bung scandal but Dein also had to sell some of his Arsenal shares.

This was to finance a court case in which he tried to recover debts from a commodities dealer whose company had collapsed costing Dein's business, London & Overseas Sugar, a fortune.

Dein eventually got most of his money back but the episode led him to abandon his other business activities in favour of Arsenal.

The rest is history.

Dein persuaded Wenger to become manager after Bruce Rioch's year at the helm and Arsenal went on to do the League and Cup double in 1998 and again this week.

Neutral football fans will worry that although Manchester United's monopoly on silverware has been broken, the Old Trafford cartel has been replaced by another club set to domi-nate the game.

But Dein is also proud that his Eng-lish superstars should be grateful for Dein's influence. He is also a vice-chairman of the game's governing body, the Football Association.

And it was at that role, two years ago, that he persuaded Steve Coppell-Eriksson to become England manager.

Dein's legacy we shall be even more grateful come the end of June.

IAN KING

Gunners boss's top quotes

● ON INSPIRATIONAL MANAGER ARSENE WENGER: "When he took over as manager five years ago some people said 'Arsene who?' – but he's changed football in this country.

"I call him a miracle worker because he makes an average player into a great player, a good player into a very good player and a very good player into a world class player."

● TO THE FA COMMITTEE WHEN KEVIN KEEGAN QUIT AS ENGLAND BOSS: "There's only one man for this job, the Lazio manager Sven Goran Eriksson."

● ON SALARY CAPS FOR PLAYERS: "It is unworkable. The market we operate in makes it a problem.

"People would find a way round the caps and that would destroy the system."

● ON SUGGESTIONS THE FA SHOULD BAIL OUT CLUBS HIT BY ITV DIGITAL COLLAPSE: "The FA is not a depository. It is there for the good of 40,000 member clubs."

The Sun shines, 1998.

Greg Dyke – the man who gave us the confidence to form the Premier League.

Profile
DAVID DEIN

JOB: Vice-chairman, Arsenal FC
AGE: 58, (born September 7, 1943)
EDUCATION: Orange Hill Grammar School, Edgware; Leeds University
FAMILY: Married to Barbara Einhorn for 30 years. Children Darren, Gavin and Sasha.
HOBBIES: Tennis, football
LIVES: London
PAY: Not disclosed
WORTH: Estimated to be £35million

A family affair ..

'Rocky' Rocastle's legs: serving as a coffee table and now a permanent memory in my office.

A gamble that paid off. Thierry Henry's first press conference, 1999.

Russians were applauded off the pitch at Highbury by the home supporters.

In the twelve years that had passed since the famous 1971 double, Arsenal had won only one FA Cup. I wanted to turn the dial and get a bit more energy into the place, and I felt I could offer a broader vision than was typical in English football board-rooms at the time. I had travelled fairly extensively and I had seen other countries developing their sport.

At the October AGM, my appointment onto the board was officially ratified. I came in with a bit of publicity. One headline called me 'Action Man'. I guess that gave me more resolve.

Barbara struggled to understand why I watched quite so many games but I wanted to be involved in everything that concerned the club at every level. She used to say, 'Why is it that you see the youth team, the senior team, the women's team? Every team that ever plays, you are there.'

Faced with a difficult question, you can't beat a one-liner. 'Well,' I said, 'they can't start without me. I've got the ball.'

Within a month of joining I faced my first test. By December 1983, Arsenal were in crisis mode. Manager Terry Neill had been losing his grip, and the club was now conceding games left, right and centre. I was also aware that the players were losing confidence in Terry. Although I was new in the directors' box I had previously struck up a friendship with some of the players, notably Graham Rix, Willie Young and Tony Woodcock. In fact they used to invite me into the players' lounge – a wonderful thing in those days. Football is a bit of a gossipy business and before long I was almost the agony aunt. Obviously, once I was on the board, I had to distance myself from those friendships which was not easy. The other board members would have thought it inappropriate and in any case friendship with some players would risk being seen by others as favouritism.

Terry reached the end of the road in the League Cup at Highbury when Arsenal lost to Walsall, who were struggling in the Third Division. That day we had just signed Tommy Caton from Manchester City and he was sitting next to me in the directors' box. The result was a profound humiliation. Within seconds of Walsall going ahead, after some poor Arsenal defending, the crowd starting jeering and chanting, 'What a load of rubbish!' It was time to get my first experience of sacking a manager and dealing with the effects of a team in trouble.

After the match ended we could hear a growing commotion coming from the streets. The area outside the Marble Halls down on Avenell Road was always the main place for people to congregate. Just to the right were the windows of the dressing room, and one floor up from there the boardroom. We could all get a very clear sense of the atmosphere outside. An unhappy crowd made their feelings known, chanting 'Sack the board' and sack me. That was an eye-opener, to hear somebody chanting, 'Dein out! Dein out!' because I'm suddenly a figure of the club. I wanted to go to the window and say, 'Give me a chance, mate, I've only just joined!'

Then a brick came through the window. I couldn't believe that somebody had actually thrown a brick through the boardroom window. Luckily, it didn't hurt anybody. But the fans were angry and wanted us to know about it. We made a decision there and then that Terry had to go. He had run his course. Peter and I had the job of dismissing him.

We needed somebody to take over. Don Howe, Terry's assistant, came in as nightwatchman. He was a coach of very high repute. He had played for Arsenal in the 1960s and when he retired went straight into coaching, first with the reserves and then the first team, where he was a vital foil for manager Bertie Mee during the great period when Arsenal won the 1970 Fairs Cup and the 1971 double. After managing West Brom and Galatasaray he returned to Arsenal to assist Terry.

Don was very faithful to Terry. He didn't want to miss the opportunity to take over, but he thought it was wrong that we fired Terry and I remember it being important to him that he made his point to us. Don could be quite outspoken. However, while he was a fine coach he wasn't a great decision-maker. Being manager required a different skillset. Yet, we took a gamble on him. Although he started off as a caretaker, we gave him the job after a few months – and obviously everybody wanted it to work.

Don came to me one day and said, 'I've been looking at this player in Scotland. I've seen him three or four times, and I really think he's talented. Would you like to come up to Aberdeen with me?'

I said, 'Sure. Happy to do that, Don, if you want another opinion, for what it's worth. I mean, I'm no football scout, but I'm happy to come with you.'

We were going to see Gordon Strachan and Don was insistent that we were careful and kept a low profile. He didn't want our interest to come out in the press. And we thought we could manage to keep it under the radar. In those days you could buy plane tickets in false names. As we arrived at Aberdeen airport, the British Airways ground staff threw open the door, saw Don and said, 'Come to see the wee man again?'

'Well done, Don,' I said. 'You kept that quiet, didn't you?'

123

We did see Gordon Strachan and we should have bought him. We were a bit slow in getting off the mark. Manchester United blew us out of the water – as they did painfully often in my time.

Don was well-respected by the players. Everybody liked him, because he was genuine, hard-working, very knowledgeable, a good football man – but he was not right to manage the club. He brought through some outstanding talent from the youth team. Tony Adams and David Rocastle, in particular, made their debuts and began to make strides under Don. Arsenal briefly topped the league in October 1984. But the team was off the pace in terms of trophies. Don resigned after a couple of years and it was back to appointing a caretaker, with Steve Burtenshaw keeping things ticking over until the board was in a position to appoint a new manager in the close season of 1986.

I had this idea to get Alex Ferguson, while another board member suggested George Graham. George did tick a lot of the boxes. He looked the part and, as a former player from the 1971 double team, he knew the Arsenal values. That held a lot of sway with the board. Some notably bigger names were mooted including Terry Venables and Johan Cruyff; but in the end it was really between Alex and George.

The board thought George could do the job. He was young, he was aspiring, he was hungry. He was elegant and always well turned-out. He started lower down to learn the ropes of management. He knew a lot of the lower-division players, which was an asset in England, to try to mould something with smart recruitment.

But while George had the Arsenal connection, he had yet to cut his teeth in the big time. He was at Millwall in the lower divisions, and that was his first managerial job. I thought it might be a risk. Alex, on the other hand, had more experience and more success. His Aberdeen team had been a revelation and won impressively, including in Europe. So I floated the idea of a double act – that we bring Alex in as number one with George to be his number two. The combination could be a dream ticket, the two Scotsmen combining a lot of qualities with the potential to be even more ambitious in the top division of English football. I knew Alex and knew the chairman of Aberdeen, Dick Donald. I sounded him out delicately to see if Alex would be interested.

In the end, I went along with the decision to appoint George. To Peter's credit, we always tried to get a unanimous decision on contentious issues. George wanted more money than we ended up offering. I remember him saying, 'This is not what I was looking for but if I am successful, then I won't be cheap!' True to his word he would come to the office the day after winning a trophy to remind us.

Between the summer of 1983, when I joined the board, and 1986 when we appointed George, we had gone through three managers – four if you include caretakers. My first few years had been eventful. A lot of action. A lot of change. I tried to absorb what we had learned – what is important in management, what to look for and what the warning signs are – but every case was different. Obviously they need leadership. Can they lead a group of players? Are they a good motivator? But there are many other questions. Are they clever enough to outsmart the opposition? Are they good tacticians? Are they good communicators? They've got to front the press and often be the spokesman for the club. Do they have an engaging personality? Do they have integrity and are they trustworthy with the club's finances and transfers?

There are a lot of ingredients and, increasingly, as the game has become more globalised, communication skills have become more important. Back in the 1980s, there were barely any foreign players in the team. It was predominantly British and Irish and the majority of the team shared similar cultural references, upbringings and lifestyles as well as language. Nowadays the manager has had to learn to deliver his message to a range of players from different backgrounds and nationalities at the same time.

In George's first full season, 1986/87, Arsenal won the league cup (then called the Littlewoods Cup), and had a wonderful run that culminated in a tumultuous, two-legged semi-final against Tottenham which went to a highly charged replay won late on by David Rocastle. Arguably, we were rather lucky to prevail, and I remember Irving Scholar, the chairman of Spurs, shook my hand graciously and asked, 'How many get out of jail cards do you have, David?' We became good mates and still are today.

And then as underdogs we beat Liverpool in the final. In those days Liverpool won just about everything. The match-winner was Charlie Nicholas. It was a hot day at Wembley with the crowd in great voice and the game delivered an upset in our favour. To me it felt like that was a turning point. It showed that we could do it. After being in the doldrums for many years we'd actually achieved some silverware. It was significant for George. It meant a lot to the club. It was a big moment for me as my first experience of a trophy since joining the board. It was an important platform to build on.

It was also a high point for Charlie, who was our star player. He was extraordinarily talented, but George was always pushing him to do better. George was a disciplinarian. Charlie had joined

Arsenal in the summer of 1983, around about the same time as I was negotiating to get on the board. He was Arsenal's biggest signing – £750,000 from Celtic – and he arrived in London with the reputation of being one of the most exciting talents of his generation on the pitch and as 'Champagne Charlie' off the pitch. He had a flamboyant sense of fun. The girls were falling at his feet. Arsenal put him up in a quaint hotel near my house in Totteridge and he was virtually running the place after five minutes. Charlie was a wonderful character.

At one of the early games, I was sitting next to Peter Hill-Wood, and after about five minutes Charlie got the ball in front of the directors' box and started juggling it from his right foot, left foot, dropping his shoulder, going past one man, another one, doing a nutmeg. And I turned to Peter Hill-Wood and said, 'Do you think he's right-footed or left-footed?' and Peter Hill-Wood took out his cigar (you could smoke in those days) and said, 'We paid for both.'

But another side to Charlie was his warm character. Every club gets letters from people who are ill or suffering, and I received one from a mother who told us about her son, Russell Brown. He was seventeen years old and a postman. He had been riding his moped, had an accident and was in a coma in Homerton Hospital. The medics didn't know whether he was going to make it or not. His favourite player was Charlie Nicholas. The mother asked if Charlie might do something for him.

I buttonholed Charlie after training. 'Charlie, read this letter,' I said. 'I've rung Homerton Hospital and they said we can go and see him.'

Straight away he said, 'Mr Dein, when can we go?'

Charlie and I made an appointment. We went to see this kid Russell and what I witnessed seemed a modern miracle.

Russell was lying in his bed, in a coma, and the consultant explained that if he didn't come out of his coma soon his chances would be slim. Charlie immediately started shaking Russell's shoulders and said in quite a loud voice, 'Wake up, wake up, we're playing Spurs on Sunday. Wake up, Russell. Wake up, Russell.' Charlie wouldn't let go. He said, 'Come on, Russell, come on, Russell.' Amazingly, as we're looking at the boy, I could see his eyelids flickering open and then close fully again. It was a very poignant moment.

The following day, I received a call from Homerton Hospital. They told me Russell opened his eyes again. Since then, every Christmas, I get a card from Russell with the two magic words – 'Thank you'. I would like to contact him again and find out how he is.

George was quick to start renovating the team. He was very shrewd when it came to spotting players – that was a big strength of his. He quickly developed a team based around an outstanding crop of young, homegrown players, mixed with talents he handpicked for their character and promise from clubs which were less glamorous than Arsenal.

Out went Charlie and in came Alan Smith. Out went Viv Anderson and Kenny Sansom – England international fullbacks – and in came Lee Dixon and Nigel Winterburn from Stoke and Wimbledon. Steve Bould was another steal who didn't come with a big reputation but went on to make one as a fundamental part of what became a legendary Arsenal back four. Rix moved on and George brought in Brian Marwood from Sheffield

Wednesday. Steve Williams was a popular player with the fans but he left and Kevin Richardson arrived from Watford.

George liked to have players he could instruct and mould, who had the desire to climb mountains for him, and he was smart about the kind of personalities he introduced. After a much less enjoyable trip to Wembley to defend the Littlewoods Cup, which went terribly – we threw away a lead and lost to Luton – George really shook up the squad, and something obviously clicked.

It was very exciting and, during the 1988/89 season Arsenal went on a great run to get to the top of the league around Christmas time. To feel that we had a strong chance to challenge for the title – really, for the first time since the 1971 double – was a credit to George and the players.

The season was interrupted in the most horrific way with the Hillsborough tragedy. Arsenal could have wrapped up the title before the final game with two home matches the week before, but the boys let nerves get the better of them. A defeat to Derby and draw at home to Wimbledon handed all the initiative to Liverpool. It was a remarkable set of circumstances to have the top two – in this case Liverpool and Arsenal – face to face on the final day, at a point where everyone else had finished all their games in the whole of English football. It was like the entire league season and a cup final rolled into one, very intense, ninety-minute game.

I am not particularly superstitious. I remember one director who never changed his socks whilst we were winning – I kept away from him! My only idiosyncrasy was I would never eat before a game. Perhaps I always felt that, maybe, there was a chance of getting selected . . . at Highbury they would serve cocktail sausages at half-time which became my lunch, but I couldn't eat before a match.

With this conclusive game, either side could win the league but, of course, Liverpool, being the force they were at the time, were heavily favoured. Liverpool had won multiple leagues throughout the decade, had just won the FA Cup and were going for the double in front of their home crowd. We were on a dip in form. It was a mountain to climb. The general feeling was that we weren't going to do it. We were going for the ride, hoping for the best but fearing the worst. I have to give George credit. He always believed we could win. I thought that was impressive. We chartered a plane from Luton and I brought Greg Dyke, then the programme controller for ITV; this was a title decider going live on his channel.

Anfield were very gracious, as always. They had a very nice board. The game itself is written into the English footballing history books. It was a moving occasion, being so close to the Hillsborough disaster. Our players carried bouquets of flowers onto the pitch which they gave to the Liverpool fans before the game kicked off. It was a gesture which the Liverpool fans warmly applauded.

At the end of the game, Brian Moore, commentating for ITV said, 'Maybe the most dramatic finish in the history of the football league.' Or, indeed, any league. Needing to win by two clear goals, which most people thought was impossible, Alan Smith headed in the first just after half-time and Mickey Thomas seized the moment with virtually the last kick of the season in stoppage time. When he did his double somersault, decorum went out of the window. Directors don't tend to celebrate, out of courtesy to the opposition. I couldn't resist. I just catapulted myself off the ground, punching the air, shouting, 'We've done it!' When I came down to my seat, there was Peter Hill-Wood quietly puffing at his cigar. He turned around to me and said, 'Never in any doubt.' That was another wonderful example of English understatement.

We savoured the moment and took our time before returning home. The Liverpool board were obviously very, very disappointed, but dignified nevertheless. It was hard because they were odds-on favourites to win the game that night.

A few minutes after I arrived back at my home, I received a call from Peter Hill-Wood. He'd had a very nice liquid lunch and dinner and then some champagne. He said, 'David, how do I get out of Luton?' He was still going around the airport perimeter.

That weekend, there was an open-top bus parade and a quarter of a million people came out into the streets of Islington. It was a reminder of how big Arsenal were and how much potential there was. It was only six years since I joined the board and my mind flashed back to losing against Walsall. Within a few years, all of a sudden, we've just won the league. Quite a transformation. I felt incredibly proud.

SUCCESS AND ADVERSITY

During my early days on the board in the 1980s, managers called the shots when it came to transfers. They would decide on a player, do the bulk of the negotiating and the directors ratified the decision. The board always had to be asked for money for any transfer and the manager would make the case for who he wanted to bring in and how much he thought it would take to do a deal. In general we would try to back him.

Sometimes I would pick up the phone to another director for a conversation about a player – there were always a lot of feelers being put out. There were only a few agents in those days and they certainly didn't have the power they would go on to have, so it tended to be clubs talking to clubs, directors to directors, or managers to managers – and it was so much easier. Transfers in those days were a breeze. Ken Friar, David Miles and I were on hand to take care of all the business of a transfer once George had organised the who and how much.

It was always the kiss of death for a director to propose a player to a manager. Invariably, the manager would respond, 'Well, do you think you're qualified to judge?' So I would never do that. I might ask what a manager thinks of a certain player but I would never try to foist a signing on any manager.

I can't understand how some clubs run if the owners buy the players and say, 'Well, here are the players. Now, coach, make him play.' I find that odd behaviour. As the manager is going to be judged on his performance he's got to choose who he buys and who he sells.

In the summer of 1990, Arsenal recruited three new signings for George. He was adamant that David Seaman was an improvement on John Lukic, and he arrived from QPR. Andy Linighan came from Norwich to provide cover at centre back. Anders Limpar was a free spirtit, a talented winger signed from Cremonese in Serie A. We never quite knew what we were getting as in those days there was far less international scouting and very little televised coverage from overseas. Channel 4's *Football Italia* was the first of its kind, a breakthrough for broadening horizons in football consumption, but that didn't arrive until a couple of years after Anders. As I was always interested in what was going on beyond our own shores, I was enthused to see someone who would bring something new and he absolutely did that. He was very quickly a fan favourite.

All three players played a part in the club winning more silverware. David Seaman, of course, went on to become one of the most revered and decorated goalkeepers in the club's history. Anders was dazzling in his first season, an influential part of the team that won the league in 1991, only losing once along the way. Andy Linighan scored the winner in the 1993 FA Cup final. George had a Midas touch in the transfer market for a while and we never had any reason to doubt his judgement.

I always got on well with George, I must say. He was tough, but fair. As a player, he was an artist, a technician. They called him 'Stroller' because he would take his time. He was a very talented player. As a manager he wasn't to be messed with – he was strong, he was tough, he was pragmatic, he was a winner.

Barbara introduced him to her friend Susie and they eventually got married. As couples there was a certain friendship, but it was a little bit sensitive because I was the vice-chairman and he was the manager: it's always difficult to get too close because you know one day you're probably going to have to sack him! You've got to be a part of each other's life but also apart from it. I always felt that it was tricky.

That 1991 title was particularly memorable for two incidents which proved a serious test of character. In October, Arsenal were involved in a brawl at Manchester United. They tended to be very emotionally charged games between the two teams. It all boiled over and suddenly everyone bar David Seaman was sprinting in to get involved and it looked like a free-for-all. Unfortunately, Arsenal's name was dragged through the mud, some critics went a bit overboard talking about punishments as severe as relegation. But both clubs were charged with bringing the game into disrepute. We fined a number of our players. The worst offenders were Paul Davis, Nigel Winterburn, Anders Limpar, Michael Thomas and David Rocastle, and we disciplined George Graham internally, hoping that would take some of the sting out of it. We tried to be proactive, admitted wrongdoing and took action. It was an attempt at damage limitation. We announced at a press conference held by Peter, with George sitting solemnly next to him, that the money from the fines would go to charity.

'Twice in two years is too often,' he said, referring to a similar incident involving Norwich City. 'The name of Arsenal has been sullied and that is why I have taken this action.' We had hundreds of letters the following week from different charities asking if they could also be in for a windfall!

Our sanctions were evidently not enough for the FA. We retained the brilliant Mark Phillips QC. He really does have two brains! (As already mentioned, he went on to play a significant part in the legalities when we formed the Premier League.) I went to the November hearing with him to represent Arsenal. The brawl wasn't pleasant. It didn't look good at all. But that's the passion of football sometimes, and you've got to deal with it afterwards. In addition to a fifty-thousand-pound fine, Arsenal were docked two points and Manchester United one – an unprecedented sanction. The different punishments were explained by the fact that Arsenal were involved in the previous incident with Norwich City. We had to pick up the pieces, take the punishment and get on with the business of trying to win the league.

George tried to use the controversy to create a greater sense of siege mentality. But an even more sensitive blow was just around the corner. In December, captain Tony Adams was sentenced to a spell in prison after crashing his car while over the alcohol limit. To this day I think Tony was, in many respects, a scapegoat because he was high profile and the incident happened just before Christmas. He did something very silly and dangerous but fortunately he didn't hurt anybody. Being famous and the festive timing of it did seem to have an impact. Tony's judgement was very much under the microscope. On 19 December I was among the directors who went to Southend crown court to give character witness statements. The judge weighed it up, banged down his gavel and announced a sentence of four months in Chelmsford prison for drink-driving.

His mother yelled, 'You can't do that to my boy.'

It was a very difficult day. I was so disappointed for him. It was terrible for Tony and put the club in the spotlight for all the wrong reasons. As a board member and a fan, that's difficult as well. How do you measure the profile and image of the club versus a duty of care to the player? There was a big debate when he came out about whether or not he should retain the captaincy, having shamed the club and, even more profoundly, whether his contract should be cancelled. Some members of the board believed that justice had to prevail and that we couldn't as a club be associated with criminal acts. They wondered if he should be out of the door. I was on the other end of the debate, defending him. He's done wrong and he's gone to prison and that's his punishment. When he comes out, he has to be re-engaged, rehabilitated and supported.

I said to the board, 'What do you want to do – punish him twice and then banish him or cancel his contract?' To me, that was unthinkable. I spend a lot of my life these days giving people second chances. The seeds of that thinking were taking root even then.

I sat on disciplinary hearings with the FA at the time. I was used to seeing misdemeanours coming up in front of me and having to adjudicate. Moral dilemmas are seldom easy. Arsenal ended up supporting Tony when he came out and I was glad we did. He served a reduced sentence and tried to stay fit in prison and in February was back playing and trying to push the team towards the title. He was, and still is, a natural winner in life. He's a big personality. He's a leader of men. He carried on, although it would be a few years later that he was even braver when he confronted his drink addiction and changed his life and the lives of countless others that he has since helped.

It is easy for people to have an idealised view of footballers, expecting them to be perfect role models, especially nowadays when their earning power seems so extraordinary compared to the fans who come through the turnstiles. They are all human too, with personal challenges and feelings just like everyone else. Tony ended up being such an inspiring example.

There was a widespread drinking culture in English football at the time and, not long after Tony confronted his own situation, Paul Merson came out in public with his own issues. Now we had a player talking openly about drugs and gambling as well. Paul was a troubled soul at the time. You don't suddenly take to drugs, heavy drinking and gambling otherwise. It is an escapist route from something else. I was always sympathetic. I knew the players very well. I wanted them to succeed. I wanted to understand their mentality. Obviously, I wanted them to be successful, but I wanted them to be happy in their job with peace of mind, not least because it's such a short career.

In a different way, one of the biggest characters of that era, another who went on to be a shining example of how to turn your life around and never give up, was Ian Wright. We signed him in 1993. He was twenty-eight years old at the time, a latecomer to the professional game and it nearly never happened for him after several rejections in his youth. He had virtually given up on his dream when Steve Coppell at Crystal Palace took a chance on him and plucked him from non-league football. As someone who had spent two weeks in prison when he was young, Ian has spoken often of how he might have ended up on the wrong side of the tracks. He really is the most heartwarming success story – a wonderful player and an exceptionally wonderful guy.

When we looked to sign him he was making waves in the top flight of English football. His agent at the time, Jerome Anderson, was a big Arsenal fan and mentioned to George the possibility of a deal. That's the way football transfers often work, through inside chatter and recommendations – and it was around that era that the agents were starting to become influential. Jerome was one of the nicest and easiest to deal with. When it came to commission he said, 'Pay me what's it worth.' Today they say 20 per cent of this, 10 per cent of that, a chunk off here, God knows what there. We had a good relationship as Jerome looked after a lot of our players and, as an Arsenal supporter, he had a natural enthusiasm for any deal.

I remember asking George, 'What do you think Ian's worth?' He came back, 'Two million pounds and don't pay more than two and a quarter million.' You could never say that George was extravagant when it came to spending money. He would want to get the best possible price – understandably. I said, leave it to me. It was time for an important conversation with Palace's chairman, Ron Noades, who sat with me on some of the Football League committees. He wasn't everybody's cup of tea and could be prickly but he was a good football man and a good ideas man. It was an awkward conversation because he didn't want to lose Ian. In fact, I tried to be clever by enquiring for Ian's strike partner Mark Bright first of all, to try to soften the negotiations.

I asked for a price for his two forwards.

'Not for sale,' came the reply.

'Come on, Ron, everyone has a price, what is it?'

After a pause, he said, 'I wouldn't sell either for a penny under £2.5 million.'

'Ron,' I said, 'I am offering you £2.5 million for Ian Wright. I know you are a man of your word.' There was a long pause.

'David, you have offered me £2.5 million. He's yours.'

It turned out to be one of the most rewarding deals Arsenal would ever do. The icing on the cake was that the press were wrong-footed: they were hosting George Graham while I was thrashing out the deal at base camp. We always liked to keep our business as under wraps as possible to make sure a deal did not get hijacked by another club.

Ian is larger than life. He has a wonderful sense of humour, loves to laugh and has a great smile. He is so engaging, just a joy to be around. You can't help but like him immediately. When I was in the dressing room I knew when Ian was coming in. You could hear him from the car park.

After Arsène first arrived, I said 'How's Ian Wright getting on?' He said, 'I don't understand him, I train him all week and on a Saturday he does what he likes!'

He would always play tricks. Sometimes in the dressing room Dennis would tell tales about his exploits. Dennis and Ian had pegs next to each other. He said, 'Mr Dein, do something about Wrighty.' I asked what the problem was. Dennis pulled up his boots to show me. Ian had put shaving cream in them. Another day Dennis told me Ian cut his underpants halfway up so when he put them on they split in two.

At contract renewal time I would call Ian into the office and he would say, 'Mr Dein, where do I sign?'

I would ask, 'Don't you want to read it?'

He would reply: 'I just want to play for the club.' And that was Ian. You don't see that any more. It was just remarkable.

I was very close to Ian and still am. He refers to me as his father and I refer to him as my son. Ian was just really special. I feel genuinely extremely fortunate and honoured to have made his acquaintance and I'm so delighted and proud of him and what he's achieved in life.

It meant the world to Ian, when he joined Arsenal, that he played alongside his dear friend David Rocastle. David was also special, in every way. Directors are not supposed to have favourites. Unashamedly, though, I will say that I had a favourite and it was Rocky. I had first noticed him watching the youth team. I remember coming home and saying, 'I've just seen a Brazilian playing for Arsenal but he's from south London.'

One day Barbara bought me a wallet and, instead of including a picture of the kids, she inserted a photo of Rocky. She knew how much I adored him. We opened up a superstore in Finsbury Park station called Arsenal World of Sport and I had waxwork models of Tony Adams and David Rocastle commissioned by Madame Tussauds for the front window. After we sold Rocky to Leeds, the dummy was redundant and I decided to play a trick on Bill Fotherby, the CEO of Leeds United, who had given me a hard time with the negotiations. I sent the waxwork up to Elland Road an hour before Rocky travelled up, with the instructions for the driver that he had to tell Bill that he was delivering David Rocastle. A few hours later, an irate Bill called to say, 'Deino, what the fuck is this?'

'It's a replica,' I replied. 'Bill, what do you expect for £2.5 million?' To this day I have a table in my office with the legs from Rocky's wax figure.

It was not easy to make the deal to sell him when the time came because he was universally loved. But George made the call, knowing that his injuries were likely to cause him more and more problems. George felt the time was right to sell him. It broke my heart – he was my hero.

A few years later, Rocky's passing at the age of thirty-three affected all of us. It was tragic. He had come back from his last club in Malaysia and he had been diagnosed with a terrible disease, non-Hodgkin lymphoma. Towards the end of his life I went to visit him at his house in Ascot. I was greeted by his wife Janet and she told me Rocky would be down in a minute. I saw an image coming down the stairs that shocked me. Instead of the strapping, twelve-stone athlete, here was Rocky looking very frail, having lost a lot of weight. I could scarcely believe my eyes. We spent some time reminiscing about the wonderful times at Arsenal. I took him a No. 7 shirt with his name on it, signed by all the players. I felt he was almost reconciled to what was happening. It was a profoundly sad moment. He was a top-class person, a gentleman, a prince and a majestic player and will always be loved and remembered that way. To this day, some twenty-one years later, the crowd still chant his name.

The team through the George Graham years was exciting and extremely determined. The mix was right, the manager knew how to get the best out of them and it was a very successful period for the club. It was a testament to their character that Arsenal won the title in 1991 even though we had been docked two points as part of the FA punishment for the episode at Old Trafford and had to do without the captain for several weeks in difficult circumstances. That title might be eclipsed in people's memories because it didn't have the drama and glamour of 1989, but it was a wonderful achievement. The Invincibles would rightly become legendary a few years down the line but the

1991 team lost only once (a little unluckily, while Tony Adams was away, as it happens). They were very close to history themselves. Around that time there was a banner that would hang on the North Bank claiming 'George knows' and he certainly had developed a powerful aura in the game.

A series of cups followed, with the FA Cup and League Cup double in 1993, and then a memorable tour of Europe in 1994 which culminated in victory in the European Cup Winners' Cup. It was a phenomenal achievement. Arsenal's CV doesn't have as many European trophies as it should – we will come to the big omission later – and that night in Copenhagen, when the Parken Stadium was turned into a Danish Highbury we had so much support, it was very special. We played a very dangerous Parma team which had Gianfranco Zola, Tomas Brolin and Faustino Asprilla leading their charge. We were missing Ian Wright, and great resilience was required. The pressure was on and the team delivered a classic 1–0 to the Arsenal performance, thanks to a goal by Alan Smith.

We had enjoyed success domestically but this victory enabled us to prove something else to the football world in general. It was a huge occasion for the club. It was also big for George to win a European trophy, his sixth trophy in eight years. It was dynasty stuff and George's star was shining very brightly at the time.

We were doing something right and we had to build on it. That was always my impression because I know how fragile the game is. As a director you have to keep fairly level-headed, you've got to think of the future. I was always saying, 'Well, how do we grow on that? How do we improve?' The Premier League came into play then, with the growth of TV, sponsors and everything else. It was even more important to maintain and build upon what we had achieved.

George's system was becoming more functional as Arsenal became more of a cup team. The famous back four with the explosive Ian Wright up front was not able to dominate in the league as Manchester United began to take control under Alex Ferguson. David Rocastle was gone and Anders Limpar, a little maverick of a winger, was on the way out (much to the disbelief of my daughter Sasha, who burst into tears when we had to sell her favourite). But it was difficult to criticise too much because George kept delivering silverware.

In the summer of 1994 we explored the possibility of signing David Ginola from Paris Saint-Germain. The opportunity arose while I was at the World Cup in the USA. It was a very different kind of World Cup experience; in the summer and very hot and they had watering machines that you could walk through to freshen up. Instead of police they had the navy doing crowd control, in smart white outfits, saluting everybody as you came in. 'Have a nice day. Enjoy yourselves. Welcome and nice to see you.' It felt very different to the more aggressive police style of Europe. I remember mentioning it to the FA at the time. It made for such a pleasant, relaxed atmosphere. It was almost Disney-esque.

I began to socialise with people from different countries as I could see this was going to become a global game. I was friendly with the former France international Jean-François Domergue. He happened to be the technical director of Paris Saint-Germain and he rang during the World Cup. 'David, I know you well enough. I thought I'd give you the heads-up. We're going to release David Ginola.'

I said, 'Oh, really? That's interesting.' I was staying in the same hotel as George and I mentioned it to him later at the swimming pool.

George thought for a moment and said, 'I can't buy him.'

'Why not?'

George had that twinkle in his eye as he replied, 'He's far too good-looking.'

And do you know? To this day, I don't know whether George was serious or joking. Ginola ended up joining Kevin Keegan as a centrepiece of the Newcastle revolution in the mid-nineties.

In the winter of 1994 the good ship Arsenal, guided by George Graham, hit the rocks. 'Bung'. The word had never been heard before in football. A 'bung' was something you put in a bottle. All of a sudden, it was about to become common parlance in footballing terminology. Ken Friar said that George had told him that £425,000 was put into his bank account which he didn't expect and didn't ask for. George had dealt with the Norwegian agent, Rune Hauge, in the purchase of two players from Scandinavia – John Jensen and Pål Lydersen. Hauge was not unknown in English football, having already negotiated deals to bring Peter Schmeichel and Andrei Kanchelskis to Manchester United. I had met him a few times. He was not an imposing guy, very average, not a strong personality. But obviously he had contacts with certain players from his region.

It is important to understand how transfers worked back then. George was the main driving force, with a great track record of spotting and recruiting hits. If he needed backup on the financial, legal, negotiating or administrative side, both Ken Friar and I were on hand to offer our support. Ken had been involved at Arsenal since he was a boy and nothing usually got past him. My business background and contacts were all part of the big picture where needed.

Hauge had paid money into George's bank account without the club's knowledge and George came to Ken to own up to it – to front up, as his lawyers recommended. He wanted to put the wheels in motion to pay that money back to Arsenal and because it was a taxable situation it needed to be discussed properly. It was not a situation that we as a board had come across before. We held an emergency meeting and members were polarised. Some members immediately wanted to dial 999. I was not one of those. The talks went on for a few days. It was unpleasant; you can imagine Arsenal Football Club, being seen as the Bank of England club, are expected to do what is right, to set the right example. My view was two things: one, what are we going to achieve by taking the strongest action against George which would only make it into a more high-profile situation? And two, can't we deal with it internally?

After what George had achieved for the club, I felt he deserved some consideration. I call it a duty of care, but you could argue the same in reverse. Did he care about us when he accepted the money? It was complex and sensitive. I'm always a great believer in giving people a second chance. I was a dove rather than a hawk. But it was impossible to keep it low-key in the end. Before long I was in a restaurant when I got a call to say it was hitting the newspapers.

We went to the Premier League about it in the first instance and let them run with it. Rather than it becoming a criminal complaint, we made it a football complaint, so, to me, that was a damage limitation exercise. I wanted to keep it within the football family.

George continued his duties for a few weeks while the investigations were underway. Even though there were alarm bells ringing all over the place he continued to make signings – John Hartson, Chris Kiwomya and Glenn Helder arrived in a flurry. It was a very strange time. But deep down, I think we all knew that George's position was untenable. He had effectively taken money from the club even if he defended himself by saying it appeared as an unsolicited gift. It was particularly difficult for me because I liked him – and still do, enormously. It hurt me to be in this position. I thought he'd let us all down badly. But where money is concerned, people do funny things.

It was clear that a long suspension would be part of the punishment given by the FA. On 21 February 1995, the board relieved George of his duties.

When all was said and done, there was a feeling in football that it could have been any manager caught up in that situation. It was rife in the culture of the times. He was the one who got caught. Finances around the football industry were not particularly sophisticated in those days. Until fairly recently, the takings from the turnstiles had been collected in a cardboard box and walked down to Barclays in Finsbury Park by a member of the ground staff. You do hear on the grapevine there are still horror stories and corruption even today – not necessarily involving managers, but within the wider world of football, considering how much money goes around the game.

There was shellshock around the club when George was dismissed, but we had to keep our heads. George's assistant Stewart Houston was offered the caretaker role to finish the season. It was not the best time to take over. The team were in unfamiliar territory in the lower half of the league table, but did have momentum in Europe with another run to the Cup Winners' Cup final. Unfortunately, the final could not have contrasted more with the joy the previous year against Parma. We lost to Real Zaragoza in the dying moments of extra time with a bit of a freak goal floated over David Seaman by Nayim from the halfway line.

George, having been such an imposing figure at the club, was a hard act to follow. The board played safe and chose another Scot with a disciplinarian image, Bruce Rioch. We made up for it with some bravery in the transfer market. In the summer of 1995 we pushed the boat out, obliterated the record transfer fee and paid £7.5 million to welcome Dennis Bergkamp. It was a huge deal for a global star who would go on to have a seminal impact on the club.

In the aftermath of the scandal around the bung, it was obvious we had to implement a new regime in terms of transfer negotiations. Where Ken and I used to be there in support, with David Miles backing us up, we became much more hands-on across negotiations. Ken and I were the two constants as far as the board was concerned, in that we were the ones who were at the club all the time, dealing with the day-to-day running of Arsenal.

Bergkamp was one of the first major deals we tackled. Dennis was not too happy at Inter in Serie A and his agent, Rob Jansen, who worked with Jerome Anderson as his counterpart in London, was putting out feelers. Knowing a player of that calibre was available it would have been madness not to follow up. I always felt as if Dennis was the first brick in the wall of the Arsenal rebuild into a more modern, ambitious organisation. When Arsène arrived a year later, there were significant influences on and off the pitch to change the mindset of all the rest of the players and, indeed, the club as a whole.

I remember going over to Inter Milan to try to negotiate the deal and I was met by an extraordinary guy. He was Italian nobility. Visconti di Modrone entertained me royally at his palace. He was Inter's vice-chairman to the owner, Massimo Moratti. We just hit it off. He was a gentleman and we did the deal with a very civilised negotiation. In a way, it suited them as well as us as Dennis had been under a lot of pressure at Inter, where settling was difficult.

Arsenal had never signed a comparable player. We paid three times more than the previous record fee – for Ian Wright – to get an overseas player with a global reputation. We'd had Anders Limpar and John Jensen but they weren't on the scale of Dennis, educated at Ajax and then a star signing for Inter Milan. The mood was changing, football was changing. These were the sort of deals that captured the transformation I felt the English game was going to have to embrace, by being adventurous and ambitious, and venturing into a brave new world that was more multicultural and more sophisticated.

There was an extraordinary moment on the day we signed Dennis. We spent some time with him and his agent inside Highbury signing all the contracts and finalising all the arrangements. As the ink was drying, Rob casually dropped into conversation that Dennis had a fear of flying.

'Rob, we have just signed all the documents, how can you tell me that now? You could have told us before!' I exclaimed.

He said, 'I am sure he will listen to you with your charm.'

I made it my business to find out everything there was to know about potential treatment for this phobia. We quickly discovered that British Airways run a course, including time in a flight simulator. They reckoned 98 per cent of people were cured of their fear of flying.

I called Dennis into my office. I had all the details on a piece of paper. 'Dennis,' I said, 'Rob tells me you don't like to fly. What's the problem?' He explained that he had been involved in a couple of emergency incidents, once in the youth team with Ajax and once at the World Cup in 1994. I started to tell him about the fear of flying course. He put his hand up to interrupt me. I could see beads of sweat on his brow and he went pale. 'Mr Dein,' he said, 'I don't want to fly. I won't fly.'

I had to make an instant decision. Do I stop talking about it? Do I try to persuade him? He had only been with us for two days. Do I provoke a confrontation when I could see it meant so much to him? I wanted to get the relationship off to a good start.

'Dennis, I am here to help you,' I said. 'Don't worry about it. You are not alone. There are a lot of people who don't like to fly, but maybe one day you will think about it. You have children, you might want to go to Disneyland or somewhere. You let me know if ever you think about taking the course – just knock on the door. If not, this will be the last time I speak about it.'

That was it. We never spoke about it again. I believe that incident cemented our relationship.

Dennis was one of many fine players who signed his deal with my 'contract pen'. It has quite a history. It sits by the side of my bed and, every time I put on a jacket, it is the first thing to go in. It dates back to 1998–99, when I was invited to my old school, Orange Hill grammar. I went to give out prizes and to deliver the end-of-term address. Afterwards, the head girl gave me a

Mont Blanc pen. I held it up and told the students that from that day on every major contract would be signed with it. This school gave me my education and I planned to pass on the message to every new player that they have to remember the school kids and make sure they sign every autograph and not forget where they came from. I use that pen, and always pass on that story. It carries some of the values of the Arsenal motto – to remember who you are, what you are, and who you represent.

The first season under Bruce was not particularly smooth. As exciting as it was to watch the Wright-Bergkamp partnership begin to blossom – David Platt also arrived from Sampdoria in Serie A – behind the scenes there was an atmosphere that suggested Bruce might not be the long-term answer.

Barbara bumped into him at the training ground one day when she had been invited to see the physio Gary Lewin to check out an ankle problem. She asked him how he was getting on. Bruce exhaled deeply and said, 'This is a very big club . . .' That felt revealing. The pressure and expectation at Arsenal was more than he was used to.

Bruce was a good man but he came into Arsenal with a 'sergeant major' attitude that might have been successful at his previous clubs Bolton and Middlesbrough but didn't work with the big players at Arsenal. Ian Wright, still the star of the show on the pitch, poured his heart out to me about his relationship with the manager. Bruce was finding the players difficult to handle. It had become quite confrontational, although he was a decent coach. Ian said, 'I just can't get on with this manager. I am going to have to leave.' He had a transfer request in his hand ready.

I said, 'Ian, you can't do that!' The mood music was reaching a crescendo. I levelled with Ian: 'You will have to leave this with me. I can't say any more for the moment. Just carry on playing. It's all you have to worry about.'

As a director you have to be very careful. You can't have a kneejerk reaction to every player's grievance. Some get dropped; they are not playing well, they lose form and so on. But when a key player says he wants to hand in a transfer request, that needs to be taken seriously. I had heard from other players that they didn't like Bruce's methods and didn't feel motivated to play for him. I had to relay that to the board for discussion. The verdict in the end was unanimous. Come the end of the season it was time to make a change.

Bruce was relieved of his contract and Ian stayed, going on to break the Arsenal goal-scoring record. The board gathered again to discuss a potential new manager. My hopes for a radical choice were gathering momentum.

RED AND WHITE . . . AND SILVER

G et. A. Winning. Team. That was my maxim. It was my raison d'être. It was at the front of my mind every day I went to work at Arsenal, as if it was tattooed across my forehead. Having assembled a winning team in 1998 – an outstanding one at that – it then became about maintaining the winning habit. As everyone who has ever been successful in any aspect of life knows, reaching the top of the mountain is one thing but staying there is quite another.

After winning the double we were striving to repeat the feat the following season. Arsenal and Man United were both pushing on multiple fronts. The first unpredictable twist occurred during our FA Cup run that season. In the fifth round we were drawn against Sheffield United at Highbury. It was 1–1 in the seventy-fifth minute and one of their defenders kicked the ball out of play so that one of his team-mates could get physio treatment. What happened next stunned everybody in the stadium.

Etiquette dictates that we would throw the ball back to them. Ray Parlour threw it to Kanu, assuming he would gently pass possession back to their goalkeeper. Kanu didn't. Kanu had not long been in England and claimed that he totally misunderstood the situation. He cantered upfield and crossed the ball for Overmars to score. Our fans didn't know whether to celebrate or not. It was not just an unorthodox goal, it was unsporting. I watched it in slow motion in the directors' box and it felt unjust but referee Peter Jones had to award the goal – giving the ball back is only an unwritten rule and there was nothing that would permit him to disallow it. It was ungentlemanly but the referee's hands were tied. Sheffield United's players were furious, their fans were burning with rage and manager Steve Bruce looked like he was about to explode. Sheffield United were so affronted he wanted to take his players off the pitch. It was pandemonium.

Watching this unfold I was horrified. Arsenal Football Club could not win a game like this. Instinctively I jumped out of my seat and dashed down to Peter Hill-Wood. 'Peter, we can't win a game like this. I think we should offer to replay the game and have a rematch.' He looked at me and said, 'David, I agree.'

Time was pressing. There were only roughly ten minutes to play. I set about lobbying each of the directors to see if they were all in favour of replaying the game. There was no guarantee we would get that outcome but at least we had to offer. They all agreed unanimously. With that I stormed down to the tunnel. I have never done that before or since but this was an unprecedented situation. I wanted to be there when the players and managers came off the pitch.

Arsène was one of the first to appear in the tunnel. 'Arsène,' I said, 'we can't win a game like this. We have to offer to replay the game. What do you think?' He immediately agreed. There was a commotion between Steve Bruce and the officials and then Steve started marching over. He was like a fire engine coming straight at me, bright red in the face, with steam coming out of every orifice. I knew I was going to get abuse, I could see it coming. There was a lot of chaotic noise and I had to shout. Before he could open his mouth I yelled, 'Steve, we are offering to replay the game!' With that he stopped in his tracks and gave me a big hug. His face softened. He asked, 'Can we do it?' I told him I would certainly do my best.

We had to act quickly. I knew that Nic Coward, the joint executive director of the FA, was in our cocktail lounge. Fortunately, I had a warm relationship with him. I shot up to the lounge and told Nic that the credibility of Arsenal and football itself was at stake. I asked him if he could rally round the FA Challenge Cup committee to get permission to replay the game. Nic and I went to a quiet spot in one of the offices and he started to make calls. He called David Davies, his co-executive director, who went on to contact the head of the committee, Terry Annabele. For the first time in the history of the Football Association they made a decision in thirty seconds! They had seen the game and agreed the offer of a replay was the way to go, even though there were no regulations to cover an incident as unusual as this. They decided to make the executive decision on behalf of their colleagues on the committee, which was necessary as it could have taken them ages to get hold of all the other members. All credit to David and Nic for saving the day. We had no time to lose, knowing how the media circus was ramping up to unleash their worst on us for this betrayal of fair play. BBC 5 Live were coming on air any minute and we expected to get killed by the fans and wider football community if we couldn't make it right.

We got word to Arsène and he announced our offer to replay the game to the press. We also announced that tickets from the original match would be valid and we would let everyone watch the rematch at half-price. Then the fun started. Later that day I got a call from the chairman of Sheffield United. He was quite happy to replay the game but felt that it should be at Bramall Lane. I had to think quickly and point out that this was a rematch, not a replay! It took a long time to convince him over the phone that we would play again at Highbury. He then queried our decision to sell the tickets at half-price and asked about their entitlement to 25 per cent of the ticket revenue. We had a lively discussion about money. Just when we thought the matter was settled we received a letter from the VAT man saying that they would miss out on tax if we gave away discounted tickets. What started as a good deed began to rebound on us. I had opened Pandora's box, but we eventually found a formula for peace. As far as the rematch was concerned, we won the game 2–1 (the same scoreline), but without any further drama.

This was not the worst nightmare I was involved in when it came to the FA Cup and Sheffield. Back in 1973, when I was just a regular fan, Arsenal had a semi-final against Sunderland and the neutral venue was Hillsborough. As a treat I decided to take my niece and nephew, Carole and Alan. As we approached the platform at St Pancras it was announced that there would be no catering available on the train. I put the young kids on the train and got them settled in while I nipped off to get sandwiches and drinks. I thought I had enough time but as I got back to the platform I almost dropped the sandwiches as I saw the train pulling away. It left five minutes early. My niece and nephew were on that train going up to Sheffield by themselves. My brother and my sister-in-law would kill me!

A British Rail worker told me to get the next train to Sheffield – although that was going to a different station as the kids were on a charter nearer to Hillsborough. A policeman noted down the kids' names, ages, appearances and I went into recovery mode, taking the next train to Sheffield. There were thousands of people milling about at the ground. I was shouting their names, looking frantically, making enquiries, and I suddenly hear 'Uncle David!' and in the back of a police car were my niece and nephew giggling away, having the best time ever. The London policeman had alerted Sheffield constabulary, who sent a car to meet them off the train and look after them until we were reunited. I was so relieved. Just to top the day off, Arsenal lost. I remember writing a thank you letter to the Chief of Police in Sheffield expressing my gratitude for their efficiency. I often use the phrase 'People are quick to criticise and slow to praise'. The police deserved a lot of praise for their actions that day.

Football's fine margins were clearly illustrated when it came to the climax of the 1998/99 season. After the Sheffield United rematch, we won our quarter-final and faced a highly charged head-to-head against Manchester United in the semi-final. The teams were so well-matched it went to a replay and we returned to Villa Park for what became an iconic match at a pivotal moment – us chasing the double and them the treble. Arsenal v. Man United really was the game of games in English football in that era.

There was a problem getting to the venue, with gridlock on the M6. We didn't think we were going to make it in time. That was a bad start but the game itself had everything; it was full of emotion, ebb and flow, on a knife edge. We should have won it and contrived somehow to lose it. That missed penalty in stoppage time must have been pure theatre for the neutral but it was heartbreaking for us. It was typical of the perfectionist that Dennis is that he decided not to take a penalty again afterwards. I can't imagine how often our players went through the Ryan Giggs goal again in their minds, wondering how on earth one of them didn't stop him. Lee Dixon says that he still has nightmares thinking how Giggsy cruised past him. That one game made a tremendous impact, geeing up United and piling on the pressure. We ended up missing out on the chance to retain the title by a point. Man United cleaned up that season.

We had a busy summer addressing key personnel in the squad. Supporting Arsène, keeping the playing squad under constant review and making sure every deal was struck to get the best possible outcome for the club, was never dull. It required a certain flexibility to react in different situations because you never knew what was around the corner with players and their entourage. A perfect example of that took the form of a young striker by the name of Nicolas Anelka beginning to fulfil his huge potential.

Having joined us in 1997 as a seventeen-year-old, he exploded onto the scene during the double season. His pace was ferocious, his finishing was fierce. Nicolas was a quiet boy but on the pitch he made his presence felt. He was unfortunate not to go to the 1998 World Cup in France but it was obvious his chance would come and the following season he became a regular for his country. He was also Arsenal's top scorer by the age of nineteen and was voted young player of the year in England.

One day his brother, the lovely Claude, rang me up, about a week before the season was finishing. He said, 'I'd like to come and see you and Mr Wenger.' We set up a meeting at Sopwell House hotel after training one early afternoon. We were sitting at an oval table. Nicolas came in, wearing a tea-cosy hat and earphones, and we suggested he remove them. He was with his brothers, Claude and Didier and one other relative or adviser.

I started off, 'Well, you've called this meeting, Claude. What do you want to say?'

And he said, 'Nicolas is leaving.'

Oh, really?

'Yes. He's leaving.'

It required a measured response. 'Well, Claude, he's under contract,' I said. 'He can't just leave. He has a four-year contract and he has another two years to go. We pay Nicolas if he's injured, if he's sick, if he's off form, if he's not in the team, he still gets paid. Contracts work both ways.'

And then he came out with this wonderful line which will haunt me to my dying day. 'A contract is a piece of paper.'

I was less than impressed. 'You can't say that to me. You can't. It's a legal document. It's there to be respected. Nicolas cannot just leave like that. He can't walk out on it.'

He replied, 'He's leaving tomorrow and he will not be coming back.'

I said, 'Well, Claude, that puts him in breach of contract, which is very serious. I ask you to rethink.'

He was adamant. 'No, you don't understand. He wants to leave. He has to leave.'

Meanwhile, Nicolas had his head down, did not speak a word, from beginning to end. The rest of us were going around in circles.

Arsène then addressed Nicolas directly and asked him what he wanted to do. Nicolas looked up sheepishly and said he wanted to leave.

Clearly, they'd made up their mind and I had no doubt they had been 'got at'. Arsène and I left the room for a minute. I asked Arsène what he wanted to do. He thought for a moment and then he nodded his head, saying, 'David, let him go, and get as much money as you can for him. If he doesn't want to play for me, let him go.' We went back inside the room and told Claude we would have to discuss it with the board.

As they were leaving the room, Arsène tapped Nicolas on the shoulder and said to him in French, 'I hope, Nicolas, that one day, you may think I helped your career a little bit.' He formed his thumb and forefinger into a space of a couple of centimetres in size. And off Nicolas went, head down.

I said, 'Arsène, there's something behind this. It's Barcelona, Real Madrid, or AC Milan.' Sure enough, the following morning, well, what do you know? The president of Real Madrid, Lorenzo Sanz, rang me up. I was just waiting for the magic words 'Nicolas Anelka' to come out. After a few pleasantries there it was. 'We need a striker and we were thinking about Nicolas Anelka . . . ' Oh, what a surprise. Welcome to the party.

It was time to play hardball. I was consistent in my message. Not for sale. Not for sale. Not for sale. He started the bidding at twelve, thirteen, fourteen, fifteen million pounds, increasing and increasing. Come to daddy, buddy, keep coming. We were waiting and waiting – and then the moment came; it was time. I was in the south of France, and I invited the chair and vice-chair of Real Madrid to St Tropez to meet on my boat (*Take It Easy* – a perfect name for this situation) and it was a perfect setting. It was very relaxed. We ate in the warm breeze and, eventually, I got them up to £23.5 million. When I felt I had squeezed all the juice out of the orange, I told them we would accept their offer. And that was that.

It was perhaps the first sale that Arsène didn't really want to do. He knew Nicolas could go on to achieve great things and he would have preferred to keep him at the club. He was an extraordinary talent. We did well financially, but that was never, ever our motivation. We're not in the business to make money out of players. We're in the business of getting a winning team. Arsène would have developed his career in a completely different way to the path Nicolas chose. To think that he went on to move from club to club – thirteen moves, what a waste of talent. No doubt he's a wealthy boy and so are his companions, but perhaps his achievements could have been more stellar. Funnily enough, several years later they met at the Belles Rives hotel in Juan-Les-Pins, Antibes, and Nicolas pleaded with Arsène to take him back.

By maximising the price we ended up with a considerable profit on a player we bought for half a million pounds. With the proceeds we were able to purchase a replacement for Nicolas who went on to be an all-time Arsenal icon and also build a new, modern training ground which Arsène felt was imperative for the club to progress. We also recruited Davor Šuker, who had a wealth of top-level experience, to help in the goalscoring department. I said we have lost the Sulker and signed Šuker.

Arsène identified Thierry Henry as the perfect choice to take on the role in the team in which Nicolas had performed so well. He had hoped to have both of them together by signing Thierry to play alongside Nicolas but that was not to be. The two young French players had grown up together in the Clairefontaine national development centre for the French Football Federation based just outside Paris. They were friends. They were also both blessed with electric pace and power and played in forward positions. Although Thierry had been a winger more often in his young career at Monaco and Juventus, Arsène felt he had the desire and intelligence to be repositioned as a more central attacker.

We had to move quickly. I was sitting on the G–14 group of clubs with Roberto Bettega, the main man at Juventus, and we had a good relationship. A connection and mutual respect was already there. I mentioned that we were interested in Thierry. He played a bit hard to get but, in the end, agreed to a sale. That was a pretty civil deal.

Shortly after signing, Thierry came into my office at Highbury for a chat to see how he was getting along. I said, 'I'm going to give you a little present, Thierry.' We had just released a video of Ian Wright's goals. It was called 'Re-Wright-ing the Record' and celebrated Arsenal's top scorer of all time. 'Just try and imitate this guy in his scoring.'

He politely accepted the gift and said, 'Mr Dein, I'll do my best.'

He really bought into the club, its history and its values. He was ready to do what was needed to blossom into one of the best players of his generation and a symbol of Arsenal Football Club. Thierry was not exactly a nobody when he joined us. He was a World Cup winner – as a young player with Monaco – and had already been involved in transfer scenarios with many of the world's top clubs. Real Madrid wanted him when he was a teenager, although Monaco did not sanction the deal. Then he went to Juventus and when that move didn't pay off he was not against reuniting with the manager who gave him his debut, Arsène, alongside his compatriots Patrick Vieira and Emmanuel Petit.

Nobody should ever underestimate Thierry's intelligence. He challenged himself always. He continually strived to get better. It was a wonderful attribute. Just ask Arsène which player took up most of his time. Before the game, during the game and after the game, Thierry was analytical and a perfectionist. He was also a model pro because he looked after himself, ate the right food, trained very well, got on with the rest of the squad, behaved like a gentleman – very, very polite and respectful. He was a joy. I had a wonderful relationship with him and, indeed, still do. He's a very special guy and a very special player. We were really blessed to have him and for Arsène to be there developing his career.

Thierry once told me about being at the checkout of his local Waitrose and an elderly lady gave him a double-take. She pointed a finger at him and said, 'I recognise you.' Thierry politely nodded, then she said, 'You're the man in the Renault advert!' Thierry smiled and said, 'Yes! And I play football a bit too!'

We also bought our first Brazilian player in the same season we welcomed Thierry. Sylvinho was another indication of how much was changing – new signings once came from Sheffield Wednesday and Charlton and the latest batch arrived from Juventus in Italy, Corinthians in Brazil and Real Madrid in Spain. Our game was going global.

Yet again, it would be a season of going close but silverware evading us. We reached the final of the UEFA Cup against Galatasaray which was played at Parken in Copenhagen, the scene of a wonderful triumph under George Graham a few years before. Unfortunately, this event was marred by crowd disturbances between our fans and the

Turkish supporters. We always had one of the directors on duty the night before the game in case of an emergency and that time it was me. Sure enough, at three o'clock in the morning, I got a call from the police. There had been an incident. One of our fans had been stabbed in the back half a dozen times. He was in hospital.

When I saw him, the fan was in a sort of incubator with a lid on it. The doctors explained what they knew – he was in a bad way. I asked if it could be fatal. Thankfully, the wounds had not penetrated any vital organs. As we were talking, the fan opened his eyes, recognised me, and spluttered, 'I've got to get to the game!' I asked him if he had a ticket, and he said it was coming with one of his friends in the morning. I told him I would do what I could to make sure he was comfortable and looked after. I asked the doctor if there was any reason why he couldn't be released. They were satisfied that, if he wanted to discharge himself, they wouldn't keep him as his life was not in immediate danger. They patched him up. I told the fan that I would try to find him some tickets and contacted David Miles – he always had two up his sleeve. We ended up providing seats on a VIP bus to the stadium and a pair of the best VIP tickets.

Afterwards, the chief of police who travelled with us asked, 'Do you know who that was?' I didn't. He explained the fan was an old football hooligan. He had been out drinking, doing a pub crawl until the early hours, goading the opposition, got himself stabbed and ended up with the VIPs.

The game itself is best forgotten. We had more than enough quality on the pitch to win. The defence had done it all before, the Vieira–Petit midfield was seasoned and feared by now and, further forward, Overmars, Bergkamp and Henry were there, with Kanu and Šuker coming off the bench. But nothing clicked. It went to penalties and ours went all over the shop. The only player to score for us was Ray Parlour.

It didn't help that we took the penalties into the Galatasaray end and their fans are not exactly known for being shrinking violets. As each of our players came up to take the penalty, they were welcomed with loud whistling and abusive gestures.

For three consecutive seasons we finished second behind Manchester United and contrived to lose two cup finals and a memorable semi-final, in each case painfully late. In the summer of 2001 we made one bold addition to the squad which turned out to be transformative.

Approaching the captain of Tottenham, our closest rivals, was hyper-sensitive. It was common knowledge that Sol Campbell was going to be out of contract and a free agent but he had the world's clubs to choose from. Crossing the Seven Sisters Road was a huge deal with significant repercussions. The biggest hurdle, in a sense, was the first conversation, the first meeting. It took some work behind the scenes to set that up, and then suddenly we were looking each other eye to eye, knowing exactly how much was at stake, shaking hands and saying hello.

His agent, Sky Andrew, was an important intermediary and a good guy. He played it very straight and very discreet. When he set up meetings, nobody knew about them. When Sol had meetings with other clubs – and there were several big-hitters across Europe – he didn't tell me who. We knew that he was naturally being courted. But all the time I think he was quietly doing whatever he could to give us a fair chance to land Sol.

The meetings were long and deep and generally took place at my house in Totteridge. It had to be clandestine. We would walk round and round the garden, late at night and at his request. It was all about building trust and getting him to feel comfortable and being confident in joining us. We spoke about life, his life, his upbringing, his ambition, what he wanted to be. We'd shoot the breeze about anything.

I think the most important skill that I had in my locker when dealing with Sol was patience. We had to play the game at his speed when he was ready to engage. And it was just a question of gaining his confidence, getting it into his mind that he was making the right decision. Playing the Arsène Wenger card was important because he was going to improve his career. Never underestimate what that meant. Most of the meetings were between Sol and me but, as things developed, Arsène came too, which was very important. All our patience and perseverance eventually paid off.

Miraculously, we had managed to keep the negotiations away from the prying eyes of the press. When the day came to announce his arrival, our media department sent an invitation to the journalists without mentioning Sol's name and some of the papers thought it was going to be a low-key signing and didn't bother to send their number one journalist. I stage-managed the event at London Colney, our training ground. Sol stood behind a closed theatrical curtain, in the Arsenal home kit, his arms folded. When we opened the curtains Martin Lipton of the *Daily Mail*, a Spurs fan, couldn't contain himself and yelled out,

'Fuck me! It's Sol Campbell!' Everyone in the room was completely shocked.

I couldn't resist a touch of humour and said, 'Of course, as we all know, Sol has come from Spurs. If he had come from Dover, we would have had Dover Sol!'

In Sol's first season, 2001/02, Arsenal won the double again. The team repeated the feat Arsène masterminded when he first arrived, triumphing in both Premier League and FA Cup. The league campaign showcased his attacking philosophy because they scored in every single game. It also demonstrated an extraordinary resilience in that the boys did not lose any away matches. Maybe that was a seed of the idea that it might be possible to complete a season without losing at all. With some more fine-tuning, who knew?

By now Thierry was making strides as one of the most feared and admired forwards in the Premier League. Dennis scored one of the most stunning goals you could wish to see up at Newcastle. Anytime Dennis is mentioned on TV, the clip of that goal is repeated. It was pure poetry in motion. Patrick and Sol were dominant in midfield and defence. It was the last season for two fine servants in Tony Adams and Lee Dixon, who had a wonderful send-off, and you could see how the team was evolving from the 1998 team, with Lauren and Ashley Cole emerging as full-backs to be reckoned with, Freddie Ljungberg and Robert Pires becoming more influential. A word, too, for Sylvain Wiltord, who popped up with the winning goal to clinch the title at Old Trafford. Manchester United were not too thrilled to concede the league in front of their own fans but our team was full of colossal characters who could withstand everything they threw at us.

The following season we collected another FA Cup. By then Arsène had been with Arsenal for seven seasons, winning five trophies, developing a habit for being in the Champions League every campaign. Fortunately, there was no seven-year itch and he was as motivated as ever to strive for more.

BUILD IT AND THEY WILL COME

In my role at Arsenal I was always keen to know what was going on, and what could be improved, across all areas of the club. My office at Highbury was behind the Clock End in the building that housed the players' lounge, a mezzanine suite for hospitality, and the JVC centre (an indoor pitch sponsored by the Japanese electronics company), sometimes used by the players and often by the community. My office had a row of windows that overlooked the back of the old Gunners shop and the entrance to the car park, so I could keep an eye on the comings and goings.

It was good to feel I was at the heart of things, but every now and then it had another value: spotting things that shouldn't be coming or going. For example, I remember coming in one morning on a match day. I always used to get there early. I had the keys to the door. I was on the phone, absently looking out of the window, when I saw one of the chefs walk along and take off his tall white hat. It had a frozen chicken underneath. He picked it off his head and surreptitiously put it in the boot of his car. I called Ken Friar and told him to give the caterers a call and tell them there was fowl play going on. One of their chefs was on the hey diddle diddle.

In my early days, Arsenal were a close-knit operation and

everybody knew everybody, but as the club developed, staff numbers began to rise. The club I walked into in 1983 felt very different in 1993, and had made another giant leap by 2003. During a period of success and growth, first under George Graham and then Arsène Wenger, it became clear that we needed to move with the times off the pitch as well as on it. Among the major strides we made were improvements to the stadium, building a top-class training ground, the introduction of commercial and marketing departments, kick-starting the community hub and the Charitable Foundation. We modernised the academy, increased the international fanbase and, something really close to my heart, we established a women's team.

Walking around the Emirates today makes for a very different experience to the old days at Highbury. The first major evolution came in the early 1990s with the obligation to turn the North Bank into a modern all-seater stand in line with the recommendations of the report that followed the Hillsborough disaster. That was a massive move because the North Bank was the heartbeat of the club: fifteen thousand people standing cheek by jowl. There were protests about abandoning the old terrace, but the truth is it was archaic, and in any case it had to go. Instead there was to be a two-tier seating-only stand.

But that would cost us fifteen million pounds, and we didn't have the money. Fortunately, I was friendly with the chairman of Glasgow Rangers, David Murray. He was a man I liked and respected – humorous, gutsy and adventurous. He had initiated a bond scheme at Rangers together with the Bank of Scotland to finance the redevelopment of Ibrox and he suggested something similar might work for us.

The fans would have the right to buy their own seat for life, and for those who did so, their season ticket price would be fixed for the next ten years. Your name would be inscribed on your seat and it was yours. Our bond scheme had two price points, £1,500 for the more central views and £1,100 for the rest.

Since I proposed the idea, I fronted the marketing. With the benefit of hindsight, it wasn't the best idea for me to promote it. The backlash was ugly and personal. I received hate mail. The fanzines slaughtered me, week after week. One front cover had my face as a dartboard, ready to use as target practice. Some of the material they published was so offensive that in one case I had to reach for lawyers. Loyal team followers were affronted that they were being asked to pay for their seats, as well as continuing to pay for entry. It was loudly argued that we were rich and should be paying for the redevelopment ourselves. I had liked to think I was a fairly popular figure in the club, but now I had become public enemy number one.

One day I went to meet Barbara at a Greek restaurant around the back of Bounds Green – Tottenham territory. I was in my car and, unsure which way to go, I wound down my window and asked this guy for directions. He was really muscular, with tattoos everywhere. Suddenly I had his arm reaching through the window and he pointed at my nose. 'I know who you are,' he said menacingly, 'and I don't like what you're doing.'

'I'm sorry about that,' I answered, 'but do you know the way to Myddleton Road?' He replied with his middle finger.

That was not the end of it that evening. While we were at the restaurant, word must have got around about me being there. After the meal I found my car had been broken into and my briefcase stolen from the boot. I was just trying to do my best for the club – how else were we going to raise the money to go all-seater? – but there was no mistaking the vitriol of some of the fans.

The Bank of Scotland agreed to underwrite the scheme in the event that we couldn't sell all the bonds, and when it came to our AGM a shareholder asked how many debentures we had sold. At the time it was around half. In his inimitable fashion, Peter Hill-Wood came out with one of his classic quips: 'We need a few more suckers,' he chuckled. There was a fair bit of uproar in the house at that.

In the end we sold around two thirds of the bonds, and, for all the drama, it turned out to be a successful venture. Eventually the stadium was a sell-out and the secondary market blossomed. Before long a £1,500 bond was trading at three thousand pounds. Even better for those who had invested, there was a refinancing of the club and everyone got their money back – as well as benefitting from cheaper season tickets for several years.

While we were planning the new North Bank I took a detailed interest in the design, and one thing I was firm about was increasing the number of toilets, even at the expense of space for seats. I wanted football fans to be comfortable, to be able to get to the toilet and have a cup of tea, or a beer or a sandwich at half-time, without it being a stress, or a choice between nature's call and something to eat or drink.

The architect, Rod Sheard, later invited me to an architects' awards dinner and mentioned that his company were up for a prize. 'And we've got a special award,' the presenter said, 'for the best toilets in any sports ground. And it goes to Arsenal Football Club.'

Rod sent me up to collect the prize: a mini-toilet which had a little lever on the side. When you pressed it down it made a flushing noise. It was one of the more unusual trophies Arsenal won.

I came up with the idea to commission some artwork of what the new stand would look like to screen off the construction site, hiding the dumper trucks, cement mixers, cranes and so on. An artist designed the mural and we installed it before the first game of the 1992/93 season. On the Friday morning before the opening game, the boys were training at Highbury in front of the mural to get used to it, and I went down to watch. Kevin Campbell came up to me. 'Mr Dein,' he said, 'that's very good but there are none of my brothers there.' He was right, and I should have spotted it myself. An all-white, all-male crowd that was not a reflection of our fans, and was simply not acceptable. I thanked him and promised we would do something about it right away. In fact the artist was summoned and overnight made substantial alterations.

Not that the artwork improved our football. We lost the first game, against Norwich city, in front of the mural 4–2. 'The game was so bad,' I reflected, 'that fifteen people in the mural walked out!'

Once Arsène came along, the focus turned to the training ground because that's where the hard work gets done. Arsenal had for years rented pitches in London Colney, owned by University College Hospital. The associated changing rooms and so on were very basic, and Arsène could barely believe that a club of our stature did not have training grounds of our own. Sometimes at London Colney, we would be kicked out because the medical students had a match. Yet while a stadium, if you're lucky, gets used thirty times a year, the training ground is used every day of the year. For Arsène this was a big priority, and he was very focused on getting the training ground right.

As it happened, not long after he arrived there was a fire at the training ground, leading to much tongue-in-cheek speculation about whether it was arson or Arsène. That gave us the impetus to buy land and get building. It just so happened our new centre was next door to the old one.

The whole thing was Arsène's brainchild, down to the last teacup. It was one of the first facilities of its generation, refined and geared towards providing a perfect environment for a top player. We did a lot of research with sports teams around the world to establish best practice, and Arsène ensured the design inspired high standards and elite performance. Many teams from across Europe came to visit and observe. Of course, since then others have done bigger and better, but in the early 2000s ours was a showcase of modern football thinking.

It was fortuitous in a way that it came right on the back of the Anelka sale. We were never usually flush with money. We never, in our wildest dreams, expected to sell a player who cost half a million for twenty-three million pounds. The profit very neatly covered the cost of Thierry to replace Nicolas with enough spare cash – twelve million – to build the training ground.

By now, Arsenal's progress was happening at such a pace that it was obvious we were outgrowing Highbury, our beloved home. We all knew we had to move. Every time I spoke to the box office manager, Ivan Worsall, we had a running joke.

I'd say, 'What's the waiting list like?'

He would say, 'Oh, 45,000 . . . 55,000 . . . 65,000 . . .'

The fans had a seemingly insatiable demand for seats. And if you've got a queue of people around the block, you have to ask yourself, how do you expand?

We were competing against Manchester United, whose grounds routinely held 60,000–70,000 people, while our capacity was now virtually half that. As recently as the late 1980s Highbury had packed in as many as 55,000 for the most attractive fixtures. But the advent of all-seater stadia changed all that. By the mid-1990s we were down to 38,000. Even so, moving would be a wrench. I loved Highbury. We all did. Some almost worshipped it. Some people even buried ashes of loved ones in an area behind both the Clock End and North Bank goals. This threw up a problem when we moved to the Emirates stadium. The astute stadium manager, John Beattie, sensitively arranged for a memorial garden to be built in an exclusive area in the Highbury Square development, which was built on the old stadium site. But our ground was boxed in by local housing which made it impossible to expand.

And as much as we'd rather stay, relocation was nothing new for Arsenal. Historically, of course, the club was founded south of the Thames in Woolwich, then one of the most famous military bases in England – hence our name, the Arsenal, and our nickname, the Gunners. In fact we had played at a few other grounds as well, and then famously uprooting in 1913 to build the stadium in Highbury. In the 1970s, before I joined the board, a historic board meeting between the custodians of Arsenal and Spurs had discussed a revolutionary idea of sharing a stadium at Alexandra Palace. It would have made good sense, splitting costs, saving money at a time when football was struggling to stay solvent. But while it was economically attractive, emotionally it was a very different matter. We all agreed on the board that the connection with Highbury and Islington that had developed over the best part of a century was too strong to disregard. We wanted to stay within the borough, and as close to Highbury as possible. But much as we searched it was very difficult to find a big enough piece of land nearby. We needed roughly six acres for the stadium alone.

Islington council were helpful but, even so, it was tough negotiating with them. I felt they needed to be put under a bit of pressure – the threat that we could move out of the borough. At the time, one of my friends was Jarvis Astaire. He was a big property man and an equally big sports enthusiast. Amongst other things he was vice-chairman of Wembley PLC, which owned the famous stadium, along with Wembley Arena, and an office block called York House – and a greyhound dog track in Rhode Island, USA. He also had all the valuable car parking surrounding Wembley stadium.

Jarvis told me that the company was in financial difficulties and were looking to sell off their assets. Putting on my entrepreneurial hat, I started thinking – how could we grasp this fantastic opportunity? After all, we were looking hard for a stadium ourselves, and Wembley is iconic. Yet moving Arsenal across London and taking over the great national arena seemed a step too far. So initially I thought of the FA. As the governing body of English football, which stages lots of cup finals at Wembley, it was a natural move for them. They paid rent to Wembley PLC for what were called 'staging rights', allowing them to stage England matches and other games there. Let them buy out the assets from the company, sell off any properties they didn't need, and retain the stadium and the car parking. Simple!

I approached the FA board. I got comprehensively outvoted.

They felt they were not in the property business and their priority was to look after 40,000 football clubs. So then I thought again. Is it really a bridge too far to think of Arsenal acquiring the stadium? Wembley has good transport links and they are used to getting 90,000 people there, whereas we had 50,000 on the waiting list, so we had a decent chance of filling it. We could become the anchor tenant, with Arsenal instead of Wembley PLC subletting staging rights to the FA, and we receive the income. This could be a win–win situation.

But would it work politically for Arsenal to own the national stadium? That would be controversial to say the least. I've never been frightened to take a proactive approach – and if nothing else a Wembley option might increase the pressure on Islington council to help us more. It always helps to have an auction.

I put it to the Arsenal board. I have to say there wasn't a lot of enthusiasm for it, that was for sure. The majority were fixated on keeping Arsenal as close to Highbury as possible, staying local to its community – and of course that was the ideal. In fact we had played our Champions League home games for two seasons at Wembley – that was in the late 1990s when Arsenal first qualified for the European competition under Arsène. It was an experiment to satisfy demand for tickets, a problem that was exacerbated because the attendance at Highbury was reduced by UEFA. (They take a chunk of tickets for their guests and dignitaries and, in addition, the first few rows all around the stadium were out of use because of advertising hoardings promoting UEFA's partnerships.) We had been struggling to get 30,000 usable tickets for our fans. But our time at Wembley was not remembered with enthusiasm. It hadn't really felt like home, and if anything the Wembley factor had actually inspired our opponents. Little wonder the board's response to my idea was broadly negative. Even so, we had nowhere else to go. Therefore, we kept the Wembley option on the table.

King's Cross entered the frame. There was a lot of disused railway land behind the station and a vast regeneration scheme was planned. In many respects it could have been an excellent venue, not least with its superb transport links. But the £3 billion project had been bogged down for years over competing visions, financing and planning consent. The problem was that time was against us. We were haemorrhaging revenue every week compared to the likes of Manchester United. That too stayed on the back burner. What about something purpose-built, near the M25? That was even worse than Wembley in terms of public transport which is favoured by our fans.

For a while we were stuck. We were going down cul-de-sacs and we had run out of ideas.

As it happened, an Arsenal season ticketholder, Antony Spencer, who was in the property business with his partner Tony Green, was introduced to me by my pal Geoffrey Klass. Anthony Green & Spencer had been exploring possibilities for a possible stadium move. Antony had studied his A. to Z. and superimposed a shape the scale of Wembley's footprint on the Islington area, and realised Ashburton Grove could be the answer to everybody's prayers. He brought in photographs and plans to show Ken Friar and me. The presentation included the line, 'Arsenal should move to Arsenal', meaning that we should stay within the borough.

The idea turned out to be an inspired one. Here was an under-developed site of fifty acres on Highbury's doorstep. It was an industrial estate with over three hundred small businesses and, believe it or not, two waste transfer stations and a council rubbish dump in the middle of it. It ticked every box. The only problem was that we would have to buy out all the local businesses or relocate them to new sites. Once we identified the area, the council were four-square behind us. Islington were desperate to keep us in the borough, and it owned 80 per cent of the Ashburton Grove site. Fortunately, they helped us with the delicate process of obtaining the remaining 20 per cent. Needless to say, the council made sure they got something in return for their support. Arsenal had to commit to redevelopment projects and social housing. They made us sing for our supper, and I can't blame them. Arsenal Football Club became the largest development project in the borough.

At any rate we were on our way to a new home just around the corner, with all the challenges that such an ambitious project would throw up.

One of the expansions I am most proud of from my time at Arsenal is women's football. The key mover was Vic Akers, who went on to play a wonderful role at Arsenal. Not only was he the kit man for the men's team during an era of memorable success (and *everyone* knows the kit man, since, like a physio, he is a sounding board for anything and everything); women's football at Arsenal was his brainchild.

One of his colleagues in the community department, Alicia, played football at a time when the women's game was very low key. Then another couple of young local footballers, Sarah Ryan and Michelle Curley, made enquiries about whether we might start a team. (Sarah went on to manage the Gunners shop and Michelle played for England.) Vic approached me to ask how the club might feel about creating a women's team, and I promised him I'd do my best. I took it to the board, on the proviso that Vic could organise and run it. Surprisingly, they gave their blessing.

We got a team up and running and they started in the lowest levels, and then we grew to having two, and then three teams and began to attract better and better players. At first I was happy to be a supporter in person, to act as a sounding board and provide a starting point to help to grow the game. But before long I was enthused, and it was time to put more emphasis on development and support for the team.

Vic was always complaining. 'I'd like to expand it, but we can't get the sponsorship. We can't get a kit.'

'Leave it with me,' I answered. And I managed to persuade our kit manufacturer to build it into our men's team allocation.

The next thing was to pay expenses. The board agreed to find £200,000 a year to subsidise the women's team, and that was a major, major stepping stone. Considering what we were putting towards players' fees and salaries in the men's team, that £200,000 would give us a lot of bang for our bucks. Even so, there were such limited finances in the women's game that the players were virtually paying to play. So we supported them by finding them jobs in the club – in the box office, the stores, the laundry or the warehouse – anything that could keep them from having to abandon professional football. For those who came from outside London, we were able to put them up in the flats above the entrance to the West Stand. We tried whatever we could to keep Vic's vision alive and to put Arsenal at the forefront of women's football.

It was amazing how we grew from the grassroots to becoming

so successful, winning every major honour in the women's game and, in 2007, becoming the only English team to win a European trophy in the Women's Champions League. We really were the first club to take women's football seriously. We made sure that they had good coaches. We gave them space and a time where they could train at London Colney. We did a deal with Borehamwood FC for a venue to play in. That morphed into playing at Highbury occasionally, when we had a big game. It evolved and it grew, and it was wonderful to see.

I became a bit of an outspoken champion for women's football and tried to get other teams to follow our lead. Thankfully other clubs have jumped on the bandwagon and it has definitely taken off in its own right. I was fortunate to be able to attend many games during the Women's World Cup in France in 2019 and it was a magnificent tournament which put women's football well and truly on the global stage. All the stadia were filled, and all the Lionesses' games were shown on BBC. When I was interviewed afterwards I happily pointed out, 'The train has left the station and it is gathering speed!'

Overall, it was a fascinating period, with Arsenal becoming one of the most pioneering clubs in Europe. We were on a roll . . .

SVEN'S ESCAPADES

'**W**omen,' replied Athole Still, simply. Now that was a reply I wasn't expecting. I'd just asked the charismatic agent whether his esteemed client, Sven-Göran Eriksson, had any weaknesses.

To explain, Athole and I were killing time as we waited for Sven at Lazio's Formello training ground on the outskirts of Rome in October 2000. Athole's one of the good guys – sadly the bad agents mostly outweigh the good – a real character and he kept us entertained by singing a couple of arias from *La Bohème*. I had no idea that Athole was an opera singer – he started at the Royal Opera House, trained at the Guildhall, sang at Glyndebourne and now was performing for the small party from the FA at Formello. I was just as surprised at his information on the FA's number one target as England manager. Women! 'OK,' I said to Athole. 'We can live with that, I guess!' Sven certainly lived up to the reputation over the next five years.

The FA's pursuit of Sven was entertaining. By chance, Athole had been a guest in the royal box at Wembley on 7 October the previous year, when England lost to Germany and Kevin Keegan resigned in the dressing-room loos. Athole spotted me with Adam Crozier, the FA's chief executive and Noel White, chairman of the International Committee, deep in conversation. Athole's smart and, guessing what we were discussing, immediately called Sven in Rome, telling him he was sure Keegan had resigned as England manager. 'There's a job for you,' Athole said.

'My God. What a challenge and what an honour,' Sven replied.

This was moving quickly. Athole called me as I drove back to my home in Totteridge. 'Athole, say nothing of this,' I said. 'We'll speak tomorrow.'

I love times like this when you have to be decisive. You can't waste time. It's the national team here, so who's going to be the best person to take the country forward? For me, there was only one man. Sven-Göran Eriksson. I spoke again with Athole the morning after the Germany nightmare the night before when England had lost 1-0 to Germany in the World Cup qualifier at Wembley.

I knew I still had some persuading to do within the FA. Adam was quickly onside, which moved us along. He could see England needed fresh ideas – and foreign ideas – shaking things up. England had gone stale under Kevin, we could all see it. Adam immediately formed a seven-man selection panel and Howard Wilkinson was placed in caretaker charge for the qualifier in Finland four days after the Germany debacle. When we landed in Helsinki, the panel gathered in the hotel to discuss our options. I knew I had to persuade the other members of the selection committee, like Noel White, Dave Richards, David Davies and Peter Ridsdale about Sven. Noel wanted Johan Cruyff. Somehow, a photographer got a picture of the flip-chart Adam had with names on it, and the papers highlighted Cruyff.

The great Dutchman was definitely in the conversation but the main contenders were Sir Alex Ferguson, Gérard Houllier, Arsène Wenger and Sven. The impression I had of such a proud Scot as Ferguson was that he would only take the job if he could get England relegated, as he mischievously once said. There was more chance of finding the Loch Ness monster than getting Ferguson to renounce his heritage. Gérard was too embedded in Liverpool. Talk in the papers about Arsène and England was a non-starter. I had warned him of the likelihood that the FA would come knocking on his door.

Arsène didn't hesitate. 'I'm here to do a job at Arsenal,' he said. 'I am by your side.' People claimed I had a conflict of interest. But don't forget, I couldn't stop the FA asking Arsène if they wanted to. Anyway, I knew he wasn't interested, despite the press constantly linking him with the England vacancy. I was pleased when Adam also told the press that I left the room whenever Arsène's name came up with the selection panel.

'Let me just clear this up once and for all, Arsène has stated many times to various suitors that he believes his future is with Arsenal Football Club,' I told the press. 'There is no point wasting our energies on somebody we can't get.'

David Davies, an important figure in discussions, mentioned Terry Venables. 'We can't go back, David,' I said. I loved what Terry did in leading England to the semi-finals of Euro 96 but we needed to step into the future. Ditto with Bobby Robson. We had to be radical.

'We should go foreign,' I told the FA. I knew from Arsène's impact on my club how a foreign coach can change attitudes, diets and results. Sven could transform England, I felt. I just had to convince the others. I explained I'd always been impressed by

Sven, ever since I watched his Benfica side take Arsenal apart at Highbury in the European Cup on 6 November 1991. No amount of fireworks left over from Guy Fawkes night could have matched the show Benfica put on in extra time. George Graham was twice a title-winner and Sven outwitted him. Watching Sven in the dug-out, he seemed totally in control. He's good, I thought. Just as I knew that Arsène would eventually manage Arsenal, so I felt England could have a progressive non-Englishman in charge.

I felt the case for Sven grow even more as Adam listed the criteria for the new manager. 'The right person must have a consistent track record of success,' Adam said. Well, Sven certainly did. He was the reigning Serie A coach of the year in a division with such famous names as Giovanni Trapattoni, Marcello Lippi, Carlo Ancelotti and Fabio Capello. 'He must have dealt with big-name players,' Adam continued. Another tick. 'He must be able to deal with the media pressure,' Adam added. Well, Sven had worked in Italy for fourteen years and was well-known and liked for being unfazed by the intensity of the media interest. He could surely cope with the intrusive English press, couldn't he? I mean, the Italian press are hardly tame.

I knew the idea of a foreign manager would enrage the English press and many fans. Even the England captain, David Beckham, said, 'The England team should be managed by an Englishman.' I heard all this and sighed. I'm fighting history here, I realised. I'm calling for revolution. I worked on the traditionalists at the FA, who were in the majority. They were scared to take such a big step.

I tried to explain why thinkers were needed. 'It's a modern form of management. English football needs that. How do you motivate players earning millions of pounds a year? It's an art form. I don't believe players at that level respond to being shouted at. That's in the dark ages now. It doesn't work any more. You have to rationalise management at an intellectual level.' Sven was a deep thinker. 'Look at the table,' I said to my FA colleagues after we'd drawn against Finland. 'We're bottom. We need someone to galvanise the players otherwise we've got no chance of qualifying for the World Cup.'

The FA rarely moves quickly and we had a long debate over several meetings. But in the end, I convinced my colleagues at the FA that Sven should be our man, our Plan A. 'There is no Plan B,' Adam agreed.

Adam and I flew out to Rome and headed to Formello. Our first job was to win over Lazio's president, Sergio Cragnotti. The meeting got off on a good note as Athole sang *La Bohème* as Cragnotti walked up. We exchanged pleasantries and then got down to business. 'Will you release Sven?' Adam asked. I couldn't believe it! It was a surprisingly easy conversation to get Cragnotti's blessing. He was a very civilised, fair-minded man and he certainly played fair by Sven, whose contract expired that June. We were closing in.

When we finally met Sven, at Formello in 2001, standing on the touchline, I liked him immediately. I thought he was a very relaxed guy with a nice sense of humour. We needed somewhere to continue our conversation in private. Fortunately, my daughter Sasha was studying in Rome and living in a tiny flat, perfect for our discreet meeting. We wouldn't get busted by the paparazzi who seemed to follow Sven and Lazio around. Sasha lived above a restaurant, we had food sent up, and got down to business. Adam and I explained the job, the pressures, and the quality of the players, and our passionate aim to get back in the qualifying race for Japan and Korea in 2002.

We discussed figures and Adam and I drafted a contract for around two million pounds a year on a five-year deal which Sasha typed and printed off from her computer. We did the deal and history was made. 'I can't say no,' Sven told us. 'If I did I'd regret it for the rest of my life.'

I wasn't surprised when news about our agreement with Lazio leaked from Italy on 30 October. And I certainly wasn't surprised by the strong reaction. 'If this doesn't work out then every one of the FA selection committee should resign,' former England manager Graham Taylor said.

Bobby Robson weighed in. 'It's a crying shame we couldn't find an Englishman.'

When I next arrived at the FA offices at Lancaster Gate, I had to pass an England fan dressed as John Bull waving a placard telling us to hang our heads in shame.

Sven's first press conference was always going to be lively. It was tense and inhospitable. The press tried to trap Sven. 'Who is Sunderland's left back?'

He answered, 'I don't know now but I will very quickly.' I actually thought Sven handled the question well, pointing out that he would have plenty of time to scout and learn every player.

'Who is Leicester City's goalkeeper?' came the next missile.

If the press intended to try to embarrass Sven, it didn't work. He kept smiling. Actually, that press conference was pretty upbeat, exciting, despite the resentment that it wasn't an Englishman sitting up there.

Sven arrived quicker than we had expected. Lazio's form deteriorated, Sven resigned on 9 January 2001 and England's new manager soon arrived in London.

'Come to a game as my guest at Highbury, Sven,' I told him. 'You'll enjoy it.' And I noticed he did! When Sven came into the boardroom, I was standing with my wife Barbara and one of her attractive friends, Sarah, who happened to be divorced. Sven was quick out of the box and immediately asked Sarah what she did for a living. 'I design lampshades,' she said. Sven immediately answered with a smile, 'I need some lampshades!' I said, 'Sven, you're living at the Royal Lancaster hotel!' Athole was right in tipping me off!

His first test – well, the start of England's new era, really – was against Spain at Villa Park. I was so proud, and I'll admit a bit relieved, when I saw how Sven just filled the players with belief, organised them, and sent them out to win, which they did 3–0.

Some England players remained in the pro-Venables camp, I knew that; but I felt a change after we beat Greece in Athens on 6 June. Sven had the country believing again. Maybe we could qualify! We had to catch Germany first. People forget we went into that famous game in Munich on 1 September as complete underdogs. The odds were against us. All I could hear on landing in Munich was, oh, Germany have lost only one World Cup qualifier before, the Olympic Stadium's their fortress and their fans are not only expecting victory but talking by how many. Well, pride comes before a fall, my mother always said.

Being on the FA's International Committee, I attended a function organised by the Deutsche Fussball-Bund (German Football Association) the night before the game. These events can be pretty staid affairs but I actually enjoy them. I'm representing England and it's important to engage with the opposition. I like to find out how their league's doing and pick up ideas. The International Committee was such a huge and rich part of my life. I loved all the rituals, the fun, the drama. We used to go to training at the stadium and Noel White and I would lap the track as the lads trained. Noel was wonderful, passionate about football, always friendly and surprisingly adept at the piano. I always smiled when people said, 'You're really an Arsenal man, Noel's really a Liverpool man.' England mattered deeply to us both.

I became very close to Noel. We were such good friends that I rushed north to see him when he fell ill in 2019. I could see his life slipping away. As I was leaving, Noel clasped my hand and nodded with a tear in his eye. I realised I'd not be seeing him again. His wife Jean asked me to deliver the eulogy at Dunham Forest golf club near Altrincham. Of course, it was packed, standing room only and no surprise, as Noel made so many friends in and out of football.

'If I'd known it was going to be this crowded, I'd have put in a turnstile!' I began. I started with a joke because Noel would have loved that. He had such a brilliant sense of humour. I found my eulogy again when we left our house in Totteridge and I felt very emotional reading it back and thinking of my old friend, a real England lion. 'As we all know, Noel was a gentleman and a gentle man,' I told the mourners. 'He was softly spoken, passionate about the game and respected by all who knew him. A dear friend – not expensive, just dear. He was a stickler for detail, and one of the few members of the FA council who actually bothered to read the entire contents of the minutes of the previous meeting! He would regularly put up his hand and correct the company secretary for grammatical and sometimes factual errors.'

It's important to understand that many of these 'FA blazers', as they were known, are real people with a real passion for football. Noel was a great servant to English football and a great lover of life. He was never a faceless bureaucrat, he was wonderful company. 'To amuse ourselves on trips,' my eulogy continued, 'we would have quizzes on music and records. These were the days of 78s, 45s and 33 r.p.m. with songs on both sides. Noel was extremely knowledgeable, having been in the sheet music business with his old friend Peter Swales of Manchester City. If ever there was a dispute, we would call on Bill Kenwright, our mutual friend, to act as arbitrator. Once when it was my turn, I asked Noel what was Tab Hunter's big hit record. He unhesitatingly answered, "'Red Sails in the Sunset' on the A-side and 'Kiss Me Quick' . . . on the backside!" That was Noel's humour!'

Fifteen months later and in Munich for a fixture with Germany in their backyard, this was going to be a huge test for Sven's credentials. In the thick of all this, I loved seeing Sven so serene and calm. He looked to me like a man heading off on holiday. I liked that Sven wasn't caught up in all the history of England and Germany. He just focused on getting the selection and tactics right. Sven simplified things for players, as all top managers do. He played them in their club positions – there was no messing about, trying to be clever. Sven simply tapped into what their club managers did. He made Ashley Cole left back. Where does he play for his club? Left back. Gary Neville right back. Sol Campbell and Rio Ferdinand centre back. That game in Germany, Steven Gerrard played his Liverpool role. Emile

Heskey supported Michael Owen. And they destroyed Germany, 5–1, and even Heskey scored as the England fans sang.

What also excited me for the future was that Sven put out a very young team. Ashley Cole was twenty, Gerrard and Owen were twenty-one and Rio was twenty-two. Here was Sven building for the future while also delivering in the present. Munich was a game-changer for his reputation and also for the England players, who put down a real marker that the team could compete on a big stage. Being in the Olympic Stadium that evening was one of my best days on the International Committee. I'm an England fan so I took huge pride in seeing them play so well. I felt a surge of optimism and vindication too. Sven was the right call. After this and every win, I'd look at Adam and mouth, 'There was no Plan B!' As we left Munich, I was asked what the result had done. My answer was simple. 'Sven has put oxygen into a body that was comatose. He's given us fresh air, he's given us belief, he's given the nation hope.'

And he really had. Sven was public hero number one, even more so after Beckham's amazing free kick against Greece at Old Trafford that took England to the 2002 World Cup. After a difficult period, everything on the inside with England was measured and positive.

External distractions, though, were not so controllable. The Ulrika Jonsson story broke before we went to the World Cup in Japan. Sven got going with the Swedish TV presenter, and her au pair duly came out with some revelations. His relationship with Nancy Dell'Olio became front page news particularly when she showed up at a cocktail party at 10 Downing Street in a fire engine red catsuit. She palled out with my wife Barbara and David Davies' wife Susan and the three of them really got on well. What I loved about Sven is that he just took all these headlines in his stride. When things started getting lively in his private life, Sven just laughed at the reaction. Another criticism was that Sven was too enamoured of David Beckham and his fame. I like David, and my take is that Sven really respected David as a person and rated him as a player, and that's spot on. If you look at the stats, David was one of Sven's most consistent players. He played fifty-seven times for Sven, was captain every time and that's how highly Sven regarded him.

I always admired how David handled the attention. To his great credit, he was never a big-time-Charlie, he was always part of the group, just a very level-headed lad. Fame and fortune didn't change his attitude. Because of the global icon he has become it is really hard to realise that he's the shy boy next door. One year, Barbara and I went to a wonderful little island in the Caribbean and we bumped into David and his wife Victoria. He talked to everybody, so nice, never fazed by being photographed, just well-mannered. David's a kind person and that's why Sven liked him – that, and of course the fact that he was a bloody good football player.

Beckham's fitness was front-page news after he broke his metatarsal before the World Cup. But nothing was going to stop him playing against Argentina in Sapporo. Beckham's a strong character but I knew from talking to him how he had to live with all the pressure and criticism following his red card against Argentina at France 98. When he drove in his penalty in Sapporo, I was overjoyed. I knew how much that moment meant. He's a proud man and very patriotic, and that was undoubtedly redemption for him.

I felt that the 2002 England group had a strong camaraderie. We progressed to the quarter-final and a glamorous tie against

Brazil in Shizuoka on 21 June. I sensed the team's confidence growing. I know Brazil had the three Rs – Ronaldo, Rivaldo and Ronaldinho – but Sven and the players didn't see them as invincible. We saw how the team struggled against Belgium in the round of sixteen, not scoring until midway through the second half in Kobe, a game we all went to watch. So we really fancied our chances.

The day before the game a monsoon came in and we all thought it would be great to play Brazil in rain rather than scorching heat. But I awoke to an unforgiving sun piercing the curtains. 'This is not ideal weather,' I said to myself. I still believed, especially when Michael raced through to give England the lead. I thought, This is it, we have a real chance of winning the World Cup. If we could just hold on. If we could just get past Brazil. It would be Turkey in the semi-finals. I really believed. But then Rivaldo scored just before half-time. When Ronaldinho then put that free kick in over David Seaman's head, my heart broke for the big goalie.

Ever since he came to Arsenal in 1990, I've admired David so much as a professional and a man. He just radiates happiness. Everyone loves David. So to see him in tears, and then apologising, really got to me. Come on! David didn't need to say sorry. But there he was in front of a camera, heartbroken, inconsolable, actually being so brave as to come out and speak. I talked to him back in the hotel. He was my player, a football child of mine, in a way. A moment of personal hell like that could never destroy a career as big as David's. I went up to him, well, to all the players, for moral support. I sensed they just wanted to be left by themselves and I respected that. Everyone was hurting. I just wanted to encourage them, to lift their spirits and then quietly withdraw.

I sought out Sven. 'You've made the country proud,' I told him. He thanked me but I knew he was hurting too. Management is a very lonely place. For those on the FA like myself, we were very aware of who motivates the manager – especially in defeat. My role was to support Sven. The closer I got to managers, especially those like Arsène and Sven, the more I realised the emotion of defeat lasts longer than the joy of winning. Exits from a tournament always stay with me. On the flight back from Japan, Sven's right-hand man, Tord Grip, got his accordion out and tried to lift the mood but it was difficult. We came home heavy-hearted.

When a door closed on one drama with England, another one opened. I knew how bothered the FA were when reading of Sven's dalliance with Chelsea a couple of months later. They got a tip-off that the *Sun* was about to run a story that Sven met Chelsea's chief executive Peter Kenyon to discuss becoming their manager. Seriously? Where's the loyalty? I had to get involved that Saturday. I went to Sven's house in Regent's Park, north London, to find sheer pandemonium outside with reporters and TV crews; you could hardly move. The media maul rolled on down to the Valley when Sven went to watch Charlton Athletic. We'd had a challenging Friday evening and Saturday morning, as Sven had his phone turned off until mid-morning. When reached at last he had advised people at the FA he was going to leave for Chelsea. Sven seemed completely unperturbed by all the fuss. I sort of admired how he could rise above all the chaos – chaos he had caused.

Sven and Adrian Bevington (head of media at the FA) came back to my house in Totteridge for a conference call with Athole,

David Davies and Mark Palios, who'd succeeded Adam as chief executive. I don't think Sven and Palios were close. But I was close to Sven, and I said, 'This is England, Sven, you can't dance at two weddings. You have to make a decision about what you want to do.' I mean, I knew Sven was technically in breach of contract because there was a catch-all as he brought the FA into disrepute. Sven was very honest and just told us he was flattered by Chelsea offering him a lot of money.

We worked on him and managed to convince him he still had plenty of work to do with England. Sven committed to stay. I always see the best in people but it was a worrying moment. I know a lot of people perceived what Sven did as a betrayal of the national team but in his eyes he was a football manager, a global manager. Clubs wanted him. I know Sven also had other approaches, including one from Real Madrid. Still, it made a change from Real chasing Arsène.

England always kept me on my toes. There was always a drama or three. Rio Ferdinand missed a dope test at Manchester United's Carrington training ground on 23 September, through sheer forgetfulness. But the FA were expected to insist that Sven couldn't select Rio, and the players threatened to go on strike. I heard the clock ticking louder and louder towards our huge Euro 2004 qualifier with Turkey in Istanbul on 11 October. This was definitely one of the most difficult periods in my time with England.

Sven's players reported to our base at Sopwell House hotel and the United contingent was particularly angry over the FA's treatment of Rio. 'Innocent until proven guilty,' was the repeated comment from Gary Neville. Rio had not even been charged yet. The players had the support of Gordon Taylor, the chief executive of the PFA (Professional Footballers' Association) and Sir Alex, a powerful combination. Sir Alex was apoplectic with us. He rang Sven early one morning, screaming down the phone. 'You can't select Rio!'

Sven replied, 'You'll have to call and yell at someone else.' Dear Sven, that took some guts.

We were in a tricky situation. The FA knew the risk of disqualification in playing a UEFA qualifier with a player potentially at risk from a drugs ban. Relations between the squad and the FA deteriorated. It hurt me to see all this tension and mistrust. I knew from talking to the players how popular Rio was. He's a really nice guy and I believed him. I also felt for the FA staff who were both close to the players and loyal to the organisation. They were being asked to arrange a meeting for the players, who wanted it in private, away from the FA. In addition, we were heading to Istanbul without fans as they were banned following the abuse directed at Turks in the home game; and now there was a chance that we might be going without players, too.

Our flight to Ataturk airport was on Thursday 9 October and we needed to know urgently who'd be on the plane. The players met on Tuesday evening at Sopwell and voted to strike and I know it was supposedly unanimous but at least a couple of players expressed reservations. Gary Neville drove everything. He was opinionated, but I knew he just felt strongly for Rio, his clubmate. Gary and the players were pilloried by the press, and woke up to headlines like WHO THE HELL DO YOU THINK YOU ARE? What a mess, I hated seeing England like this. But I'm an optimist. I always felt the players would get on the plane. I had this strong feeling that common sense would prevail and thank

God it did. Rio very sensibly helped enormously by sending Gary a message of thanks and telling him and players to go to Istanbul. Never has hearing, 'Boarding complete' made me smile so much on a plane.

The players played fantastically well on the Saturday night in an incredible atmosphere at Fenerbahce's Şükrü Saracoğlu Stadium, full of Turkish fans and no English ones. They got the draw, a fight in the tunnel, and I must admit there was astonishment amongst the International Committee that apparently Heskey threw the best punch. Emile's so mild-mannered, he wouldn't hurt a fly but that was the players in Istanbul. Attack one of us, you attack us all.

The Euros in 2004 was another big opportunity for England but again we fell short, going out on penalties. I never complain about referees, they have a hard enough job, but I only just managed to hide my frustration when Urs Meier disallowed a Sol Campbell goal that would have won our quarter-final against Portugal. Sven was typically calm at the final whistle, in contrast to Portugal's coach, Luiz Felipe Scolari, who was very boisterous in the tunnel at the Stadium of Light, banging on the walls. England's dressing room was a morgue, no surprise, the players were heartbroken, but I noticed Sven insisting on going to the referee's dressing room. We all feared he would have a go at Meier, who explained to Sven that he ruled Campbell's header out because of an apparent infringement by John Terry, supposedly impeding the Portuguese keeper, Ricardo. I felt it was so harsh but I was still surprised by Sven's response. He went round the room, shaking the officials' hands, saying, 'Well done, well done, well done.' Then left.

Shortly after we returned from Lisbon, forensic details of Sven's latest escapade landed with a thud on the FA's doormat on 18 July. The *News of the World* had chapter and verse on Sven's relationship with Faria Alam, David Davies's PA. People within the FA had suspicions and some within the building used to say 'Danger' when mentioning Faria's name. In fact, she was colloquially known as 'Fire Alarm'. It wasn't a secret that Sven was attracted to her. Every time I went to Soho Square to see David, Sven was always hanging around in his office. I didn't need to be Poirot to detect what was going on.

Faria told the FA that nothing was going on and an official statement on the Monday afternoon rubbished the story. David Davies contacted Sven, who also said, 'It's nonsense.' As he explained later in his own book, Sven 'didn't mean it wasn't true but that the question was nonsense'. Sven felt his private life was his own business and I had some sympathy, but this was directly impacting on the FA.

Anyway, it seemed to go quiet but my peace was disturbed on 25 July by the *News of the World* headline I BEDDED SVEN AND HIS BOSS. Heavens above, I couldn't believe what I was reading. Faria had also slept with Mark Palios. They were all single, by the way, but it was such a mess. It was a bit incestuous. I was left trying to sort out who was doing what with whom! The FA had to retract its earlier denial, which was so embarrassing. I now read speculation of a 'third man' at the FA, another Faria conquest. Since she was David Davies's PA he was a natural suspect but that was rubbish. I was buttonholed by a group of journalists who incessantly asked me the same question. Eventually, I couldn't resist, I said, 'OK, do you really want to know?' They all surged forward in their seats. I paused. 'I'll tell you. There is no "third man". It was Sven – twice!' They appreciated the humour.

Sven seemed typically unperturbed as we headed out to the pre-season Amsterdam tournament to watch Arsenal. On the Sunday, just as Arsenal were about to play Ajax, the latest *News of the World* bombshell dropped from a great height. Not another one? I found Sven and got him up to my room. 'Sven, this is serious, I've just had a call from Adrian,' I told him. 'You and I go back a long way. I've got to ask you straight, are you having an affair with the FA receptionist?'

Sven's eyes rolled. 'No, but I'd like to!' That was good old Sven.

I knew the storm would leave some damage at the FA. The headlines, and the misleading statements, were just too much. At 6 p.m. on that Sunday, Palios tendered his resignation, adding, 'I do not accept I have been guilty of any wrongdoing.' I felt for him, he was a very able CEO, but he felt it was the honourable thing to do.

The *News of the World* struck at Sven again on 15 January 2006 with a Fake Sheikh story landing out of nowhere. The story had all the hallmarks of its undercover reporter, Mazher Mahmood, here posing as an owner of a football academy. Sven had made unguarded comments and it seemed that he tried to persuade the Fake Sheikh to buy Aston Villa, saying he'd be their manager for five million pounds a year. I stared at the story in disbelief. What was going to hit us next? Sven even said he could get David Beckham to quit Real Madrid for Villa. Well, I guess both have a bullring. Sven had to apologise to players, including Michael Owen who he suggested was not enjoying Newcastle United. As with the Chelsea flirtation, I put his entrapment by the Fake Sheikh down to naivety. Sven got sucked in.

Brian Barwick, the FA's latest chief executive, called me the following day and we decided to stick with Sven. But we knew a second week of Fake Sheikh revelations were coming and when I read them, I really feared for him. Sven claimed knowledge of irregular transfer deals at three clubs. I mean, I was now speechless. On Monday 23 January, the FA's compliance unit interviewed Sven and Athole about the claims. Just 'gossip' was their reply. There were six hours of talks with Sven, Athole and the FA at Soho Square. Sven argued strongly that he shouldn't have his contract terminated. I knew the feeling within the FA was that Sven's position was untenable. It was sad, I liked him, but he just couldn't continue. Sven had made himself a figure of fun in many people's eyes. We decided that he should go after the World Cup in Germany. Sven is still sore about this. He was adamant that he didn't say some of the things that were reported.

The only time I ever saw Sven annoyed was when Sir Alex called him at our base in Baden Baden at the 2006 World Cup. Fergie was furious that Wayne Rooney was going to play at the World Cup, with England gambling on his recovery from a recently broken metatarsal. 'You're finished,' he screamed at Sven.

Sven lost it. 'F★★k off,' he said, which was seriously unlike Sven. 'Alex, I will pick Rooney. Have a nice holiday. Ciao, bye.'

Overall, I believe Sven was a success. England went from seventeenth in the FIFA rankings to fourth under Sven. He confounded his critics. He proved himself. He lost just one of his twenty-four qualifiers, to Northern Ireland, and guided England to three quarter-finals. Of course, he wasn't perfect. He was flawed – as we found out.

I felt that we should go for Scolari as a replacement. He certainly knew how to beat us so surely he'd know how to inspire us? But Scolari got cold feet at the media intrusion and we eventually turned to Steve McClaren, Sven's number two. A nice guy – but sadly he did not succeed.

It has been described as the impossible job. It is certainly one of the loneliest jobs, and with so much on the line and such intense scrutiny it is a relentless challenge. The FA's task in choosing and supporting their man is never easy.

SIMPLY THE BEST

For all Arsène's qualities, privately, he was a very sore loser. If we went out for dinner after a defeat it was very strained. Invariably, I found myself talking to myself. It was a monologue not a dialogue.

He had this habit of saying, 'Oh, what were you saying?' and it was obvious his mind was elsewhere; on why this player didn't get across or that player let his man in; or the impact of each of the individual decisions, actions, or inactions that, to use a well-known example, allowed Ryan Giggs to run all that way without being stopped. And that's without talking about referees' poor decisions.

Going out after the game was a ritual. Some of the time it was wonderful. At Highbury we would go to San Daniele, a local Italian run by two brothers, and we would eat spaghetti and shoot the breeze. Some of the players did the same. The atmosphere in there was a buzz and it was a special place to wind down after a game. Patrick Vieira or Robert Pires would come in and get a round of applause and then everyone would leave them to their meals in peace. The atmosphere of family and positivity was magical and boosted us all. Conversely, the post-match dinners after a bad defeat never tasted good.

I had such faith in Arsène that, if he felt a season without defeat was achievable, despite considerable scepticism when he first mentioned it publicly, he had my backing. It had not been done since the late 1800s in England so I wasn't particularly expectant, but I knew that if Arsène put his mind to something it certainly felt possible, if not probable.

The players who delivered the Invincible season of 2003/04, both as individuals and as a group, had exceptional qualities. They were guys of character, of personality. They were all winners with extremely high standards that they demanded of themselves and each other. Once the trust grew and they gelled, the played together like a wonderful orchestra.

During the magnificent World Cup in Brazil in 2014, I hosted our three Brazilian players, Gilberto Silva, Edu and Sylvinho at La Figueira in São Paulo. I was sitting next to Gilberto and asked him to tell me something about the Invincibles. He paused for a moment and then stood up and told me this story. The team would be lining up in the tunnel before the match always – superstitiously – in the same order. Just before going out on the pitch, Patrick, the captain, would turn his head, look down the line and nod at Jens behind him. Then Jens would turn his head and pass the nod to Lauren, and so it went all the way down the team from front to back. They didn't need a word, their eyes said it all, that they were going to do it today. They were ready for anything. As if choreographed, they'd look across to the opposition who felt fear. It was very powerful.

When I look at the figures that we've had at Arsenal through the years, in every generation, you may generally have one really outstanding player. But with the Invincibles, we had a team of outstanding players. This team has a special place in Arsenal hearts and it is an insightful example of how to mix all the right ingredients to make a winning team.

Jens Lehmann

Jens arrived as an experienced pro to replace David Seaman – not easy gloves to fill but he had the mentality to do it. He is an unusual guy, extremely focused, passionate and determined. He does not want to be beaten. He gets very annoyed and is a very sore loser, a bit short-tempered. Before a game he would have this routine, bouncing the ball against the wall and catching it whilst moving side to side. It was all very intense. He would get himself geed up as if he was going to box. Ten minutes before kick-off it was as if he was preparing himself for a world title fight. He got himself psyched up, ready for battle. That attitude permeated through the team. He was a good leader and a good lad who I still keep in touch with. You'd have him in your team every day.

Jens always reminds me of one of my maxims about my life in football: in the end it is all about tickets. It would be impossible to calculate how many tickets for events I have tried to rustle up for people over the years. I will always try to look after people who are important to me. Which brings us to Jens and the 2014 World Cup final. Germany had just beaten Brazil 7–1 in the semi-final in one of the most astonishing results in the tournament's history. The morning after I got a call from Jens.

'Mr Dein, obviously Germany did very well. We're in the final. I'd like to come with my wife. Can you get us seats?'

I immediately asked, 'Well, what about the DFB [the German Football Association]? You're a former player.'

He said, 'No, they won't help their former players.'

I replied with my usual line when I had a mission to attend to, 'Leave it with me.'

I reached out to some contacts at FIFA to see if anyone could help to get two VIP tickets for the final for Jens Lehmann.

Sure enough, they said, 'Yes.' When I told Jens the good news he was delighted but then told me he couldn't get a flight out to Brazil.

'Jens, leave it with me.' I managed to get him a flight which would arrive on the Saturday before the game and come back the following Tuesday. Half an hour later he phoned me back and mentioned he couldn't get a hotel. I told him I would see what I could do.

That day I was flying to the third and fourth place game with Gary Lineker on board. I asked if he happened to know if the BBC had any room in their hotel. Gary came to the rescue and I told Jens he now had a hotel room. He was extremely grateful.

The day before the final Jens called me at about midday from the BBC hotel. He mentioned that he and his wife Connie like cycling but his hotel could not help him to locate any bikes.

I said, 'Jens, leave it with me.' I knew everyone at the Fasano hotel where I was staying, as we had been based there for a month and they got hold of a couple of bikes within an hour. When I told Jens I invited him and Connie to lunch before picking up the bikes. We were eating at the rooftop restaurant and on the next table were a group of Germans. They recognised Jens. I leaned over and said, 'Hi, guys, you're obviously here for the match.' We got chatting and it turned out they had come on a private jet and were going back straight after the game. I said, 'You don't have room for two more people, do you?' They said, 'Yes, as a matter of fact we do.' I said, 'Jens, you could be in luck here . . .'

From the simple question, 'I would like to attend the match,' came the flight out, hotel room, bicycles, VIP tickets for the game and a private jet back. You need a bit of luck in life.

To top it all off, the Germans won.

Lauren

We signed him from Real Mallorca. He was one of those in whom Arsène saw something beyond what he had been doing for his old club and he was transformed into a fullback even if that wasn't his favoured position. Lauren was a quiet guy with a big heart and a really strong character. He was a genuine boy, a team player, and a very talented footballer. He had great strength and was very rarely injured. The Invincible team did not carry a lot of problems in that way. It is funny but when you've got a team that's winning, they all want to play, and when you've got a team that's losing games, some of them want to hide. I couldn't imagine Lauren – or any of the other boys for that matter – would ever want to hide. It wasn't in their nature. Lauren was one of the players who reacted the strongest to the flare-up at Old Trafford – he was all in for protecting the team.

Lauren had the courage to volunteer, although it wasn't his job particularly, to take a penalty when he had to. He had taken a very important one against Tottenham in the 2002 title run-in. It was scarily straight down the middle and not that fast, but he was as cool as a cucumber. Lauren is a person you can trust with anything.

Kolo Touré

I think of all the Invincibles as my children and to this day when we exchange text messages Kolo calls me 'Dad', Barbara 'Mum' and I call him son. He is a wonderful boy and he had a very endearing personality which made you want to look after him. He was not very experienced when he arrived from Ivory Coast, initially on trial. Arsène had contacts there with a local academy, ASEC Mimosa, which was in partnership with his old friend Jean-Marc Guillou and he was recommended and seized his opportunity.

I had been to the Ivory Coast quite a bit and the fact I spoke French to him was helpful at the time, and aided him in settling down. Pastoral care was very important, particularly with younger players arriving from abroad. They've got no friends, nobody to help them. It's very important the club takes them under its wing at that stage. Before we had a player liaison, we would take care of as much as we could, making sure they got a nice house, with someone looking after them.

Kolo was just charming, a good trainer, and desperate to do well. He was willing to play anywhere for the team. He didn't mind whether he was right back, left back, centre back, midfield. He just wanted to play. Everything clicked for him in the summer of 2003 when Arsène tried him out in a pre-season game at centre back next to Sol. Almost by accident a tremendous partnership began and Kolo ended up being the most used outfield player in that legendary season. When you realise that centre back pairing cost next to nothing, with just a few hundred thousand compensation for Kolo and Sol on a Bosman, and add the modest fee for Lauren and Ashley, being homegrown, it really is a wonder. That Invincible back four was put together for a relative pittance.

Sol Campbell

We have a special bond because of the delicate nature of the transfer that brought Sol to Arsenal. The slow burn of our discussions was very meaningful and dependent on being very trusting, honest and understanding. When he was unveiled the drama and the magnitude were spectacular. To this day it seems amazing we were able to pull it off under the radar.

Sol is a deep thinker and was an outstanding footballer and defensive leader. He could have gone to any club in his peak years and choosing Arsenal was not easy for him. We made sure we gave him plenty of protection before his first game at White Hart Lane as an Arsenal player, which was very hostile. There were bricks thrown at the team coach and the reaction of their fans was quite frightening. Sol handled it, even though at times you wonder whether he could have saved himself some personal turmoil and abuse had he taken another path. His inner strength was remarkable.

Once we were into the Invincible season we had a routine. I'd say, 'How are you, Sol?' and he would say, 'Mr Dein, we've got to keep it going.' That was his mantra, all the time, 'We've got to keep it going.' His single-mindedness was a real asset.

It must have been one hell of a moment for him to actually win the league at White Hart Lane, of all places, but it was typical of his intense, winning mentality that he and Jens had an argument in the dressing room because of a stoppage time penalty given against Jens which meant the match ended in a draw.

Ashley Cole

Ashley was a bit of a special case in that Invincibles team. He was the homegrown beacon. He'd been there since he was a little boy and there are pictures of him when he was small in his Arsenal gear. As well as being a phenomenal left back, combining fierce competitive spirit with brilliantly timed technique, he was a nice boy, a humble, local lad. I recall when he was first called up by England. I was on the FA International Committee and got an early warning and happened to be at the training ground when he got the news.

I met him as he was coming off the training pitch and said, 'Congratulations.' I was looking at him very closely and he said, 'What are you looking at?' and I told him, 'I'm looking at your head.'

He said, 'Why?'

I said, 'I just want to make sure it hasn't got bigger.' He went on to be one of the best England defenders ever.

I still have regrets when it comes to Ashley because Arsenal could have handled it differently. He should never have left the club. He was an Arsenal boy through and through. We had an opportunity to re-sign him, and we let him slip, we didn't do it. We could have done, but we didn't offer him the money that he was looking for and it was so silly.

It is a shame he is not recognised more within the club – because of the tapping up, the way it ended and the successes he later had as a Chelsea player. He still should be recognised as an Arsenal legend, as a major part of that team and that era.

Martin Keown

Martin is very intense and as genuine as the day is long. He will always speak his mind. Every time I had a contract renewal meeting with him his body language was such that he was always leaning forward intently and he'd look at you with eyes wide open, glaring. 'I know how much Steve Bould and Tony Adams get,' he would say before we even started negotiating. It always took the wind out of my sails! He's definitely a character and he really proved his worth during the Invincible season – with his presence in the dressing room, as much as everything else. It was wonderful to have him in the team because you knew you'll get everything from him. He will run through the brick wall.

There is a famous picture of Martin bearing down on Ruud van Nistelrooy in one of the most pivotal moments of the 2003/04 season. It summed up how Martin would stop at nothing for the cause. He was fired up because we didn't lose the game, and he wanted to make his point to van Nistelrooy as the team were irate. They felt his gamesmanship had played a part in Patrick being sent off. Martin is a very straight shooter. He doesn't mince his words. You know where you stand. Once again, he has the traits of a natural winner and is also a good guy. He was old school. Don't forget, he started his career at Arsenal, coming through in the 1980s alongside Tony Adams, David Rocastle and the rest. George let him go to Aston Villa and then Everton; however, he brought him back, thankfully. That is an unusual scenario but Martin went on to play a huge role over many successful years. He was Arsenal through and through. That does mean something. If you bring the players through the ranks I'd like to think there is an extra warmth in how they perceive the club, and maybe a little bit of gratitude that we gave them the chance.

Robert Pires

I called him the Bank of England because, when he had the ball, he'd never lose it. Your money was safe. You knew he wouldn't do anything silly. He would always be looking, and he had the great vision. He knew where Thierry and Dennis were, the runs they would make. He'd find them. He was quite fast, a great passer of the ball, very accurate, and such a clever player. He read the game very well and possessed a lovely genial character. He was involved in twenty-one goals, either scoring or assisting, during the Invincible year.

Robert is just a wonderful guy, easy-going, extremely polite, extraordinarily talented. He did not get enough credit for his role, in my opinion. To me he would always be one of the first people on the team sheet. He made his life in England and stayed on for a long time in Hampstead with his family. It was a blessing for Arsenal that he continued to play a role at the training ground, keeping himself fit and being around to share his wisdom for years after his retirement.

The fact that Pires was bought for six million pounds from Marseille, when he was aged twenty-six, just hitting his peak and was already a World Cup and European Championship winner, ranks as one of the best pieces of business of any era. He was a central piece of the jigsaw.

Patrick Vieira

Although Arsène was not officially our manager the summer we moved for Patrick, he absolutely drove the deal. He knew plenty about Patrick, who came through as a teenaged captain at Cannes while Arsène was managing down the coast at Monaco. He recognised that he could be a transformative talent and when he heard that AC Milan made him available, we had to move rapidly. Patrick was on his way to sign for Ajax when Arsène contacted him to intercept the deal.

I had enough trust in Arsène to run with it and arrange the transfer with AC Milan. But I won't forget the first time we saw him properly. He was a substitute against Sheffield Wednesday and came on to have one of the most remarkable debuts I've ever seen. All of a sudden we thought, Wow, this guy is incredible. What have we landed here?

Ray Parlour goes on record as he was injured during the game and got substituted for Patrick and, after seeing how Patrick was playing, he turned round to Pat Rice on the bench and said, 'F★★★ me, I'll never get in the team again!'

After a few weeks people said, 'Well, we may not know much about Arsène Wenger, but at least he brings good players.'

When it comes to skill and stature not many can get anywhere near Patrick. He was a tower of strength but also a gentle giant. He is very polite but he has got his own mind. He took over the captaincy from Tony Adams and it was demanding to wear that armband after such a colossal figure in the club's history. The way Patrick took it on and gave it his own slant was really something special for the club and a great advert for multiculturalism.

Patrick led by example and he was a fighter. Well, we had to defend him a few times in disciplinary hearings. Not long after he arrived there was a spitting incident with Neil Ruddock. At the FA hearing in that case our QC, Mark Phillips, argued that the trajectory of the spittle demonstrated it was not directed at his opponent, but was aimed towards the floor. Ruddock had called Patrick inflammatory names and the reaction was difficult, but we did our best to get the punishment reduced.

The fans like a bit of a naughty boy but his will to win was outstanding and the example he set, as both a leader and an outstanding player, was remarkable. As time has shown, he was virtually irreplaceable.

Quite apart from his playing ability, just to communicate with him was always a pleasure. You would be lucky to have him as a friend. He's got great warmth, humour and integrity.

Gilberto Silva

Arsène and I had been watching a Brazil game with a view to acquiring another player and, after about twenty minutes, he spotted immediately someone else with quality he liked. That was Gilberto. His transfer was a nightmare. His club didn't want to engage at all after I travelled all the way to talk to them. I didn't know what I was letting myself in for. I went to Belo Horizonte, Brazil, and met the president of Atletico Mineiro. He said, 'Thank you for coming, but I'm not actually going to sell him. Let's have a good time, let's have dinner.'

We went for dinner and they didn't want to know. I must have stayed four or five days, trying to get him to enter into some kind of negotiation. I had to go through one of the president's colleagues, who was a senior shareholder and ran a bank. Once I finally managed to lock him in there was a chink of light. I virtually had to sleep on their doorstep for a few nights until they engaged. When we agreed terms I metaphorically handcuffed Gilberto as we were leaving. We flew to Austria to meet up with the group, who were on a pre-season training camp. I said to Arsène, 'Here's your player.'

There was a solidarity tax we had to pay to the development club at the time. The Premier League introduced a scheme where the team that developed the player would get part of the transfer. We dropped a line to the Brazilian federation, the CBF, to find out who should get this percentage of the fee. Five clubs put their hands up. They all claimed to have developed him. Meanwhile, when we asked Gilberto he said, 'No, I was working in a sweet factory for most of the time.' These sort of things happen, especially when dealing with overseas clubs.

Gilberto is one of the calmest, kindest, most humble and respectful people you could meet. He is so understated, but a wonderful player who appeared ninety-three times for Brazil. People don't realise quite what a superior player he was. I remember after a month or so, I said, 'What do you do in London? How do you keep yourself amused?'

He said, 'I go down to play street soccer in Brixton.' He got involved in it because that's where he started in Brazil, playing street football. He found out that there was a street soccer league in Brixton and he wanted to help them. That was Gilberto.

Freddie Ljungberg

Freddie's arrival was another instance of Arsène making the identification and then leaving it to me to do the rest. He made an impression during an international game. Sweden played against England and Arsène saw that he was a young, intelligent player causing England's defenders some problems with his movement. Arsène said, 'I like Freddie Ljungberg,' and that was it, he had passed the baton to me. Freddie was being watched by a number of European clubs so we needed to act decisively. We did the deal with Halmstad for three million pounds, which turned out to be another golden deal considering the quality of the player and the service he gave.

Freddie was flamboyant. He'd always come in with these funny coats, with extravagant colours. He was loved by the girls, especially once the Calvin Klein adverts took off. But because he looked so stylish, people underrated quite how serious he was about his football, determined and dedicated. He was absolutely on it. He was a great player who had a knack for timing his runs brilliantly.

I was pleased for Freddie when he returned to join the coaching staff. It is not a coincidence that so many of this team wanted to go into coaching in some capacity. They were all very switched on and very intelligent and addicted to the game.

Edu

I have a soft spot for anybody who signs for Arsenal but you know when you're buying a Brazilian, you are lucky to get them. You've got a fair chance that they will have good balance, that they will have good rhythm, that they will have good technique. It's ingrained in them. God gave them a gift. Because they've got a ball by their feet very early in life, and the sun, the sand, the culture – it is instinctive.

The actual transfer of Edu was dogged by bad luck. Signing him was far more complicated than we had reckoned when we first approached Corinthians. We were told by his agents that there was a work permit problem. Many Brazilians have got European ancestry and are entitled to get what is normally either a Portuguese or Italian passport. Edu was said to have had

Portuguese heritage and a passport which meant he could come in under EU regulations; buying players with a South American passport was far more stringent.

At one o'clock in the morning on the day he was to arrive, my phone rang. 'Hello, this is the immigration office at terminal three, we've got one of your players here. Mr Edu. Well, I'm afraid he's got a false passport.'

I immediately went to Heathrow to deal with it in person. I said, 'Hold on a minute. Is there nothing we can do to at least get it sorted out, because apparently he's entitled to it?'

The immigration officer explained there was no exemption and that it would have to be sorted back in Brazil. Despite my pleading for a stay of execution and our lawyers getting on to it, we didn't get anywhere. Unfortunately, he had to go back.

They kindly let me in to see Edu, who was understandably confused and upset. I said, 'Edu, we will resolve it. I want to tell you don't worry.'

The following morning I spoke to Arsène. He was concerned, naturally. But his first thought was for Edu. We relayed the message that we would wait for him and would help to get it sorted out. He had been embroiled in a scam in which he was given a passport number that didn't exist, in an effort to speed up the process of issuing the document and save a few months of waiting.

It also impacted another of our players at the time, Sylvinho, a left back who was the first Brazilian to ever play for Arsenal and had been with the club for a couple of seasons. Who will ever forget his left-foot rocket shot at Stamford Bridge in 2000? He came in before the scam had been detected and, once we realised the issue with Edu, we didn't mess around. We took

Sylvinho's passport to the Portuguese embassy to find out whether it was genuine. It wasn't. We had to move quickly and managed to get him out to Celta Vigo.

Edu was a charming boy, a stylish, upright player who was skilful and had stature. It was not easy to get into our central midfield with Patrick and Gilberto around but he made a fantastic impression and appeared in thirty of the league games during the Invincible season. I am delighted that Edu has returned to Arsenal as Technical Director. With his knowledge and personality, he should do a great job.

Ray Parlour

I have a love of humour, so I used to love Ray. He could have been a comedian; he is naturally funny. His one-liners are legendary and he was an important piece of the squad jigsaw because we had a lot of overseas players and he got them all mixing together, which was essential. He would teach the boys cockney rhyming slang and bet them to use it in television interviews with a straight face.

He and Martin were on neighbouring treatment tables not long after the Manchester United incident at Old Trafford in 2003. Both players had been given long bans for their part in the emotional overspill at the end of the game. Seeing me enter the dressing room, Ray turned to Martin and said, 'Martin, Mr Dein's here, you know he's got good mates at the FA. He's going to appeal against your ban.' Martin brightened at the news, before Ray went in for the killer. 'Instead of five matches he is going for an eight-match ban.' Martin started growling. Ray did enjoy winding him up.

He was also a phenomenal club servant. He and Martin were

the only Invincibles who had been part of George Graham's successful teams; they straddled two wonderful eras. Ray was homegrown and he was in the first team for thirteen years. The way he bonded everyone and kept spirits up was important. He was a special kind of glue in the dressing room.

Dennis Bergkamp

As much as Arsenal will always be grateful for Dennis, there was a bit of gratitude on his side that we went that extra mile for him and were not about to put him under pressure for his fear of flying. He wasn't comfortable at Inter Milan and we got him out of a hole there. I think he really appreciated that. The crowd and everyone at the club immediately adored him.

Pound for pound, that transfer of £7.5 million has got to be one of the best in the history of the club for what he gave – not just in terms of world-class ability but in symbolising a new Arsenal. People say that he changed the way Arsenal played; its philosophy. He was just an extraordinary talent. He was a game-changer, a genius with a ball. There were times when, because of his vision and intelligence, he would do something to make me think, I've just seen something I've never seen before, something that felt impossible. He played like an artist. To make it even more impressive he did it without a big ego. He was always very calm, very modest, very matter-of-fact, it was just normal to him to be so naturally gifted.

When Arsène joined a year after Dennis arrived, it was obvious they were perfect for each other. Here was a meeting of minds and ideas. Dennis was highly intelligent, both in football and in life. Maybe that explains how he was able to so easily bring the best out of the players around him, and in particular his two most prolific strike partners in Ian Wright and then Thierry, as well as the best of himself.

Thierry Henry

Bringing in Thierry wasn't easy. He had not been long at Juventus and it was unusual for a club to bring in a promising talent – Thierry was young but don't forget he was a World Cup winner by then – and discard them after just a few months. The timing of a deal was never an exact science but this was one we had to go for. Clubs are always going to make you work hard for a transfer.

Roberto Bettega of Juventus was a colleague of mine at UEFA committees, making facilitating a meeting easy. I travelled to Turin for a meeting. That was one of my tactics. I would offer to go to a club when we were interested in their player, to let them have the home advantage. That already clocks up a few brownie points. I was always ready. My passport always went into my pocket first thing in the morning, because I didn't know where I was going to go in the afternoon.

Arsène and I would always agree beforehand on a price that we were prepared to pay so that, when I went into the meeting, I'd have that figure in the back of my mind. I would start, we'd see whether they would negotiate, do our best to come down, and Arsène and I would be in constant touch throughout any negotiation.

The Canadian Mounties used to have the slogan, 'We always get our man' and that resonated with me. If I was going, I couldn't come back without the player. Even if it meant paying a little bit more, I would advocate doing it because if I'd gone so far, I wouldn't let a little wriggle room spoil the deal, particularly if I knew that Arsène wanted the player and he fitted in with the squad. There was too much at stake. You can be too clever in negotiating if you're not careful.

Signing Thierry for less than ten million pounds turned out to be a gift. He elevated our team and was a central part of what people all over the world thought about Arsenal for a decade. When Thierry had the ball, instinctively you moved forward in your seat with expectation. You felt something was going to happen. You were not quite sure what, but you knew he would do something wonderful. No matter what part of the field he was on, he could always glide because of his blend of speed, skill and balance. You don't get too many of those in a lifetime. If you're very lucky at a football club, you may see one genius. Having Thierry in the same team as Dennis, Patrick and all the rest underlined how special it was.

To play alongside Dennis was good for Thierry. Dennis didn't have the demanding ego that Thierry had and having someone to look up to in the team who had Dennis's profile and personality helped Thierry to channel his gifts without him getting affected. The way he developed at Arsenal, from turning up at the age of twenty to becoming the club's record goal-scorer in some ways defined that period. At times during the Invincible season he was unplayable, nobody could get near him and he had the confidence to shoulder the responsibility to be a difference-maker. You could almost see him thinking, I'm going to make this happen. I'm going to show the magic. It felt like anything was possible when Thierry was playing.

He was analytical about his own performances. 'What did I do? I want to see the game again. I want to see the videos.' He was such a consummate professional that he would go to

Arsène's office straight after the game, rattling off questions: 'What did I do wrong? What could I have done here? Should I have gone this side? Should I have made an earlier run?' He would look to Arsène for guidance because he believed in him. Arsène was his professor.

Kanu

Kanu had special ability. He played with special joy.

He had been diagnosed with a heart problem when he was younger and we had to ensure he went through very rigorous medicals. When he came over to London for his tests we spent the day together. My knowledge of Nigeria helped us to bond during our conversations. I drove him to three different heart specialists. I remember asking the medical staff, 'Do you think he is OK for a four-year contract?' That's a funny thing to say to a doctor. It was a bit bizarre. When we got the all-clear we were thrilled. The deal to bring him in from Inter was on.

It is fairly common for players to cheat about their age. As we were driving away from Harley Street I turned to Kanu and asked him if I could throw in a personal question. He said sure. 'Kanu,' I said, 'how old are you really?'

There was a pause. He looked at me, smiled, and said, 'Mr Dein, how old do you want me to be?'

Sylvain Wiltord

Sylvain's agent, Ghislaine Dugueperoux, was challenging. It wasn't easy to do the deal from Bordeaux, but we got there and, after we sealed the deal, the club kindly presented me with a case of wine from the region. Keeping Ghislaine happy was also tough. She was on my case regularly. She would ring me up and tell me to tell Arsène where he should be playing, insisting he should be down the middle and not on the wing. She would waltz into my office smoking, which I was not keen on. I politely told her to get her coaching licence!

I have always believed it is a good thing for a player to know how much an agent gets. It should be an obligation. I used to insist on that. When we went through the contract with Wiltord, Ghislaine took it out. She said, 'We don't want that in there' and I said, 'Oh yes, we do.' I insisted we kept it in after a game of mental poker. She did the best for her client and didn't do badly herself!

Sylvain arrived when there was a strong French presence in the group, joining Vieira, Petit, Henry, Pires and Grimandi just after France won the Euros in 2000. His stock was high, having scored in the final but it was telling that one of the aspects that attracted him to Arsenal, as well as having so many compatriots around to help him to settle, was the club's growing reputation in the Champions League.

Sylvain was part of the French revolution and he was always bubbly and funny, bringing energy into the group. Creating a team is like an orchestra bringing together the qualities of different instruments – you need the cello and the trumpet and the timpani. They work together to create the harmony.

José Antonio Reyes

I went to meet our Spanish scout, Francis Cagigao, in Seville as we wanted to sign José. His agent, Jesus, also handled bullfighters and thought he would entertain us by taking us to see one of his clients at work. Being an animal lover, I thought it was repugnant. The poor bull has got no chance. I am sure that there is a lot of skill involved but I was more interested in the football player than the bullfighter. That said, the atmosphere of being in Seville, a beautiful city with passionate fans, was a theatrical backdrop to the transfer. When word had it that we were signing Reyes, it made for a very intense occasion.

At Sevilla's stadium, thousands of people turned up with banners and voices ready. They chanted for Reyes to stay. They blocked our car; we were surrounded by people who thought we were coming to steal their family jewels; getting him out was very dramatic.

He was one of the most coveted young talents in world football and likely to have gone to Barcelona or Real Madrid – but we got him. We signed him in the January window of the Invincible season – we were strengthening while we were at our peak, which sent out its own message. We were still prepared to improve the team even when we were doing so well. But Arsène was never satisfied. He would constantly ask himself, 'How do I improve the team?'

Reyes was a great player and he was much loved within our group. Tragically, he was killed in an horrific car accident in June 2019, travelling between his home town of Utrera and Seville. He was just thirty-five.

Pascal Cygan

We signed him from Lille and he was very reliable. He was more of a reserved personality, calm and likeable, and willing to serve the team. He always realised he was going to have to fight for his position and he had some serious competition at centre back. Nevertheless, he fitted in well with the group. He was valued, popular, and ended up with eighteen appearances to qualify for a winners' medal, no mean feat for a squad player.

Gaël Clichy

Gaël came as a teenager from Cannes at a young age and at a budget price of £250,000. With Arsène's Monaco connections he knew everything that was going on in football along that coast. Damien Comolli, our French scout, watched him and agreed with Arsène that this boy had a future. We were beginning to look at younger players with potential around the early noughties to try to continue competing at the top, in the knowledge that we would soon have to cut our cloth more carefully because of the new stadium project. Gaël came in at a similar time as Cesc Fàbregas, Philippe Senderos and Robin van Persie. That was not a bad group to be getting on with. Gaël was a gem of a boy. If he was your son you would be proud of him. He came in after Ashley so he had big boots to fill. He was committed and a very solid pro.

Jérémie Aliadière

Jérémie joined us straight from Clairefontaine, the French Football Federation's academy system, the envy of the world at that time. At such a young age he had to be patient to get game time, considering the calibre of forwards at the club. It would not be easy for any youngster to displace Thierry, Dennis, Kanu, Sylvain and José. We really were fortunate to have assembled such an array of talent. He sometimes used to ask me, given the attacking depth, if he could make it at the club. I told him that was up to him. He was not short of working hard and giving it his best shot.

Arsène believed in Jérémie and he mostly played in the League Cup games as he was developing; in fact, he won the best young talent award in that competition during 2003/04. Overall, it must have been an extraordinary experience for him to be around that squad in that season and to gain enough appearances to earn a Premier League winners' medal.

There were a couple of very special days as we closed in on the prize of invincibility. First of all, winning the league at White Hart Lane was memorable. Even though there had been some agreements between the two clubs to try to keep everything calm and avoid provocation should we get the result we needed, things don't always go entirely to plan. The team couldn't help running towards our fans in the corner to share in this iconic moment.

Later, leaving White Hart Lane, I was getting into my car in the car park when there was a knock on the window. Alan Davies, the actor, comedian and very well-known Arsenal supporter was on his own, deep in enemy territory. I asked him how he was getting home. He said, 'I don't know yet, I am frightened of getting ambushed!' We could both hear a rumpus in the streets outside. There was trouble and police realised there was a problem; Arsenal fans were celebrating and let's just say the Tottenham supporters were not too happy about Arsenal winning the league on their turf. It was getting a bit rough and I told Alan to jump in the back. He squeezed alongside the family, having to lie flat on the floor of the back seats as I drove out. We managed to get him to safety.

The season wasn't finished yet, with four games to go, so there was no way we were having a club celebration party at Sopwell House. A quiet dinner out at a local brasserie was about as far as we could stretch. Arsène wouldn't have gone anywhere further than Totteridge, for sure. A good bottle of red Malbec was on the menu. Arsène was never a champagne man.

The final match was at Highbury in the sunshine against Leicester and it was beautiful. We went 1–0 down but Thierry decided to pull everyone together to ensure they were focused. Dennis produced a signature pass for Patrick to ensure victory. Watching it all unfold it was very emotional. I was the fan in the boardroom but it was also like watching my children out there, as I had such affection for the boys.

Going through the season unbeaten was unprecedented in modern times. It happened to the club I had been supporting since the age of nine! Arsenal had achieved something very special which was applauded around the world. I felt very proud to have been part of it all – I guess it is what is known as job satisfaction.

We were blessed. We were fortunate to be there at the time to see our club (not anybody else's club, but ours) enjoy such a golden and precious era. We had a group of players who complemented each other and eventually made themselves the Invincibles. And they were plucked from clubs all over the world, handpicked components who made the perfect team. The unbelievable thing is it didn't even cost a lot of money to put together.

A PIZZA HISTORY

As the song goes even to this day Arsenal went 'forty-nine undefeated'. It could have been fifty or more, but it came to halt controversially at, of all places, Old Trafford, when our fortunes turned on a dubious decision to award Manchester United a penalty.

I headed down to see the team as I normally did after a game, only to find a fracas going on in the area between the home and away dressing rooms. I saw Cesc throw an unguided missile of pizza into the melee of Manchester United players and staff. Unfortunately, it hit Sir Alex Ferguson. A voice from the Arsenal contingent cut through the tension, 'Pizza for Fergie!' There was a lot going on down there, and in the heat of the big occasion sometimes boys will be boys.

It was one of those scenarios where it was best for Arsène to use his famous line that he 'didn't see it'. Naturally he often did, but relied upon that defence in order to protect his players.

Arsène always had a bee in his bonnet about referees. Sometimes he couldn't help himself from complaining. 'They don't like the French!' 'They don't like anyone non-English!' 'That ref is a gangster!' He was paranoid. I could not dissuade him. I knew all the referees well from the conferences where we would meet, and I would defend them. Some are more competent than others, but I will go on record as saying the English referees are honest. You can't say that in every country in the world. I would try to be a bit of a peacemaker, and he would say, 'You love the referees!' I would reply, 'I think they are decent people. They are human. Everybody makes mistakes.' Arsène is still niggled by that penalty decision at Old Trafford all these years later. Arsène and I used to philosophise about things, even talking about death. He once came up with the line about when he dies and goes to heaven, and St Peter asks him which way he wants to go, his reply will be, 'The opposite way to the referees.'

Even if the seasons that immediately followed the Invincibles were not quite as successful, they were not without high points. In 2005, we picked up another FA Cup, playing the final at Cardiff as Wembley was being redeveloped – our third in five seasons – by beating our old friends from Manchester United; although we were not the better team on the day. It went to penalties and Patrick scored the decisive kick. We didn't know it at the time, but it was to be his last action for Arsenal. That summer we sold him to Juventus. For so many years, keeping Patrick at the club had been a mission, but the football business demands a lot of difficult decisions and knowing the right time to sell a player is just as challenging as the gamble of bringing someone in. Patrick was clearly a giant loss, but Arsène felt handing over the midfield keys to Cesc Fàbregas was part of the programme to build around youth.

At a sensitive time for the club, we faced complications in the transfer market as we tried to renovate our squad when we were at risk of richer clubs targeting our players. The sale of Ashley Cole hurt us a lot.

There were two phases to Ashley's departure and neither of them reflect too kindly on the business of football. First there was the tapping up scandal in January 2005. (Tapping up, or tampering as Americans call it, is a secret attempt to persuade players to break their contracts and join another team.) Just seven months after Arsenal won the league unbeaten, from a position of sporting supremacy, but now in a state of financial weakness, we were being targeted by a club which had overtaken us as a financial powerhouse. Without our knowledge, Ashley and his agent, Jonathan Barnett, met up with a delegation from Chelsea, including José Mourinho and Peter Kenyon, and the 'super agent', Pini Zahavi, in a hotel in Lancaster Gate. It was one of these little bed-and-breakfast places, supposedly somewhere discreet. The waiter happened to be an Arsenal fan and knew what was going on. He told the News of the World, and I got a call from the editor, Andy Coulson.

'We've got something you should be interested in,' Andy told me. 'I can't talk to you about it over the phone, would you mind coming to the offices now? We've got the story, we're running it.' I dropped everything and went down to the newspaper headquarters to see the evidence, including photographs. He said, 'We have them bang to rights. We have a statement from the waiter. Your player is being tapped up. What do you want to say about it?' What did I have to say about it? I thanked him, told him I would report it to the board, and that I was leaving to prepare for our weekend match.

We had to establish our response. The board were reluctant to do anything, let alone issue a strong reaction. They didn't want to make a fuss, and they didn't want friction with another club. I disagreed. We had to stand up to these tactics.

'It is immoral!' I insisted. 'We know this goes on in the background, but this is so blatant. We can't allow this to be in the public domain at our expense. This is Arsenal Football Club. Chelsea think they can railroad us? Well, I am not going to stand for that.'

The majority of the board still wanted to skirt over it; but I was digging in my heels. The Beautiful Game must also be a clean game.

That episode was the beginning of the end of Arsenal's relationship with Ashley, a boyhood Arsenal fan who had come through the youth system to become one of the finest players in his position in the world. But he wouldn't have gone to that meeting unless he was prepared to leave. That was sad.

The tapping up incident was investigated by the Football Association a few months later. Ashley was found guilty of breaching rule K5 which prohibits players from meeting other clubs with a view to a transfer without their current club's permission. Chelsea were charged with breaking rule K3, which forbids approaching another club's player while they are under contract. Mourinho broke rule Q which governs manager's conduct. They were all fined.

I was disappointed with Chelsea's behaviour, but also with Jonathan Barnett, with whom I got on very well. But I'm afraid that's the murky world of agents. That's what happens. You can't forgive them, but in the end you have to move on because you never know when you might need them. Agents are a critical part of our game. Jonathan's agency has got several hundred players. In this case, his licence was suspended, and he was served with an eighteen-month ban.

Generally, with agents I enjoyed what I call the 'joust'. Agents have the talent and you and have to engage with them. I made sure to maintain a good relationship with them; I remember going to one of the finals at Cardiff when I invited all the agents of our players – and, indeed, some who weren't – on the plane with us. It was a gesture. I always tried to keep a good rapport with them.

There's no point in having grudges with anybody. It doesn't make things better. The same applied with Chelsea and their board. I was annoyed, but we would all do business with each other again. There's always another day.

Although there was some tension, naturally, for a while between the clubs, there was a surprise the following January when I was at the Africa Cup of Nations in Ghana. In the hotel after dinner one evening, I was sitting at the bar area and saw someone come to check in at reception. It was José Mourinho. I thought to myself that this might be awkward. To get to his room, José had to pass right by me. He saw me, I stood up, and he gave me a great big hug and something not far off a kiss and asked how I was. After putting his bags down, we spent two hours together chatting.

We spent a couple of days on the same beat and the more I got to know him, the more I liked him. He was out of his usual zone – this wasn't a match or a press conference and he was relaxed, thousands of miles away. I'm all about giving people second chances, even though his relations with Arsène were difficult. They were both natural winners. Mourinho punched him below the belt under the guise of humour. The comments about being a specialist in failure and a voyeur were insulting to Arsène, which is a pity. There is nothing as hurtful as the spoken word. I hope he didn't mean it in that way.

After the tapping up we had to bring Ashley back into the family and it wasn't easy. I felt like there was a bit of an open wound, and that he didn't feel the same loyalty, which is a great pity because he was an Arsenal boy. By the end of the 2004/05 season he was a central part of our FA Cup winning team, scoring a superb penalty in the shootout to beat Manchester United. He also played in the 2006 Champions League final. We didn't want to lose him, but clearly he wanted to leave.

The transfer to Chelsea happened eventually, and we will never know if it could have been prevented, or for how much longer. We were negotiating with him for a contract extension but at the board meeting to discuss players' salaries we hit a problem. We had offered Ashley £55,000 a week and he wanted £60,000. At a time where the stadium money was such a big deal, Arsène and I tried to push the board to go to sixty and they refused. Ashley was upset, and he was right to be upset.

The 2005/06 season was played under the weight of old and new history. The last season at Highbury was upon us and, even though the move was inevitable, maybe we underestimated how much of our soul would be damaged by such a big change.

At the same time, reaching the Champions League final was unforgettable. We had enjoyed fantastic years of travels and experiences in the competition. It was magical, competing in that elite company with our head held high for such a long period of time. When we got to the final it was a phenomenal opportunity. Just being there was extraordinarily exciting – only two clubs could ever get there in any season and for the first time in our history it was us. We were underdogs against Barcelona, but we gave it our all, a task which became even harder when Jens was sent off in the first half. When Sol

Campbell scored first for us, we thought, could this be our year? But the rest is history. It wasn't to be.

It is difficult to weigh up emotions. If you have a choice, to win the Champions League or be Invincible, which do you choose? It is not easy. Every year there is another Champions League final, but the Invincible achievement has not been equalled yet. Maybe that helps with the rollercoaster of feelings in football.

THE MAGNIFICENT SEVEN: MY FAVOURITE ARSENAL GOALS DURING MY DIRECTORSHIP

Michael Thomas v. Liverpool, 1989.

David Rocastle v. Man U, 1991.

Anders Limpar v. Liverpool, 1992.

Ian Wright v. Bolton, 1997 (breaking Arsenal's all-time goal scoring record).

Tony Adams v. Everton, 1998.

Thierry Henry v. Man U, 2000.

Dennis Bergkamp v. Newcastle, 2002.

The magnificent Michael Owen goal against Argentina in France, 1998.

David Beckham's sensational free kick against Greece at Old Trafford, 2001.

It's good to be a winner Royal Ascot 1981. Left to right: Paul Kelleway (trainer), stable lad, Barbara, DD, Kiki Kaye, Geoffrey Kaye (co-owner).

2002 FIFA World Cup, Korea/Japan. Singalong with England at 30,000 feet. Left to right: David Davies, Paul Barber, Doug Ellis, Tord Grip on accordion, Adam Crozier, Noel White, DD, Sven-Göran Eriksson.

The Three Musketeers flying around Brazil during the World Cup, 2014.

With the first team. World Cup bid, December 2010.

If Mum could see me now!

Aston Villa and Arsenal.

A very proud boy with his Honour.

Trying to sign Nelson Mandela for Arsenal during the South Africa tour, 1993.

Out of small acorns, mighty oaks grow. Alex Scott, aged fourteen, playing for Arsenal Women U16s.

Engine room of the Twinning Project. Left to right: Jason Swettenham, DD, Hilton Freund.

Rest in Peace Gérard

Bernie – best in class!

A star has fallen out of the sky. With Gérard Houllier.

The 'Food Patrol Man', saluting good table manners, with his eight 'nippos'.

Golden wedding anniversary, Turkey, August 2022. Left to right: Gavin, Maya, Claire, Edward, Marco Sasha, Leo, DD, Barbara, Darren, Sara, Olivia, Jessica, Elena, Sophie, Dylan.

BUY ONE GET ONE FREE

I'm not easily shocked, I've spent a life in business and foot-ball, and there are many sharks in those seas. Even now I find it hard to believe what happened during bidding for the right to host the 2018 World Cup. I was privileged to be part of the FA bid campaign, doing what I love, travelling around, flying the flag and presenting England's case. I soon realised we were taking on much more than we had bargained for.

Here is one story that summed up the state of play. It takes a huge amount of logistical and infrastructure planning to stage a competition on this scale, and so the decision on where it is to be staged is taken many years ahead. In this case the crucial vote would be taken by FIFA in Zurich on 2 December 2010.

Campaigning started months in advance, and on one stop we arrived in a country which was home to one of the FIFA exec-utive committee members, someone who had one of the criti-cal votes. He was influential so it was an important visit, and we had worked hard on making our pitch. After the presentation and usual glad-handing, I bumped into the chief executive of the local football association as I checked out of my hotel.

'We enjoyed your presentation, Mr Dein,' he said with a friendly smile. 'But what is in your bag?' He pointed to my holdall.

'Laundry,' I replied. I knew what he meant. I knew what he wanted, and it stank more than any dirty laundry ever could. 'We don't do that,' I said.

The FA played it straight. We knew we had a compelling bid. Everyone knew we had magnificent stadia, the right infrastructure and a passionate fanbase. We had world-renowned ex-players like David Beckham representing our bid, and all the official backing anyone could hope for – the royal approval of Prince William, and official support from the Prime Minister David Cameron. We put out a great team and we offered a top-notch proposal.

It hadn't started quite so well. I'd been brought in late to the team, in November 2009, after the FA chair Lord Triesman had let it be known that they thought the bid was failing. I'd heard about the trouble on the bid board: not just clashes of personality but systemic tensions between FA representatives and those from the Premier League. Because I'd been at Arsenal and on FA committees, I had a foot in both camps. What's more I'd chaired the G-14 group of leading European clubs, now subsumed into the European Club Association, and I had contacts and friendships in football around the world. Lord Triesman made me international president of the bid, a suitably grand title the FA hoped would appeal to FIFA.

Walking into the bid offices at Wembley, I was excited by the challenge and the quality of the twenty full-time staff, led by chief executive Andy Anson, an experienced campaigner working with a £21-million budget. I could see we had a team full of expertise, energy and complementary talents. We soon became a closely knit bunch. To this day, we've still got a WhatsApp group called '2018'.

Even so, I sensed the team's spirits needed lifting. It had just got itself into an awful mess about giving £239 Mulberry handbags to the wives of the ExCo (executive committee) members. The story was exaggerated – no surprise there! It was, literally, handbags, properly permitted within FIFA bid guidelines as 'incidental' gifts. But this was where Jack Warner, a FIFA vice-president and president of Concacaf (Confederation of North, Central America and Caribbean Association Football), began revealing to me his remarkable gift for cool hypocrisy. The Trinidadians had previously criticised the FA for not providing them with goodie bags at an earlier event, but then had the nerve to denounce the FA for attracting bad publicity to FIFA with the Mulberry bags. Warner even wrote to Triesman in florid tones, saying he was insulted by the reaction to his taking the bag for Maureen his wife: 'Therefore, there is only one recourse: a return of this gift, which has become a symbol of derision, betrayal and embarrassment for me and my family,' Jack was a likeable rogue, but for me he came to epitomise everything that was wrong about FIFA and the World Cup bidding process. He was great company, but never missed an opportunity for personal aggrandisement.

Unfortunately, we needed this rascal onside. He had a vote for 2018 and controlled the two other Concacaf votes. I was always amazed how Warner, primarily representing the comparatively small islands of Trinidad and Tobago, could influence the votes of his region, which included USA and Canada. But that was his mercurial talent. Wooing this special adviser to the Trinidad FA was a necessary evil, and so the FA started their charm offensive early.

On 1 June 2008, England flew to Port of Spain for the local football association's centenary celebration match. The press questioned why England's players were being sent 4,500 miles to Trinidad and Tobago at the end of an exhausting season. Well, although it could hardly be explained publicly in these blunt terms, in truth the answer was simple. Operation Win Over Warner.

The FA hosted a dinner for Warner and the Caribbean Football Union (CFU) in Trinidad on 26 February 2010 in the ballroom of Port of Spain's Hyatt Regency hotel. I flew out with two top members of our team, chief executive Andy Anson and the FA's head of international relations, Jane Bateman, along with one of our ambassadors – the engaging David Ginola, who was to do some coaching for local kids. We listened to Warner's words of welcome with growing fascination. 'In light of the harsh economic conditions that we are battling in the region, I am pleased to announce that the FA has agreed to formally partner with us to host the dinner. It is an offer which I have agreed to.' And he left us to pick up the £35,000 tab. It seemed a bit steep, especially as they also charged a grand for lighting. At least this could be passed off as a legitimate expense under FIFA guide-lines, and internally the FA could justify the outlay by saying the CFU should keep its money for much-needed local grassroots initiatives. But we knew that we'd been Warnered.

The following day we drove seventeen miles to Warner's home town of Longdenville with the feeling we were heading into an ambush. Our suspicions were confirmed as soon as Warner started speaking in front of some ramshackle sports facilities. Local residents suddenly appeared from everywhere. 'We are delighted and honoured to have the delegation from the FA led by David Dein and they have agreed to build us a new playing field here,' Warner announced.

'What?!' I whispered to Jane.

'Perhaps,' Warner went on, 'perhaps, David, you'd like to say a few words?'

'Ahem. Well, thank you very much, Mr President. Of course, we are very impressed with what we see here, and when we get back I will definitely put your suggestion to our board.' I mean! Jack was such a scoundrel. I then heard he had promised the locals that he'd arrange funding for a £1.2-million sports complex. I read, with a slightly weary feeling, local newspaper reports about the 'English pledge to help Longdenville'. Apparently, the FA would be stumping up fifty thousand pounds immediately to start work on what *Newsday* hailed as 'a spanking new, state-of-the-art sports facility'. Much to my surprise, I read that I gave a 'commitment' to residents when talking to Warner in Longdenville. 'Warner is the force who is making it possible,' the paper gushed.

We carried on wooing Warner. What else could we do? Four months later, at the World Cup in South Africa in June 2010, we presented to him and Concacaf again, this time in a Johannesburg conference centre. No ambushes from Jack, and it went perfectly, I thought. The Russians also made their 2018 pitch there, but their presentation was plainly not as good and their offer seemed considerably less convincing. Yet when I saw the Russians heading off with Warner afterwards, I sensed trouble. I knew that what went on backstage could be just as important, maybe more so. Indeed, the 2018 World Cup bid turned out to be a campaign that was won in the shadows.

Perhaps it was also lost in the spotlight of the British media. I was not entirely surprised by allegations made by the *Sunday Times*'s respected Insight team on 23 October 2010. The headline ran, WANT THE WORLD CUP? IT'LL COST YOU MONEY OR GIRLS. The story claimed that two of the FIFA ExCo members, Amos Adamu of Nigeria and Reynald Temarii, president of the Oceania Football Confederation, had sought cash in exchange for their votes. They were trapped by two journalists who were wired up, and were masquerading as an agency from the USA with funds available to help developing countries in return for their vote for 2022. Both Adamu and Temarii were banned within a fortnight by FIFA.

The technique employed by the *Sunday Times* is often regarded as entrapment, and is a legal minefield. Arguably only those disposed to crimes like bribery would take the bait, but equally plausibly, usually honest people can be lured off the straight and narrow. Thus, if Adamu and Temarii had been taken to court in England the prosecution would seek to prove that they habitually took kickbacks, while the defence would try to show that their behaviour had been manipulated by the journalists. I must say that I had qualms myself. To be honest, I was as concerned for the two individuals as I was about the English media raising FIFA's hackles, and the prospect that bad publicity would harm our bid. As I saw it, the national interest came first, a national newspaper's interests came second.

FIFA and its president Sepp Blatter had always loathed the English press, and I really began to worry when the chair of FIFA's ethics committee, Claudio Sulser, lambasted the *Sunday Times* for twisting the truth. In fact the suspension of Adamu and Temarii harmed us more directly, since both had told us they were very much inclined to vote for England and I had an excellent relationship with them. Of course that assumed nobody else would swing them away with inducements. You never knew. You couldn't trust anyone.

Now we were lobbying only twenty-two of the twenty-four members of ExCo. Actually twenty-one, as we already had the support of the FA's man at FIFA, Geoff Thompson. He knew all the ExCo members well and was always genuinely shocked when one of them was exposed as crooked. The thing is, Geoff is an honourable man, an FA lifer, a JP, a man of strict morals – but he was swimming in a shoal of piranhas.

As we counted down towards D Day, 2 December 2010, we got wind of another media exposé, this time from the BBC. Its investigation programme *Panorama* planned a feature on FIFA corruption. It was to be broadcast just before the vote.

I was incredulous.

'What's it called?' I asked one of the bid team.

'*FIFA's Dirty Secrets*,' they replied.

'Well, that's subtle.'

Here was a hand-grenade covered in English fingerprints about to be rolled into the ExCo voting chamber while our proposal would be in the room – a bid still very much alive we hoped, despite the *Sunday Times*. Talk about friendly fire!

Two weeks before the broadcast Andy Anson and I went to the BBC in White City to see Mark Thompson, the director general, and Barbara Slater, their head of sport. Barbara said little, and I suspected she was embarrassed by the conflict of loyalties between her love of sport and her duty to the Corporation. I focused on Thompson. I explained that we respected the BBC's editorial right to make such programmes. More than that, I had my own very deep misgivings about the lack of integrity inside ExCo. I had no problems with a well-research exposé. But

FIFA's Dirty Secrets was due for broadcast on Monday 29 November, three days before the vote. 'It's the timing that will kill us,' I said.

Thompson was adamant. In fact it was the timing that made the BBC so excited. Our World Cup bid would be high on the 'news agenda' that week – or in Mark's own words, it was 'the right time editorially'. What he really meant was that with so much buzz about FIFA in the days before the vote, the show would draw more viewers.

'Look, Mark, I understand it's a good story. You don't need to tell me that FIFA's corrupt. I get it that you're reflecting everyone's anger at them. But do it afterwards, not just before we have our big chance to convince them.'

'That's not the way we do things,' he replied. 'We can't fix the news around what suits everyone, and we can't stop stories because they're inconvenient to someone.'

Someone! 'There are sixty million people out there who want England to host the World Cup. Most of them are your licence-fee payers. You're a public service broadcaster. Don't blow us out of the water.'

'We are above all a news channel,' reiterated Thompson. 'If we have a hot story, we have to run it.'

I too was starting to repeat myself. 'Run it – but after. If we lose, then blow the whistle for a foul. In fact, it will have more value afterwards than before.'

I fought for England's bid. Mark fought for his programme.

Andy and I left the meeting in something like despair. The BBC had offered no concessions, and we had to be resigned that the show would run as planned. We knew perfectly well that, coming on top of the *Sunday Times*'s dig at FIFA, this could be the nail that sealed our coffin. On my way home, I rang Greg Dyke. He was a former BBC DG. What would he do with the programme?

'Mark's got a story, David, he's got to run it. On something like that you can't hold back.'

I carried on campaigning, but with a heavy heart. Ours was one of eleven bids from thirteen countries hoping to stage the competition (Belgium and Holland had put in a combined bid, as had Spain and Portugal) and reviewing the competition I was confident we should win on technical merit. But you have to be a realist. And my mood wasn't lifted when I saw that Miguel Ángel López, chief of the Spain and Portugal bid, warned that any more lobbying was pointless since at this stage: 'All the fish are sold'. The inference was that the deals were done. Privately, I suspected the fish stank.

I headed off to Zurich for the vote with my eyes open, but strangely, perversely, my heart still full of hope. After all, England were still favourites. Everyone could see the technical quality of our bid and our economic value. We brought royalty, political clout and stardust to Europe with our 'three lions', Prince William, David Cameron and David Beckham. I think everybody knew that a World Cup in England, the first in the home of football in half a century, would be such a special show.

I settled down at my hotel on the shores of Lake Zurich, switched on the BBC and watched *FIFA's Dirty Secrets*. I knew that, along the plush-carpeted corridors, all of Blatter's mates, all the president's men, would be tuning in too. Over thirty minutes' painful viewing, the investigative reporter Andrew Jennings accused three ExCo members – Issa Hayatou, Ricardo Teixeira and Nicolás Leoz – of taking bribes between 1989 and 1999. OK, that was more than a decade ago, but these were major FIFA figures. Hayatou was a FIFA vice-president representing Africa. Teixeira led the Brazilian Football Confederation. Leoz was president of CONMEBOL, the South American federation. The programme also accused Jack Warner of selling tickets to touts. There was nothing specific to say that the current bid process was corrupt, but that night's *Panorama* was a full-on assault on FIFA.

The moment the show finished, the FA's bid team convened. They denounced the allegations as old, previously investigated and already dismissed by FIFA. I did my best to distance our bid from the programme. 'It should have been aired on the History Channel, the allegations were so ancient,' I said with as much of a grin as I could muster. But I knew England's chances had been badly damaged. Mortally? That I didn't know.

The following morning, I got up early to begin clearing up the *Panorama* mess. I put on my best upbeat face and sat down for breakfast with Sepp Blatter at the FIFA headquarters at Baur au Lac. It was comforting to have David Cameron and David Beckham around the table. It was only a matter of time before Blatter raised *Panorama*. He said it was an attack by the English on FIFA, and asked if the English hate foreigners, and whether in particular the British Broadcasting Corporation hated foreigners. We were in a deeply uncomfortable position, and I was grateful to Beckham for his calmness and for his willingness to find a positive in a negative.

'If we win, the English media will get behind the World Cup,' he promised Blatter. I've always respected Becks, so down-to-earth, despite his fame and fortune. There we were discussing *Panorama* over pain au chocolat, and Becks was holding forth on what a party it would be in England in 2018. Cameron was soothing too, emphasising how committed the UK government was to the bid, talking up how grand a show we would put on, and emphasising how much money it would generate for FIFA. Pounds, dollars and euros were always likely to get Blatter's attention. I came away from breakfast feeling that we'd accomplished some pretty effective damage limitation. Prince William, meanwhile, was busy building bridges over eggs benedict with Nicolás Leoz, the most powerful man in South American football. I didn't really know William before the bid but I came away from Zurich feeling that the future of the monarchy was in safe hands.

Perhaps our bid was safe now too.

But then again, perhaps not. The day before the vote, I had a strong sense that things might not go our way. Alexei Sorokin, CEO of Russia's bid, joined me for breakfast. We were friendly and although rivals we had a shared experience of travelling around and pushing our respective bids.

'How do you feel, Alexei?'

'We feel fairly confident.'

And he sounded confident too, the cold certainty I associated with Russian officials from the Soviet age. It was as though Sorokin knew something I didn't. I suddenly wondered if Vladimir Putin was on Sepp Blatter's speed dial. Maybe the fish really were all sold.

But we still had 24 hours. My school motto was '*nil desperandum*', 'never despair', and David Cameron, Prince William and David Beckham had worked through the night talking to ExCo members, many of whom had given them their word. Our team continually crunched the numbers. It still looked like we could win.

The night before the vote, the FA booked two suites at Baur au Lac for late-night lobbying. We invited ExCo members from the bar downstairs that was awash with malt whisky, chatted to them, and it seemed to be going well, with some staying until after midnight, clutching further whiskies. Warner even embraced Prince William at midnight. I went to bed thinking the motherland of the game had a chance. Warner was finally onside. My last calculation that night before falling asleep was that England had eight votes. We were in the mix.

Our positivity permeated the English media. It was as though *Panorama* had never happened; as though allegations of vote-rigging were forgotten. The British reporters surrounding us wanted the World Cup to come home and made us favourites. So did their editors. So did the public.

BRING IT HOME, read the back page headline in the *Daily Mail*, with a picture of Bobby Moore lifting the trophy in '66. I had been there that day at Wembley, and even a patriot like me winced at the triumphalism. Everyone on the FA bid team was under orders to avoid any of the 'Football's coming home' rhetoric that derailed the 2006 bid. Andy Anson was very strong on the need to duck anything that played into the perception of English arrogance.

But the press was in buoyant mood. The *Mail* went on, 'England can complete an amazing recovery today by landing the 2018 World Cup . . . William, Becks and the PM put victory in sight for England.' Fair enough, they'd done the maths. And the other papers followed suit.

The last day before the vote was a whirlwind. We flooded Zurich with ambassadors, including Lord Coe, Sir Bobby

Charlton, Boris Johnson, Fabio Capello, Richard Scudamore, Hugh Robertson, John Barnes and Alan Shearer. I remember casting an eye over the names and imagining a five-a-side team. If only the bid came down to a game played under Corinthian rules!

In the closing hours the Spain and Portugal bid was seen as our biggest rival. Almost no one mentioned Russia, and the fact that the Russian leader, Vladimir Putin, hadn't shown up was widely taken as a sign they did not have a chance. Then up popped news that Putin had accused the English of conducting a 'smear campaign' against FIFA. It brought back the unease I had felt at that breakfast with Alexei Sorokin, the CEO of Russia's bid. He had been running a clever campaign.

And so it began. On 2 December, we headed to FIFA HQ to make our presentation. Netherlands–Belgium kicked off followed by Spain–Portugal. Then, at 11 a.m., show time. We were on. First up for us was Manchester City's social inclusion manager Eddie Afekafe, and his speech was deeply moving. Leaving aside all the pomp of the occasion and the high stakes, I just found it profoundly poignant to hear this young man talk about how football changed his life.

'I grew up in one of the roughest parts of Manchester,' Afekafe said, 'and some of the guys I grew up with were in gangs – some still are, some are in prison. What they didn't get, but I got, was an opportunity and that was through football.' Surely, I felt, this would strike a chord with the FIFA men, some of whom, like Warner, grew up in challenging circumstances.

Prince William then strode up towards the stage, applauded by the twenty-two ExCo members gathered in the front row. He spoke so eloquently, delivering a note-perfect message, welcoming the world. The future king was such a great ambassador for us, not simply because of his royal connections but because he also put in the hard yards to try to win voters over. William was such a natural conversationalist, a good listener and, as a genuine Aston Villa fan, in touch with the common man.

When I met him nine years later – in 2019 he gave me the MBE – we just joked about Villa and Arsenal. 'What do you think of my team?' William began. We talked about Jack Grealish, obviously.

'By the way, Your Highness,' I said, 'the word is that you played very well yesterday.'

'How do you know that?'

I had heard that the prince was raising awareness of mental health at Abbey Stadium, Cambridge United's ground. 'One of my talent scouts was watching you,' I told him. He laughed.

He was full of humour in Zurich too. After wooing a particular ExCo member William told David Cameron that he was confident he had won the member over.

'Gosh, how did you do it?' Cameron asked.

'Prime Minister, I think I offered to marry him!' William replied.

He was magnificent through the whole process. So, incidentally, was Prince Harry. They were so nice, so supportive, so very down to earth. They were good team leaders.

Cameron was up next and spoke of the passion for the game in England. We were on a roll now, I felt, especially when Andy Anson showed a video of Sir Alex Ferguson, Arsène Wenger and Roberto Mancini backing the bid. Beckham then took the stage, an easy task for him, and spoke of what this would mean to the children of England in creating a better future. All our presenting team delivered their script without any notes and with passion and sincerity. We should have won hands down. I checked the odds, and others thought so too. At that point we were 4/5 favourites, with Russia now coming up behind at 7/4. Maybe all the fish weren't sold.

At 2 p.m., the twenty-two men who would decide our fate convened in their boardroom at FIFA HQ. We heard afterwards from several members that Blatter addressed them before they voted.

'Our family has been attacked by the press,' Blatter said. He didn't mention that the offending media were British. He didn't ask that England should be punished. But he did say, 'We've been under siege. We must never forget that when we're voting.'

Shortly before 4 p.m., the delegates emerged from their private room and headed to the main hall. We immediately sought out Geoff Thompson. Even before he spoke, Geoff's drained face showed me the scale of the defeat.

'I am afraid we got only two votes,' Geoff whispered as he followed Blatter to reveal the winners.

Two?! Out of twenty-two! After our huge effort of lobbying, after spending twenty-one million pounds, after travelling hundreds of thousands of miles with our bid ambassadors, and despite royal involvement and the support of Number 10, we had managed to persuade only one person apart from our own FA member. Thank heaven, at least, for Issa Hayatou, president of the Confederation of African Football. But what about the others? Despite what was widely considered the best technical bid and the best presentation, we received the lowest votes. Elimination in the first round. It seemed to me there was only one explanation: it was a deliberate humiliation.

I put on a brave face as I entered the hall. I knew the cameras were on us, looking for any hint of the verdict. I hid my heart-ache as I took my seat on the second row, next to Prince William, with the Russian delegation to our left. FIFA's ExCo members, of course, took the front row, in the limelight. All the cameras focused on Blatter, who delivered an unnecessarily long speech. He spoke about the spirit of fair play which grated with those of us who knew the real story. He talked about how only one of the four final bidders could win.

'Football is also a school of life where you learn to lose,' he said.

I sat in my chair and stewed. Losing is one thing, Mr President. Losing fairly. This wasn't fair. As I quietly fumed, the public notary of the city of Zurich walked up and handed Blatter an envelope. Then came the theatrical moment as Blatter tore open the seal. Russia. The Russian delegation all leapt up, celebrating and hugging. We leaned over and congratulated them.

As I slumped back in my seat, I tried as hard as I could to give ExCo the benefit of the doubt. Maybe we had been victims of our own PR. Maybe there were good reasons to prefer Russia over England. If you wanted to give FIFA the benefit of the doubt, this was certainly opening up new territory. The World Cup had never been to Russia before. It was a big country, a footballing nation, so maybe ExCo members had decided to give them a chance. If you wanted to be suspicious, you'd say there was something unusual going on. You'd think all the fish were sold.

When details of the voting finally emerged, there was nothing to soften our humiliation. In the first round the joint

Holland–Belgium bid had secured four votes, Spain–Portugal won seven and Russia nine. If England had not been there in the equation, those results might seem reasonable. But England appealing to only one delegate other than its own? It wasn't just that we were promised votes that never came. It wasn't just that we were lied to. Even going back over these numbers now, many years on, I find them shocking.

Anyway, with England snubbed, Russia went on to win the bid in the second round. Thirteen votes to Russia, seven to Spain–Portugal and two to Holland–Belgium.

I don't think I'm a sore loser. I believe in sport; I love sport. In sport you have to lose as well as win – and sometimes the results surprise you. But I also believe in sportsmanship. You don't stitch things up, you don't do deals behind closed doors. During the whole bid we had felt uneasy. The stories in the *Sunday Times* and *Panorama* weren't invented. I simply didn't believe that we had lost on the merits of our bid.

In 2015, Blatter finally admitted that my suspicions had been right. He acknowledged that a deal had been struck before the vote to give 2018 to Russia.

I was almost equally dismayed when Qatar won the right to host the tournament in 2022. Qatar's success was mainly due to the powerful and persuasive performance of Hassan Al-Thawadi, who admirably let their bid. However, I could never understand why Michel Platini for France voted in favour of Qatar. Platini played the game at the highest level and was now voting to play the World Cup in forty degrees of heat at the height of summer? To add insult to injury, Platini took three European votes with him, swinging it for

Qatar ahead of the US. What on God's good earth was Platini playing at?

I was fuming. I had been quite friendly with Michel, and so was Arsène. But Greg Dyke was unsurprised. 'David,' he tried to calm me. 'It's always bloody corrupt.' Rumour later had it that Platini was influenced by France's President Sarkozy and that trade deals had been negotiated alongside vote deals. Who knows?

The only time I smiled that day was when I got a message from my son Darren, who has a wicked sense of humour. 'After travelling around the world for eighteen months, you got two votes: one of them was your own – and the other bloke probably ticked the wrong box!' I had to laugh.

The game in the shadows was soon exposed. Warner was chased down by the US Department of Justice. Even FIFA's ethics committee eventually banned him from football for life. Platini was suspended, as were others. Even Blatter was run out of football.

Of those twenty-two members, Geoff Thompson retired, and only Abo Rida from Egypt survived to join what was renamed the FIFA Council. That surely tells you a lot. I felt it should have gone further. FIFA should have been dissolved with forensic accountants appointed to clean up the mess. But instead of investing in a thorough audit, FIFA spent fifteen million pounds on a vanity project of a movie which few people saw. At least they should have spent that money on pitches in deprived parts of Africa or in the Brazilian favelas.

FIFA appointed a new leader, Gianni Infantino, who came in on the ticket of cleaning up the house. I know him well and met him the first time when he was a legal attaché at UEFA in 2000.

To his great credit, he has modernised the organisation and encouraged transparency. Whereas the old system encouraged corruption and collusion, FIFA has opened voting up to all 211 member countries, and members must each declare their votes in an open forum. He has some very able vice-presidents in Victor Montagliani of CONCACAF (North America), Salman Bin Ibrahim Al-Khalifa of AFC (Asia), Patrice Motsepe of CAF (Africa) and, of course, Aleksander Čeferin of UEFA, although they don't always see eye to eye.

At the time of writing the next big vote was scheduled for 2024 on bids to host the World Cup in 2030. Sadly, in my view, England decided not to pitch for it, even in a collective bid with the rest of Great Britain and Ireland. In view of FIFA's new system of voting I felt we would have a very good chance of winning, but the wounds of bidding for the 2018 World Cup have still not healed. In fact the idea of a further bid was attacked by politicians as 'an expensive pipe dream'. Instead, it was decided that Great Britain and Ireland should aim for Euro 2028, which was felt to be more winnable.

I hope we win, and I am a proud believer in unity and national alliances. But football is special. England, Scotland, Wales, Northern Ireland and the Republic of Ireland each have their own fans, and it is an obsession with those national teams – not a British Isles one – that permeates every household. In any case, England is too big a footballing country not to stage the World Cup again. Thanks in great part to the Premier League, English football is England's biggest sporting export. Were we to host a future World Cup, we would generate the most money of any nation apart from the USA.

In fact, we would probably gross in the region of six to eight billion dollars. Obviously, I will do everything I can to help GB and Ireland host the Euros 2028.

And as I often say, being in a minority of one doesn't always make me wrong!

THE DANCING BEAR

OK, so this may sound weird but it was a dancing bear that convinced me of the need to have technology in football. The dancing bear entered my life – and football's – when Barbara and I went to see a movie at Barnet Odeon in 2008 and sat through the usual commercials before the main attraction. One of the ads began, 'This is an awareness test,' which caught our attention. It showed eight basketballers, four in black tops, four in white. 'How many passes does the team in white make?' the narrator challenged. Barbara and I were counting, as were loads of people in the cinema, shouting out 'nine', 'ten', 'eleven', 'twelve'. And then the narrator said, 'The answer is thirteen . . . but did you see the moonwalking bear?'

Barbara and I looked at each other.

No!

They replayed the sequence and there he was, sliding across the basketball court in a black tracksuit. The ad ended with the words, 'It's easy to miss something you're not looking for . . . look out for cyclists'. This was a safety announcement for Transport for London and it really had an impact on me.

I didn't know it at the time but the moonwalking bear was based on a famous experiment by American psychologists in 1999 – in their case they used someone dressed as a gorilla. It's a startling demonstration that whatever we focus our attention on, we miss a lot of other detail, some of it glaringly important. What it told me was that the camera will always beat the eye.

Little did I realise then that the dancing bear would live with me for about ten years! I rang up a friend of mine in the advertising business to find out whether I could use the clip for my presentations and after some sleuthing tracked down the agency and got clearance.

I began using the dancing bear in my talks at conferences around the world and, whenever possible, at UEFA and FIFA events. 'We need technology to help the referees,' I kept saying. It seems strange, looking back now in 2022, that there was even a debate about the issue. 'America put a man on the moon in 1969 but we still refuse technology to check whether a ball has crossed the line.' I had to drag football into the modern world. I went on a campaign!

FIFA were initially resistant to the idea. Yet every talk I gave, I was able to add another incident.

In Arsenal's 2001 FA Cup final against Liverpool, Stéphane Henchoz's blatant handball allowed the defender to make a crucial 'save' on the line to deny Thierry. It went unseen. What should have been a penalty for Arsenal and red card for Liverpool didn't happen. Injustice!

Then in 2005 during a match between Manchester United and Spurs, Pedro Mendes took a long-range shot which looped over Roy Carroll. United's goalkeeper managed to scoop it out, but the ball was definitely nearer the back of the net than the front. Even so, the goal was disallowed.

In 2009, I watched footage of a shot from Crystal Palace's Freddie Sears bouncing out from the back of the Bristol City net after striking a stanchion. The ref gave a goal kick. The recording showed he was wrong.

In 2010 I was in Bloemfontein at the World Cup in South Africa and I'm still speechless now at how the officials could not see that Frank Lampard's shot had crossed the German goal-line. Of course I was angered because the wrong call hurt my England side, but also because it damaged football. This was the World Cup, and this was amateurish.

'It's ridiculous,' I said to the FA. 'We have to do something.'

At least Sepp Blatter was now embarrassed into taking action and, finally, FIFA became more receptive to technology.

I went to Basingstoke to talk to the Hawk-Eye guys, the people who had pioneered the tennis line-calling system, to see how their technology worked. It was very impressive. 'This has to come into football,' I said to them.

I kept banging the drum, and eventually the drumbeat got through. FIFA were turned in 2012, and the following season goal-line technology finally came into the Premier League. Not long after that, on 11 May 2015, my lifelong hurt at Arsenal conceding a goal unjustly was softened when we were able to see proof that a goal had really been scored. I was sure that Bafétimbi Gomis's header for Swansea City was pushed out by David Ospina, but the referee, Kevin Friend, simply pointed to his watch which buzzed to confirm that the ball was over the line. You win some, you lose some, but at least this time I knew it was fair.

Yet, even now, I hear people say, 'Well, it's used only once or twice a year.' Not so. Every season in the Premier League the times it is relied on is in double figures. In my book, every goal counts.

What do the match officials make of the new technology?

One day in late 2014, I was at England's magnificent coaching campus, St George's Park, where I bumped into Mike Riley, the former Premier League referee who was now chief executive of Professional Game Match Officials Limited.

'Mr Dein, our referees and assistants are here. Would you mind speaking to them at lunchtime?' he asked.

'Of course, Mike! I consider them to be an endangered species. They need help.'

I had half an hour to spare, and I could hardly just greet them and say, 'Well done, you're doing a great job!' So I quickly jotted down a poem. When I give my talks in schools, I tell the students to try to be original. Think out of the box. And that's what I tried to do that day by addressing the officials in verse.

'In days of old when cameras weren't invented;
The refs made mistakes, yet everyone was contented;
Nowadays every foul, every offside is analysed;
It's no surprise the refs are criticised!
The time has come to help these guys;
I urge you all to sympathise;
It's not an easy job, they always get the blame;
But without them, there wouldn't be a game!'

I go on to say,
'I'm a poet,
And I don't know it.'

I received an unexpected round of applause. OK, it wasn't Shakespeare but the refs seemed to appreciate it. Mike even has a signed copy on his office wall.

'It might be worth a fiver when I've gone!' I told him.

After reciting the poem, I posed the question: 'Who's in favour of technology coming in?'

Every single one of them raised a hand.

One of our most experienced officials, Andre Marriner, put both hands up. He said, 'I've had to put up with a lot of criticism in the last six months – I sent the wrong player off.'

I remembered the incident well, as it involved two of our own players: Arsenal against Chelsea on 22 March 2014. Andre had sent off Kieran Gibbs instead of Alex Oxlade-Chamberlain. I felt for Andre; a case of mistaken identity would have been solved in seconds by video playback.

I continued to campaign wherever I could, pushing for new technology with FIFA, and with the former ref, David Elleray. David was influential since he was on the FA council with me and also on IFAB, the International Football Association Board, the body that goes back to 1886 and which determines the laws of the game. Another key figure I consulted was Mike Foster, the former general secretary of the Football League – and then Premier League – who went on to be chairman of the Professional Game Match Officials Board. Here was another able and trusted administrator whom I needed onside.

I went to see Hawk-Eye again and discovered they were already working on it. The system now had a name: VAR, short for video assistant referee. I also went to see the technology in action. In July 2016 the Dutch were trialling their system and I sat in the Hawk-Eye truck outside the stadium to watch the Feyenoord game. As it happened the video assistant referee came into its own, and I was so impressed. So was the ref in charge of the game. 'I'm so pleased,' he told me afterwards.

'Without VAR I would have looked a bloody idiot.'

Finally, FIFA introduced VAR at the 2018 World Cup, where it was a runaway success.

Even so, I still wanted to make sure it became thoroughly accepted throughout the game, and that it didn't prompt a backlash. One of my concerns was the on-field review. In principle it's a good idea for VAR to prompt the ref to replay on the monitor. But that means stopping the game while the video is checked. 'Won't this take up too much time?' I asked Massimo Busacca, FIFA's assistant head of refereeing.

Massimo was an official I'd come to like and respect, albeit after a challenging start. I could never forget the Arsenal Champions League game with Barcelona on 8 March 2011. Massimo showed Robin van Persie a second yellow at Camp Nou for taking a shot a second after he'd blown the whistle for offside. Massimo thought Robin was time-wasting by kicking the ball away. He absolutely wasn't. We could all tell that Robin couldn't hear the whistle above the noise of ninety thousand Barcelona fans, and he certainly didn't deserve to be sent off. Incidents like that leave indelible grudges. But Massimo is a good referee and his work on VAR was really important. He was reassuring; if the ref needs to stop the game and check, he must have the option to do so. People will simply have to wait.

'The referee still must be the boss man,' Massimo said.

He was right, of course. But surely fans would be more accepting if they weren't left in the dark about why a decision had been taken or been overruled.

In 2021, I spoke to Massimo again. 'What we have to do, sooner rather than later, is communicate the VAR decision to the public,' I said. 'For example, was Harry Kane offside? Was it his ear, his toe? Let the fans know. Get it on TV within thirty seconds.' We needed to engage and educate supporters – and the viewers. I was an admirer of how VAR was used in American football, where the public address system was used to explain the reasons for decisions based. The only question for me was who should make the announcement.

'It has to be the referee,' said Massimo, repeating his mantra. 'He is the boss man.' And I agreed. The on-field ref is the most important person in the game and VAR must add to the referee's authority, not be seen to undermine it.

I have to admit VAR has worked better in other countries but, despite teething problems in the Premier League, and despite some persistent critics, it is definitely here to stay, and I am sure it will settle down. Whenever I talk to its opponents, I point to the evidence that referees used to make one game-changing error every three games. We should all remember that VAR is still in its infancy, the technology will definitely improve, and the on-field referees will become ever more proficient.

Curiously, another innovation I pushed for could hardly have been less high-tech. During England's bid to host the 2018 World Cup, I was in Buenos Aires in front of several thousand football people, trying to convince their representatives to vote for England. Afterwards a man named Fernando Martinez approached me and said, 'Mr Dein, you seem to know your way around global football, can I interest you in my product?'

'What is it?' I asked.

He said, 'I'm in the paint business.'

I was baffled as to what that had to do with football.

'I have invented an invisible paint that will help referees. When there is a free kick the players in the wall shuffle forward like penguins, and instead of a ten-yard gap between the free kick and defenders, it shrinks to nine, then eight, then seven!' He was absolutely right.

Fernando then produced a can of something called '9.15'.

'9.15 metres corresponds with your ten yards.'

He drew a line on the carpet with the spray where a free kick would be taken, then paced out ten yards and drew another line with the spray. It disappeared within a couple of minutes.

'This is genius!' I told him. It was another occasion for my turtle motto, and I stuck my neck out for Fernando. 'Give me some samples, and let me see what I can do.' After that, wherever I went, I talked about this magical spray. 'This will stop encroachment,' I told the Premier League, the FA, UEFA, FIFA and anyone who would listen. FIFA brought in the vanishing spray for the 2014 World Cup and the Premier League took it on straight away.

As it turned out, the product was pirated and Fernando's company had to litigate in various countries to protect its patent. As far as Fernando was concerned the vanishing spray became the vanishing pay. Sadly they got precious little for their pioneering work. Sometimes it's the second mouse that gets the cheese. However, every referee in all the top games around the world now carries a can of vanishing spray.

Football continues to evolve. For the past eight years, I have been trying to take the guesswork out of extra time. I spoke to each of the seventeen elite refs in the Premier League, and asked them, 'When the fourth official puts up the board to show how long the games should be extended – three, four, five minutes, or whatever – how accurate are you with your timekeeping?'

They were all honest that it was a challenge. One admitted outright, 'It's simply guesswork.'

Hence I've been promoting 'Effective Time Keeping', 'ETK' – or 'Pure Time'.

The referee, the busiest person on the pitch, cannot be expected to make sure every second is added on. And so many things can justify extending the match. The ball goes out of play – twenty to thirty seconds? A keeper time-wasting over goal kicks – another twenty seconds, often more? Players celebrating a goal, or a player down injured . . . VAR delays or substitutions – more seconds lost. And don't get me started on wasted time at penalties! The goalkeeper kicks the post and has a chat with the penalty-taker. Time doesn't get added on for mind-games – but it absolutely should be. It's fairer and gives proper value for money for fans, who are being cheated out of real time.

I collected hard evidence and it turned out that in the ninety minutes allowed for any game the actual time the ball is in play is between fifty-eight and sixty minutes. So an extra minute here or there can make a huge difference. I often show people the clip of Mo Salah scoring against Arsenal on 20 November 2021. Alisson played it left, Kostas Tsimikas flicked it on, so did Diogo Jota, before Sadio Mané crossed and Salah finished. The whole action from start to finish took 10.4 seconds. It was devastating and showed how quickly a goal can happen. If 10.4 seconds can be so decisive, think about a ref working out whether it is three minutes or four minutes that should be added on.

Let's get it accurate. I believe there should be a clock in the stadium with two halves of thirty minutes of pure time counting down with an official stopping and starting it. (As I tell my Spurs friends, 'Every ground needs a Clock End!') Leave the ref to focus on other things. At least that way you wouldn't get the hapless Zambian referee at the Tunisia v. Mali game at the Africa Cup of Nations tournament on 12 January 2022, blowing the whistle after eighty-five minutes – and then eighty-nine minutes in Limbe. It was crazy. The referee, Janny Sikazwe, was apparently suffering from heatstroke and of course I felt for him, but that's another reason for introducing 'Pure Time'.

A fortnight after Salah's goal – the move that took 10.4 seconds – I was at the FIFA Arab Cup in Doha and made a presentation at BeIN Sport's wonderful studios. By chance, Pierluigi Collina, chairman of FIFA's referees' committee, and Massimo Busacca, his colleague, were in the audience. After I showed them Salah's goal – and other incidents where time had been wasted in matches and never added at the end – Massimo said, 'Don't worry, David, we are going to have some trials.' Great, I thought, the game really needs to keep improving.

I am still on another campaign too. Penalty shoot-outs have become part and parcel of finals – the established way to find a winner after a hundred and twenty minutes of stalemate. I remember vividly the UEFA Cup Final at the Parken stadium in Copenhagen in 2000. It was Arsenal playing Galatasaray. The score was 0-0 at full time, and the referee determined that the penalties should be taken at the Galatasaray end. As you can imagine, the Galatasaray fans did everything to put off the Arsenal penalty takers with consistent booing, whistling and aggressive gestures whenever an Arsenal player went up to take his kick. Arsenal's penalties went everywhere except the back of the net and they lost 4-1!

Soon afterwards, when I was sitting on one of my UEFA Club Competition meetings, I proposed that there should be two spins of a coin to determine the end that the penalties should be taken and which team should go first. I am pleased to say that that was passed and is currently the adopted practice.

However, even that can be improved on. I would now like to see penalties taken at either end so that each club can take their penalties in front of their own supporters. The fourth official is a qualified referee so he can officiate at one end and the on-field referee at the other. It is fair and I cannot see a reason why it should not be implemented.

Football needs to be fair. And it needs to be seen to be fair. So going back to goal-line technology and VAR, I would like to thank the bear for dancing football into the twenty-first century.

LIFE AFTER DEATH

After leaving the club I had to decide what to do with my shareholding. I am not a good back-seat driver, and once I had left the club I couldn't comfortably sit with a lot of my personal wealth tied up in my shares while I was unable to have any input. I might as well sell them and move on. It was almost like cutting that financial link was part of the process I had to go through – the easier part, it must be said. The emotional bond was a different story.

I thought Stan Kroenke would be the natural purchaser of my shares since, following my introductions, he had already acquired 9.9 per cent from Granada. I had assumed he would still want me very much on board, but I will never forget his response when I offered him my shares: 'The landscape has changed.' I assumed what he meant was that I was surplus to his requirements. I felt abandoned and badly let down; after all, I had introduced him to the club, met him several times, including at my home, and encouraged him to become an investor in the club.

I had always assumed Kroenke had the financial capacity to be a bigger investor, and he was clearly interested in taking the club over. Let's face it, he is not normally a minority player. But he was playing a long game, and, though he didn't show an interest in my shares at the time, he was picking up tranches wherever he could. To my astonishment the rock-solid Arsenal supporter Danny Fiszman sold him a substantial tranche. Presumably Kroenke thought that Danny's shares would raise his influence with the board, whereas I was out and no longer had authority there.

Selling my shares was not straightforward. I wanted the best price but I wanted to make sure the club would be in safe hands. So I approached an old schoolfriend, Sir Ronald Cohen, who had started one of Britain's first venture capital companies, Apax Partners, to work with me on the sale process. I knew that I could trust him implicitly. He was my sounding board.

There were a few leads. My son Gavin was going out with Tamara Ecclestone, the daughter of Bernie Ecclestone of Formula 1 and an original pioneer of TV rights in sport. Bernie showed some interest himself but ultimately passed. However, he had introduced me to Khaldoon Al Mubarak who was keen on investing in the sport – and went on to become chairman of Manchester City. But the timing wasn't right.

In the summer I was introduced to Uzbekistan businessman and Arsenal fan Alisher Usmanov through an intermediary. When we met on his mega-yacht *Dilbar* in Sardinia, the first thing he did was reel off the '71 double-winning team.

Meanwhile, I was still in touch with Kroenke and although he'd been disappointingly unsupportive in the past he now invited me to meet up on his own mega-yacht for discussions. Talk about serendipity – at the same time, both Kroenke and Usmanov were in Sardinia on their boats in different locations. One minute Ronnie and I were on Kroenke's boat; the next minute we were on Usmanov's. Most disappointingly, Kroenke lowballed me, thinking that he was the only game in town. I had a figure in mind of what the shares were worth but he came nowhere near. 'This is my price,' he said, 'and if you think you can do better then you must do what is good for you.'

Alisher's approach was almost the opposite. 'What is it going to take?' he asked. 'I want to buy the whole club.'

Here I was juggling with two billionaires, with two totally different personalities, who both wanted to own the club. Kroenke was a very sophisticated player looking for value. He already had many other interests with sporting franchises in the US. Alisher, on the other hand, was a true Arsenal fan and just wanted to own the club immediately, at any financial price.

Whichever of these two men bought the club, frankly I was hoping to be reinstated. That was one of my conditions of sale: if you get control I want to run it.

Kroenke had already shown he was reluctant. Now not only did Alisher hit the table with considerably more money, but he asked me to run a vehicle to build up his shareholding. I agreed to sell my 15 per cent holding, shared equally between Alisher and his colleague Farhad Moshiri. Alisher made his intentions clear that he wanted to own the club outright, and I was happy to help for a year and see how it went. That year, I chaired Red and White Holdings for him, and we managed to build his share in the club up to 30 per cent. This gave him an important foothold because if you hold more than 25 per cent of the shares in a company, you have the right to block any financial restructuring. In fact it never gave him the power base that he wanted.

He loved the club, wanted to put money in and wanted to help, yet they never offered him a seat on the board. He was never taken to the dressing room. He was never even invited to an away game. Alisher was frozen out. It was astonishing how badly they treated him.

After a year I felt I had served my usefulness. We had hit a brick wall: we hadn't been able to acquire any further shares, and we decided mutually for me to drop out of the picture.

Kroenke on the other hand was discreetly building up his own position and, crucially, he was also ingratiating himself with the board. He was playing a long game or, as he once put it to me, was remaining patient until he could drain the swamp. Usmanov was serious opposition and Kroenke was content to wait it out. It was a very difficult period for Arsenal, with a stand-off for ownership between the two biggest shareholders, and it did the club no favours. Two factions were vying for control and no business can be ambitious and unified in such circumstances.

The turning point came as Danny Fiszman was critically ill. Just before he died in 2011, he sold his shares to Kroenke and convinced the other major shareholder, Lady Nina, to follow suit. That was the pivotal point that helped Kroenke gain control.

In an attempt to improve his position, Usmanov approached Kroenke and asked to buy his shares. Kroenke cleverly turned the tables, making it clear that he was not a seller, and offered to buy Usmanov's stake. Once Usmanov realised that there was an impasse and he was unlikely to get control, he decided to turn his attention elsewhere. He knew he wasn't going to get anywhere with 30 per cent. Kroenke bought him and his colleague, Farhad Moshiri, out. Moshiri turned his attention to Everton.

Finally Kroenke had what he wanted – full control. But only partial commitment.

The truth is, you may think you know Kroenke but you don't know him. He is difficult to get to. You put calls in and it is very rare he will return them. They don't call him Silent Stan for nothing. He is not an easy man to gauge. He is a multi-billionaire, yet he can walk around Denver and nobody notices. He owns the LA Rams and Denver Nuggets and Colorado Rapids and Arsenal Football Club. And that's the point right there: and Arsenal. That says everything. In my time on the board, Arsenal was our whole train set, in his case it is a carriage on his train. That is the root of the problem. Whereas I gave it tender loving care, he is an absentee owner who gets other people to run it. Arsenal is not yet steeped in his blood and probably not his first priority. I hope this will be addressed. Football is a living organism, one which requires personal love and attention.

There are two types of owners. Those whose money follow their love: they buy in, and, with luck, they don't lose their investment. And others who have a love that follows their money; they buy in and, with luck, they develop an attachment.

Investing in football used to be described as dead money. Today, of course, football is huge. When I first joined Arsenal the turnover was £1.5 million, today it is £450 million. And while we may have reached a plateau in UK domestic television rights I think the overseas rights will continue to grow. Within a few years of Kroenke taking control, the value of the club had tripled. In fact he turned down a bid of two billion pounds from Daniel Ek, the owner of Spotify who may well have been prepared to pay much more.

Ironically, Arsenal is owned by an American but what most

people don't know is that, once upon a time, there was a chance that Arsenal itself would own an American franchise.

In the early 1990s I got to know Alan Rothenberg, a lawyer who was driving the World Cup in 1994. On the back of that tournament, they launched Major League Soccer. It began in 1996, a few years after the Premier League was formed. He told me they were trying to encourage soccer franchises, and that during the planning phase they wanted wealthy people to come in and start the MLS in the various major cities.

I had this idea. Miami is a glamorous place – quite apart from the fact that my wife Barbara comes from there. It is prosperous, drawing people from all across America, and Dade County in which it sits has a permanent population of 2.7 million. It already had a very successful NFL franchise, the Miami Dolphins and basketball franchise, Miami Heat. I thought, What about the 'Miami Gunners' soccer team? Why not start an MLS team? As usual, I stuck my neck out and made a presentation to the board. We could have picked up a franchise for nothing. The Americans would have been only too happy to see us come in as a founder-member club. I got blown out of the water by the board. Rolling forwards a few years, when David Beckham first bought into the Inter Miami franchise, the cost was twenty-five million dollars. Last year there was a $150-million injection. These franchises are now enormous and every club is owned by a billionaire. Stan Kroenke has got one – the Colorado Rapids. We could have had the Miami Gunners for nothing.

The Kroenkes' initial problems at Arsenal stemmed from putting the wrong people in. I believe money has been wasted on frivolous transfers and that worries me as an Arsenal fan. I still have my ten regular seats and four club level seats. Every season-ticket holder is an investor in their own way and certainly an emotional investor.

There are some talented boys in there but this does not yet look like the squad to challenge Manchester City and Liverpool. Is there a road out of here?

That's a key question. The board needs refreshing. There is no diversity. There is also the matter of chemistry. Somehow that needs to be recreated. That can only be done with determination and care at the very top.

Good people have gone. People who were part of the fabric over several decades were culled in the redundancies. When I was there it had to be a family. I made sure I knew everybody across the staff personally. I would walk, once or twice a week, around every department. I would go and see the box office – how are we doing? Junior Gunners – how is it going? Travel club – what does it look like for the trains? I did this firstly because I was curious and secondly I wanted them to know I cared.

When Ivan Gazidis was the CEO there was a breakdown of communication between him and Arsène. Again, there was a disconnect between the demands on and off the pitch. I understand that Ivan got too busy, but even so he positioned himself at the training ground, which was Arsène's department. He was in Arsène's airspace. Arsène is his own man and didn't need or want the CEO watching his every move.

Ivan's way of developing the club was to hire more and more people. At one stage Arsenal had 650 staff, with executive account managers all over the place, a massive HR department, its own big legal department and dozens of partnership and commercial staff with no great deals to show for it. The club could afford it for a time, but when Arsenal dropped out of the Champions League they lost a huge part of their income, and that resulted in a culling of staff, and not just newly recruited ones. Some of the people so euphemistically 'let go' had been devoted to the club for years. Meanwhile, Ivan left the club in 2018 and, to his credit, resurrected himself at AC Milan where he won the Scudetto in the 2021 season.

After so many years in the corridors of football decision-making – not just with Arsenal but with all the various committees – it was very difficult to adapt to being on the outside. I was used to being on call 24/7. If leaving the Arsenal board wasn't bad enough, I also suffered the loss of other key positions in football as a direct consequence. I had to step down as president of the G-14 group of clubs. This was an action group consisting of fourteen, and eventually eighteen, of the most powerful clubs in Europe. The loss of my role there was a huge blow to me; and then I lost some of my responsibilities at the FA and UEFA for similar reasons. I wasn't just kicked once. I was kicked four or five times in quick succession. For decades football had consumed almost all my thoughts and waking hours. It was hard to know how to fill my time.

I still keep in touch with all the people that I used to know from football. The addiction remains. I still went to games in the aftermath, and would gladly travel to conferences and tournaments and deliver presentations. For a short time, however – and for the first time in decades – I kept away from Arsenal matches for several months, and that hurt. Then Karren Brady's dad, Terry, invited me to be his guest. 'You have to come back to the club,' he said. 'You've put so much into it.' It was surreal in a sense to go back.

I remember Robin van Persie saw me outside. He said, 'Mr Dein! What happened to you? We miss you. Where are you?' He gave me a big hug. That was an emotional moment for me. Robin couldn't understand it but I had never had a chance to say goodbye to staff, or even to the players – many of whom I'd signed and all of whom were family to me.

I was living my Arsenal life vicariously now. I still talked to Arsène all the time because he was my closest friend. Also my son Darren still represented a few of the players as their agent.

So I was there with Arsenal, but I wasn't there. At times it drove me mad. Above all else, I felt sad because I had unfinished business. The club was going through a metamorphosis. For the next few years, I travelled as much as I could just to take my mind off it. I would spend a month at the big tournaments – the World Cup or the Euros or the African Cup of Nations; that was what I knew best. Barbara was very considerate, so I could just take myself off because that was my playground. Then I would travel to wherever there was a football conference where I was often invited as a speaker.

There were offers to work at other clubs but I was not seriously tempted. One of my first calls was from Joan Laporta, who invited me to join him at Barcelona. AC Milan were interested too. Mike Ashley rang me to say, 'I need somebody to run Newcastle.' Liverpool rang offering the chief executive role. About a dozen major clubs asked me to come in and run them. And I couldn't. I felt I'd be betraying my own club. I'm an Arsenal man. I had opportunities and I turned them all down. That's blind loyalty for you.

Arsène's last home game on 6 May 2018 was the first time I returned to the directors' box. Interestingly, it wasn't the club who invited me. I was there at Arsène's personal request. And it was so nice. Linda, who ran the directors' suite for catering, gave me a big hug and a kiss. It was like being back home again and it was very welcoming, with so many people saying, 'Oh, we've missed you, it's so nice to see you back where you belong.'

I have never really been far away. I give away my ten season tickets every game to teachers, prison officers and others in the community. I use my four club seats for myself and my immediate guests. They are the next-door block to the directors' box; I chose them when we were building the stadium. At times being there is like an out-of-body experience. I'm seeing people sitting just across the aisle in the directors' box who I believe are not deserving of a place there.

Where do I see Arsenal going now? Since Arsène and I left, there has been a lot of restructuring. It was as if the club was fitted with revolving doors, with so many people in senior positions coming and going. The most recent trend is to back a younger group, with three ex-players, Mikel Arteta, Edu and Per Mertesacker, calling their own shots.

Edu was a player I signed in 2001 and I like him very much. It has been fascinating to see him taking on the technical director role, which involves player trading and being a welcoming face of the club and point of contact. Naturally, he has his own style and did a very good job with the Brazilian Football Federation, the CBF. I would say he was a bit naïve and influenced at the start when he returned to Arsenal and that not all the transfers paid off. Now that he is freer and more settled into his role he is going in the right direction, particularly with the emergence of the younger players. I wish him well.

While it's obvious that the club has suffered slippage over the past few years, there are promising signs of recovery and Arteta's young team have revived hope. Even so, we are still way off the pace set by Manchester City and Liverpool. When I was working with Arsène, invariably we would finish in the top three in the league. It hurts to see that Chelsea and Spurs have caught us up. My advice to Arsenal fans is to remain patient, as it might take a few more years to challenge for the title. Winning teams have to evolve, and there are positive signs for the future. Nothing would give me more pleasure than to see Arsenal challenging at the top.

The end for Arsène came as a shock and a bitter blow. For the news to appear suddenly, on a random morning, with several games of the season still to play was not good management. It was a knifing. What happened with him was not dissimilar to what happened to me. Yet his run had been extraordinary, not just for Arsenal but for football as a whole. We won't see that again with any manager. Even if he had come to the end of his career at the club as a coach, he should have been offered loyalty. He should have been kept on. The board should have invited him upstairs at the least. They should have made him chairman or sporting director, or whatever everyone was happy with. He made modern Arsenal. He taught the team. He inspired them. He spotted the players. He changed the mentality and style and delivered unprecedented success. Yet here he was, thrown out into the wilderness.

Of course it brought back bad memories of my own treatment. Until I saw how badly Arsène was treated I often felt it must have been my own behaviour and my own miscalculations that had caused the breakdown in relationships. But when Arsène was treated just the same – unceremoniously kicked out after so many years of passionate service and so much loyalty – I realised this pattern of behaviour had far more to say about the management than it did about Arsène and me.

Of course Arsène had seen the writing on the wall, or in his case, in the sky. The abuse he received from a sector of the fanbase at times in the last few years was difficult to see, knowing how much of himself he gave to the club. He never really showed how much he was suffering. It is very rare he shows his true emotions, but even so I could see that he was hurting, and that some of the key relationships inside the club were problematic. It was a great shame.

When Arsène left Arsenal in May 2018, he told me, 'David, I'm not quite sure what I'm going to do.' He was desperate to stay in the game, and I knew he had several offers, including Barcelona, Bayern Munich, Monaco and Strasbourg.

'Stay away from club management,' I urged him.

He was sixty-eight. I worried about him returning to a profession where the average time in post is now twelve months. I felt responsible for Arsène and I still do, to this day. Arsène is in good health, I know that; but I didn't want him to get back into the hotbed of club management and to have a heart attack in the job, as happened to our closest friend, Gérard Houllier.

Away from Arsenal, Arsène had to stay active professionally, keeping that amazing, alert mind ticking over. What would that challenge be? He has never had much time or any interests outside football, although he is a keen follower of politics. But he needed his life back.

Arsène and I spent time together at the 2018 World Cup in Russia. Soon after we arrived, both FIFA and UEFA made it very clear to me they each wanted Arsène to work for them. I was staying at the Hotel Lotte in Moscow, and FIFA were there too. I spoke to Zvonimir Boban, who was then Gianni Infantino's right-hand man at FIFA in charge of developing football. Boban had been a great technical footballer with AC Milan and Croatia and is a highly intelligent guy.

'Do you think Arsène would come to FIFA?' Boban asked me.

'I think that's the right job for him,' I said. 'That is where he deserves to finish his career – at the top of world football, shaping the world game. But you would need to think about it very seriously, Zvonimir, because I know he's going to miss the day-to-day coaching. You know, he loves being with players and on the training ground. You can't stick him in an office and lock the door, because that would kill him . . .'

Boban nodded. 'I am sure we can work it out.'

He met Arsène to chat about the role. Boban was Arsène's type of man, one of the greatest footballers of his era, and there was an immediate bond. 'I like him,' Arsène told me. 'I can see us working together. And I like Gianni.'

That was key. Arsène knew that FIFA's president, Gianni Infantino came in with a mandate to clean up the shop. FIFA had a bad name after the shenanigans that occurred during the 2018/2022 World Cup bids, with many of their executive committee being suspended and indeed jailed. What Blatter liked was power, and he devolved a lot of the real work to the people below him, especially on the Executive Committee, and it was they who abused their positions. I hear people say that

Blatter must have been guilty of sleaze himself, as head of an organisation where more than three quarters of his immediate board members were accused of corruption. I think his crime was allowing his colleagues to run their own show without proper accountability. He was drunk with his own power and needed their votes and support. Having said that, Blatter also did much to help football, including the Goal Project that provides football facilities all over the world. People do not realise how much good FIFA do.

Under Gianni Infantino, FIFA do even more good. It's an unusually complicated job being FIFA president. Infantino's got to look after 211 countries. That's 211 mouths to feed – with different tastes. What goes on in Africa is not the same as what goes on in Asia or in Europe.

This is what Infantino and Boban were asking Arsène to help with. I knew that UEFA's president, Aleksander Čeferin, was also very interested in drawing on Arsène's years of experience, and I set up a couple of meetings during the same tournament so that he could have a choice. Moscow lived up to its reputation for intrigue and secret meetings! It came down to whether he wanted to work for FIFA or UEFA.

'Look, Arsène,' I said. 'You could be head of football for fifty-five countries, most of them you know well, or you could be head of football for two hundred and eleven.' Without wishing to influence him too much, I felt that, since this was going to be his last roll of the dice, he should finish at the top of the world game where he belongs. With all due respect, as much as I like UEFA, I pushed him towards FIFA. Arsène's such a close friend that I wanted him to finish his career by cementing his legacy. 'You're a mentor to so many managers, and this FIFA role will expand that even more,' I said. I could see the Arsène Wenger manual on football coaching being a legacy around the world.

Gianni was very shrewd. He told Arsène, 'We need a true football man for coaching, to mould the future for the rest of the world. You are the best.' FIFA did have Marco van Basten doing the job, and he's a footballing legend, but I don't think he put his heart and soul into the role. I knew Arsène would give everything. He always does.

'I want to make a difference,' Arsène told me. 'I will only go to FIFA if I can really make a difference. My objective is to get more boys and girls playing the game with better coaches to coach them.'

Yes, he misses the adrenaline of being a football manager, but did he really want to stand on the touchline in the rain on a cold January night in his eighth decade? Did he need that aggravation or that pressure which is getting worse and worse? 'The game's changed,' Arsène said. 'The power's with the players.'

Arsène decided the FIFA job was the more appealing and dropped the idea of UEFA fairly early on, but then it came down to FIFA or a club job. Real Madrid wanted him. They had the gap between Zinedine Zidane and Julen Lopetegui just before the World Cup, and they were hot on Arsène's tail. I sighed. It was like the old days. I was forever fending Real off at Arsenal. They'd always chased Arsène and always coveted our players.

In my eyes FIFA were always favourite, and that's how it turned out. The job as head of global football development was too good to resist. There was still plenty of negotiating to establish the exact nature of his role before he finally agreed. It was not announced until 13 November 2019.

'I believe the new FIFA we've seen emerging in recent years has the sport itself at the very heart of its objectives and is determined to develop the game in its many different components,' Arsène said. 'I know I can contribute to this objective and will put all my energy into this.'

His role at FIFA is far-reaching. He introduced the Arsène Wenger doctorate around the world, teaching training methods and having regular meetings with elite coaches to raise standards. On top of that, in his role on the panel of the International FA Board, Arsène has an important influence on the rules that govern the game. In particular VAR has come under his remit. Arsène wants to see accuracy. He wants offsides to be a hundred per cent right. He wants dangerous tackles punished with red cards – and yellow cards upgraded if necessary after the referee has watched a replay on the pitch-side monitor.

In early 2021, Arsène told me of his plan to revise the football calendar and introduce a World Cup every two years. Certainly, the calendar needs rethinking as there are too many international breaks. We start the season in August, play four or five games, then disappear on international duty around the world. We come back, play another four or five games in September and we're off again on another international break. A dramatic rethink is necessary. Unfortunately, his plan met with tremendous resistance. It was just too ambitious, and some confederations would have to give up valuable qualifiers and so would lose considerable amounts of money. Personally, I would be in favour of a three-year World Cup – year one, a World Cup; year two, Euros or equivalent; year three, Women's World Cup, and perhaps a Club World Cup – but played at a different time of the season. Also, it is essential that UEFA – as the largest economic confederation – are consulted early in the proceedings. (I am not a great fan of the UEFA Nations League as it seems to be a manufactured tournament at the wrong time of the year. I understand the logic as it replaces meaningless friendlies.)

The root of the problem is the land grab for fixture dates by FIFA, UEFA and the Leagues. I maintain FIFA as the world governing body really needs to assert itself in the best interest of the sport, give players more of a chance to play in the most important competitions.

Actually I think we should be more radical and shift the season. I pitched my idea to Arsène about making football a summer sport. 'Could February to November work?' I asked him. It would still be a nine-month season – but we both knew there would be huge resistance. 'We're used to August to May,' everyone would say. People don't like change. And then, when it becomes established, it becomes acceptable.

I'm a great believer that people's habits change in different weather. World Cups and Euros are held during the summer. The last one I went to, the Women's Euros in 2022, was a wonderful tournament. Inside the stadium people were in shirt-sleeves and shorts. You've got a different atmosphere. It's a concept worth further debate.

I felt Arsène not only brought his knowledge of the game to FIFA but also his values. As I have said before, one of Arsène's most important attractions is that he has a strong moral compass. Everything he does is based on honesty and integrity. When you hear some of the horror stories in football, to this day, with illicit money passing hands, it's good that somebody as scrupulously honest as Arsène has come in at the top.

Honesty is such a key ingredient. When anybody talks about buying a club and appointing a manager, they occasionally ask me to help them in a consultancy capacity. The first thing I ask the owner is, 'Do you think the guy is honest?' A new manager's going to be looking after the money. 'If you're going to give him twenty million pounds . . . fifty million, or a hundred million to spend, you've got to make sure a) that his judgement is good, and b) that it's going to be a clean deal.'

It was a pity for Arsène that Boban jumped ship in June 2019 to go and work for AC Milan. They'd struck up a cordial relationship. That hurt Arsène. As it happens, Boban didn't really enjoy it at Milan and Čeferin convinced him to move on to UEFA as chief of football in April 2021. In the long run I feel that may actually be good for Arsène. Boban could be the bridge between UEFA and FIFA. Boban is intelligent enough to do that.

I know Arsène misses football, the training and the games. He misses it passionately. Every day. Because that's in his bones.

'Do you like FIFA?' I asked.

'Yes,' he said. 'I miss the competitive side, I miss the engagement with players. But yes, I'm happy in the job.'

I'm happy for him too. Of course even when Arsène was at Arsenal people were trying to poach him, and at FIFA he received offers all the time. But he has a job that has huge influence on the game and which cements his legacy for world football.

'I hope you like the FIFA job?' Barbara asked him a few months after he started.

'I have to say yes,' he laughed. 'After all, David put me there!'

THE PLAY THAT
WENT WRONG

The text arrived at 2.27 p.m. on Sunday 18 April 2021 from my good friend, Giorgio Marchetti, deputy general secretary football of UEFA. 'Your beloved Arsenal is in this bloody loop.' What?! This was the first I'd heard about a European Super League, and I was stunned.

Instinctively, I knew this would bring the football world crashing down. First I checked the story out, and it was true: twelve clubs were plotting to set up their own closed shop. An elitist Super League by invitation only, without promotion and relegation. I messaged back to Giorgio: 'I find it abhorrent, and so will the press and the fans.' Where's the sporting integrity in a self-appointed closed elite league? The idea was detestable. If it succeeded, the ESL would hijack the key dates for television. The Premier League would become a midweek league, and in effect be killed – this was the league I considered my baby, and I was going to fight for it!

The Champions League would be pushed out into the background, and I would fight for that too. After all, I was there in the room at UEFA in 1992 when the Champions League was created. Together with Gerhard Aigner, the general secretary, and Lennart Johansson, the president, and along with Team Marketing, we were building on the history and glory of the European Cup. The Champions League was not a clique like the Super League proposal. It was open and sporting and had been a runaway success.

The more I thought about the six UK Premier League clubs breaking away, the more certain I was that it would cause civil war in the English game. There would be a huge backlash from the fourteen disadvantaged Premier League clubs who might even evict the six – including my beloved Arsenal. And the fans, including most fans in the rebel clubs, would be outraged.

I am always very cautious when I am approached to do an interview for press or television and I choose my timing carefully. If I am quoted, I want it to be impactful. But when I was approached by BBC's *Football Focus* that week, I felt so incensed that I threw caution to the winds. I had to say something and I gave it to them with both barrels. I was asked by Mark Lawrenson whether I had not done something similar in creating the Premier League. I told him pretty forcefully that there was no comparison at all. The Premier League took the whole of the First Division – twenty-two clubs, not a self-proclaimed elite of six! We insisted on promotion and relegation to keep the pyramid alive. What's more, our first port of call was our own Football Association to get their blessing. The ESL was just a clique.

I'd felt similar outrage on 11 October 2020 over Project Big Picture, another plan to give privileged power to just six clubs: Liverpool, Manchester United, Manchester City, Arsenal, Tottenham and Chelsea. To me, that project just seemed unworkable and divisive. The success of the Premier League is down to fairness: one club, one vote, a two-thirds majority and TV monies redistributed by a strong and long-standing formula. That democratic pyramid must be protected because all clubs matter, and so do the grassroots. The Premier League is about heritage, jeopardy and opportunity; knowing that however well your club is doing today, it could face relegation tomorrow, and however badly it is doing now, it might one day rise to the top. Fortunately, Project Big Picture was quickly seen off.

Having said that, I do have some sympathy with the argument that the glamorous clubs are the ones driving the value and should be rewarded for their contribution. After all, they are the performers that the audience – particularly millions abroad – want to see most. But not at the expense of the rest of the clubs. Watching these so-called Super Leaguers trying to ruin the game – my game, your game, our game – I was seething. Sport's about creating the opportunity for dreams – fluctuations in fortunes and promotion and relegation must be sacrosanct. I felt a duty, almost a mission, to stop the Super League.

I texted Stan Kroenke, who was at home in Denver. 'Stan, I do hope you and the family are well,' I wrote. 'I really do need to speak to you about what's going on with the proposed European Super League. It is damaging the club. Let me know when we can catch up. Best regards.' No reply. 'Silent Stan' lived up to his nickname. I emailed the same message. Nothing. If I'd still been at Arsenal, I'd have walked away. Arsenal have to set standards, not betray them.

In fact I had found myself in that position a dozen or so years before. In 1998 a similar ambush had been mounted by Media Partners, founded by the controversial Italian businessman and prime minister Silvio Berlusconi. They had a plan for thirty-two European clubs in two divisions, ignoring clubs from smaller leagues. Too elitist for me, too much of a closed shop and that time I did threaten to resign. The European Super League was more of the same. It had to be confronted.

(Recently, I came across an Arsenal match day programme from 2 January 1989 where I said the prospect of a ten/twelve club super league was 'unthinkable'. I even said, 'it would be too sterile for words . . .')

'Unfortunately, it's more than a threat,' Giorgio messaged. 'My club is in and makes me feel ashamed.' Giorgio is a proud Inter Milan fan, and he was as enraged, and as embarrassed for his club, as I was for mine.

'It's the "G" word,' I replied. 'Not "Giorgio", "greed"!'

That night I couldn't sleep so I messaged him again at 4.30 a.m. 'I don't understand it. The clubs want to stay in the domestic leagues and then screw their own colleagues. It's totally immoral. This meal has been cooked in a batter of cash, with little thought to the final taste.'

And another thing: six English, three Italian and three Spanish clubs signed up for this European Super League; no French, Dutch, German or Portuguese clubs! What kind of European Super League is that?! The rebels said they were confident of getting another three. But though Paris Saint-Germain, Bayern Munich and Borussia Dortmund were invited to the party, they quickly realised it would be a wake. Sensible chaps, and thank God they were.

Another thing troubled me: where were FIFPRO in all this? They're the international players' union. What do the players think about it? Surely, they'd stand up against it – all those extra games, all that damage to the domestic leagues that produced them – or would they just see more money? Again, I couldn't sleep. And what a provocative time for the Super League to launch, directly before the UEFA Congress on Tuesday 20 April.

'This is disrespectful,' I messaged Giorgio. I really felt for him. I knew how much he cared about UEFA. Giorgio was one of the reasons why European football was in such a good place. The Champions League was competitive, involved a range of clubs, and the broadcasters and supporters liked it.

'My club is winning the title,' Giorgio replied, 'but yesterday night, watching the game, I hated them. This is awful. They are stealing football from the heart of people in the most cynical and arrogant way.' Like me he was hoping FIFA would be stronger. 'They should condemn them immediately.'

Despite my anger I realised that we would have to try to bury the hatchet with the breakaway six – and not in one another's heads. We had to make the clubs see sense and bring them back into the football family. I wanted to be a peace-maker; I wanted them to see common sense. So on the Monday morning, 19 April, I messaged an executive I respect who was at one of the six English clubs which was proposing the Super League. This is a guy I'm very friendly with, and I was hoping to help him as well as dissuade him. 'I foresee open warfare,' I warned him. 'The notion of the same twelve clubs being permanently invited won't sit well with the fans. UEFA, FIFA, FIFPRO may not come onboard. You have to remember what you're doing is very serious. I urge you, urge you, to reconsider. Meanwhile, you have to expect a rough time today.'

'Honestly, I need a little bit of time,' he told me.

That evening, I saw the cracks appearing in the Super League camp. Jürgen Klopp spoke against the plan after Liverpool's match with Leeds United at Elland Road that night. Good on you, Jürgen!

Then the talented player James Milner followed suit: 'I don't like it, and I don't want it to happen.' Well done, James! He's one of the game's good guys; seen it all, cares for the game and always talks sense. I felt more confident now. I felt the tide was turning.

I texted Giorgio: 'I cannot remember the last time a subject has received such universal condemnation.'

'That's what they deserve,' he replied.

These guys simply hadn't thought it through. It was amateur night in Dixie, except it wasn't Dixie, it was Denver, Boston, Madrid and Barcelona.

Everyone weighed in and it was good to see the press and fans give the Super League a good kicking. I was proud that the English led the revolt against the Super League. My spirits lifted to see fans protest outside Elland Road on Monday night and outside Stamford Bridge on Tuesday night. I hear so much about the importance of TV viewers, but what the past few years have shown is the power of those who actually attend the games. The matches played behind closed doors during the Covid-19 pandemic were totally soulless – but when fans returned it was like the sound being switched on again. The sound was certainly switched on over the European Super League.

We should never forget that the English game belongs ultimately to its supporters – and challenging the Super League was far from the first time they had made their voices heard loud and clear. I'll never forget the raw power of fans at Anfield when the cost of tickets in the rebuilt main stand went up to sixty-seven pounds. After sixty-seven minutes, a quarter of the crowd got up and left in protest. It really shook the club up.

With the Super League the noise was infinitely greater, and the message was unmistakably clear. The government heard it. Boris Johnson, the then prime minister heard it. And never a politician to miss a popular cause, Boris waded in. UEFA were very grateful for the PM's intervention, and especially his famous phrase on the Tuesday morning that he'd be willing to drop a 'legislative bomb' to stop the plot. UEFA officials kept repeating those two key words to me. 'Legislative bomb'. That was a game-changer. And Boris wasn't messing about. I heard that the government was considering blocking work visas for overseas stars for the six UK clubs. In fact if there was a defining moment, once he threatened the 'legislative bomb' that was game over.

'We owe you a debt,' UEFA's president Aleksander Čeferin told me during the Euros.

As that Tuesday wore on, I felt more and more confident. The chairman of PSG, Nasser Al-Khelaifi, issued a damning statement, criticising the twelve for acting only out of 'self-interest'. This was huge. I immediately messaged a friend at one of the English six: 'As a friend, don't be the last to pull out.'

He replied, 'Thank you, as always. I'm a fighter, and I will fight this as hard as I can.' But he was fighting on behalf of the Super League.

The best of the bunch were Manchester City, by a mile. I messaged Khaldoon Al Mubarak, the chairman of City. I know and like him immensely. 'Hi, Khaldoon. In all my career, I've never seen such universal resentment to a proposal as the Super League, from the fans, media, players, and now even a prime minister. You have done a sensational job building up your club, achieving a magnificent reputation, and gaining global respect.

Unfortunately, being part of this project is damaging your good name. Can I urge you to reconsider? I'm here for you 24/7 to discuss and assist.'

He messaged back, 'David, thank you for your advice, as always. Don't worry, we will do the right thing.'

I was confident he would. Khaldoon has good principles and I just believe he got sucked in by the others. I mean, City hardly needed the cash. What they have done in the past ten years has been nothing short of incredible – with eleven satellite clubs around the world, four of whom won their domestic titles in 2021. They are a truly classy operation.

I listened to the UEFA Congress in Montreux, where Aleksander spoke strongly. He's a black belt in judo, and I saw the fighter in him. 'Gentlemen, you made a huge mistake,' Čeferin said to the owners of the rebel clubs. Whether it was 'greed', 'arrogance' or 'complete ignorance of football culture' did not now matter, he went on. 'What does matter is that there is still time to change your mind. Everyone makes mistakes.' Aleksander's performance was masterful. Also, all credit to FIFA's president Gianni Infantino for coming out publicly and supporting UEFA's position.

City soon broke away from the plotters and the whole project collapsed. With hindsight perhaps it should not have been a great surprise that the conspiracy fell apart as easily as it did. The owners of all the breakaway English clubs were such different characters. At least when we were forming the Premier League, we went through the front door and not through the back.

The talk now was all about retribution. I contacted Richard Masters, the Premier League's CEO, and Gary Hoffman, the chairman. We'd not spoken since the beginning of April and the Project Big Picture nonsense. 'I wanted to help them restore harmony to the Premier League. 'I know the six will accept more robust legislation to ensure this unsavoury situation never happens again,' I told them, and I went on to propose a solution. 'At the moment clubs only have to give one year's notice to resign. That's set out in the FA's rule A3.5 and for your information I know that from experience. This is the loophole that was exploited when the Premier League was formed!' I urged them to amend the rules so that clubs have to give a minimum of three years' notice to resign – maybe even five years. I was confident the clubs would all accept this.

I also suggested how the issue of punishing the renegades should be addressed. 'There can be little doubt the six broke the "acting in good faith" rule,' I said. 'But they need a way back. And likewise there has to be an acceptance all round that these clubs add tremendous value to the league.' The family had to stay together.

So first and foremost, I urged them to get the rebels to give an 'absolute commitment to the Premier League'. Second, to reassure everyone else, 'get them to agree to a huge penalty – say £100-million-plus – if there is an attempt to form another super league'.

Next I addressed the tricky question of how to restore harmony between the would-be breakaway six and the remaining fourteen. There was such bad blood that I suggested 'all chief executives and owners of the six should volunteer not to attend Premier League meetings until the summer 2022 get-together'. The subject was so raw and there was so much acrimony in the air, that I thought it would take time for the tremendous hostility to die down.

Finally, I proposed an immediate 'fine of ten million pounds per club, payable as two million pounds per annum for five years' – a total across the breakaway clubs of sixty million pounds. I pointed out to Masters and Hoffman that this was 'nearly twice the penalty UEFA were considering but still only represents approximately one per cent of the clubs' annual salary bills!'

This fine should be seen as a donation to the EFL or the Football Foundation to avoid a public hanging. 'Personally, I think it would be positive publicity for them to be seen helping Mansfield Town, Stevenage, et al., as those lower division clubs are on the verge of going out of business.' I explained that I spend much of my life nowadays giving people a second chance, and whatever mistake the six may have made, they need to be rehabilitated.

The Premier League did punish the Super League plotters. UEFA sanctioned them too. 'So happy, David, this is a people's victory,' Giorgio texted. 'I'm in tears.'

However, Real Madrid, Barcelona and Juventus have not withdrawn their legal action against UEFA challenging their exclusivity to run a tournament in Europe. The threat remains!

OUT OF BAD MUST COME GOOD

On 11 July 2021 I, like thousands of others, was heading to Wembley for what should have been a glorious evening's entertainment. The Euros final between England and Italy kicked off at 8 p.m.

I left home at 4.15 p.m, got on the tube. I changed to the Metropolitan Line, non-stop to Wembley Park – and there the atmosphere could not have been more different to the semi-final. The train was so packed that I was lucky to get in the carriage, and I found myself with my nose against the door. Don't forget, this was mid-pandemic and we were all still wearing masks and supposed to be socially distancing. In any case it was surely too early for the train to be so full; there were still three and a half hours before kick-off.

There was almost a deafening chant against our Italian rivals, 'You can stick your fucking pizzas up your arse.' OK, they're excited, I thought, and I could see a few of the fans already had beers. I didn't see any drugs on the train, but I could hear the clicks and fizzes as bottles and cans were opened.

I just hoped I would not be recognised – it often happens and it isn't always a good thing. Amid the din I remembered another train journey after Spurs had played Blackburn Rovers in the

2002 League Cup final. I was coming back from Cardiff, standing with my son Gavin in a packed carriage full of Spurs fans who'd just lost. My heart sank when I heard, 'Deino, Deino'. A Spurs fan staggered towards me and I could see he was well tanked-up.

'You stole Sol Campbell from us.'

'No, no, he was at the end of his contract.'

'No, no, you stole Sol Campbell.'

I thought, I'm going to get a right-hander here. So, I tried engaging with the guy. 'Tell me, what do you do for a living?'

'I work in a car wash.'

'Where?'

'Crouch End.'

'OK. Is there another car wash in Muswell Hill?'

'Yes.'

'Well, supposing that car wash happened to be offering you more money, or maybe it had better facilities? Would you leave there if it was for more money?'

'Yes.'

'Well, Sol Campbell left because he had better terms coming to us. He wanted to improve himself, and you'd do the same.'

'No, no, no, you stole Sol Campbell from us.'

I changed tack, trying to deflect, and making sure Gavin was behind me. 'Tell me about your team today. What do you think went wrong?' Now he started analysing Spurs, and the tension ebbed away.

That was hardly an isolated event, so I was always on my guard. Fortunately, on Euros Final day, I went unnoticed on the tube to Wembley Park. They were too preoccupied, too lustily singing about where the Italians should put their dough topped with mozzarella. Perhaps with hindsight I should have noticed just how hyped up they were. We all know football has long had problems of crowd control, but we had made huge progress since the 1990s, and I really didn't expect this day, with England having reached the finals, would be anything but boisterous good fun. But when we got to Wembley Park, the intensity of that day became all too apparent. As I and my fellow passengers tried to climb the stairs from the platform, a horde of people poured down, pushing in the opposite direction, shoving and aggressively trying to get to the trains on which we had just arrived.

What on earth was going on? My first thought, as a football administrator, was that the match had been postponed. Why else would all these people be coming away from the stadium? Then I became worried. Memories of Hillsborough and Heysel came to mind. Something's happened here.

I managed to get out of Wembley Park station, struggling down the steps and through the small tunnel, only to find Wembley Way gridlocked with fans. So, that's why people were heading back into town. They had come to Wembley, savoured the experience of being outside the stadium, and – presumably ticketless – had decided to go elsewhere for a liquid dinner and watch the game. Leicester Square, probably.

There were still more than three hours to kick-off. As I pushed and zig-zagged my way through the throng, I noticed a distinct lack of police on Wembley Way. Where on earth were they? I wanted to say, 'I've got an official badge. How do I get through this crowd?' Moreover: 'Don't forget, the gates aren't open yet! If this is what it's like now, what's the crush here going to be like when more trains arrive every two minutes, each with five hundred people pouring in?'

By now, I was treading on broken glass. I got showered in beer – one of my best suits, drenched! Then somebody flung a flare. I was weaving away, like doing a Jack Grealish, trying to squeeze my way through the throng, and was beginning to feel distinctly vulnerable, hoping I wouldn't get hit with a missile. The thoroughfare was heaving with drunks; I couldn't believe the numbers.

Strange thoughts went through my mind. My UEFA accreditation was in my jacket pocket and my NHS Covid pass was on my phone; I would have to show both at the gates, but how could I take my pass or phone out in this crowd?

Finally, I reached the entrance and saw a group of UEFA officials – and there was Martin Kallen, director of events and a personable guy whom I've known for many years. 'Hi, David. You're just in time, the gates are about to open.'

'It's taken me thirty-five minutes from the tube – normally a seven-minute walk. What's going on?'

I was ushered inside and it felt like entering a sanctuary. At the hospitality area, the first person I saw was Mark Burrows, the very competent and likeable FA chief operating officer. 'Mark, have you seen what's going on down Wembley Way? It's blocked and it's ugly. There's a lot of broken glass, a lot of beer and to put it mildly people are a bit raucous. There are no police and it seems an insufficient number of stewards. In all my years coming here, I've never experienced anything like it!'

And there were still three hours until kick-off!

I explained to Mark Bullingham, the chief executive officer of the FA, who is calm, measured and a good strategist, what I had witnessed. But he was already deeply worried. 'A lot of the fans are trying to get in without tickets,' he told me.

I'd been taken aback by the crowds and the rowdy behaviour, but perhaps I shouldn't have been quite so surprised. I knew that crowd control around Wembley was a big challenge. What happened at the Euro 2020 final was a legacy of a bad decision made many years before. The FA had the opportunity of buying all of the land around the stadium and failed to do so. Now, you can't swing a cat without being on property owned by private landlords. It's difficult if not impossible to set up a security cordon when you're so closely hemmed in by residential and business property.

But even a ring of steel could not have prevented the disturbances that night completely. Even with proper policing the crowds would have been too big and many of the fans would have been too drunk. The kick-off time of 8 p.m. on a Sunday gave people the whole day off to congregate, mill around – and drink. UEFA quite rightly always insist that since the final is televised around the world, the kick-off has to be at 8 p.m., and they wanted it shown especially in the United States. Midday was no good because most of America would still be asleep.

I carried on moving between tables before the final. I chatted to the Italians, who were super-friendly, and did my best to disguise my worries – frankly my embarrassment – at the scenes going on outside. I was really concerned about the prospects of England hosting future tournaments. Indeed, my main job that day was to make sure we ingratiated ourselves with UEFA. Aleksander Čeferin, Zvonimir Boban and Giorgio Marchetti were all sitting together at a table.

'Congratulations, the tournament's gone well, despite all of the problems with the pandemic,' I said to them. 'I've been to twenty games, I've loved it, it's been a pleasure being a part of it all.' They smiled. Everyone at UEFA was exceptionally welcoming to me during the Euros, thanks to the role the English played in killing off the European Super League a few months previously. But they must have been aware of the trouble outside, and now the mood was edgy inside, too.

Part of my role as an FA ambassador is man-marking the president of other national associations. I'm not being paid, I've no private agenda, I'm doing it because I love the game and I passionately want to present the FA's case to UEFA and FIFA officials.

And to be honest – although I hate to admit this – sometimes representing England isn't easy. We're often seen as arrogant. We sing 'Football's coming home!' We boast of THE Football Association! Of course it's true. Football was played in England in medieval times. England certainly invented the modern game. We are *the* Football Association, the very first, founded way back in 1863, and we should be bloody proud of that. (For the same reason I often refer to Arsenal as The Arsenal.) But if we are to host international events we have to be seen to be welcoming the world.

It certainly doesn't help our case when England fans boo the opposition's national anthem. I've always found that to be abhorrent, disgraceful and – I use the word again – embarrassing. I just cannot understand it. It doesn't help the England team either; it just fires up the opposition. We're a football-obsessed country and I love that. Unfortunately, that brings with it an element not so much of nationalism, or even jingoism, but of xenophobia. For a tiny minority, football is war with shinpads, and in the excitement of the moment they carry others with them.

'Maybe we should stop playing the national anthems,'

somebody at the FA said to me. It's certainly been talked about within the FA, and even been tabled as a serious proposition.

But I have always disagreed wholeheartedly. 'That's giving up,' I'd say. 'If anything, play the anthems louder and drown out the mindless booing.' Those people have to be educated that not only does their boorishness sully England's reputation but it winds up the opposition.

There also has to be more robust stewarding. It's not easy to police tens of thousands of people, but somehow the good majority has to be better protected from the uncouth and ignorant troublemakers.

And it's not just their offensiveness to rival teams. That ultra-tribalism still all too often manifests itself as racism. Prejudiced, hurtful, damaging – and shaming the country and clubs they profess to support.

For me, sitting at Wembley as some fans booed England players taking the knee during the Euros, it was deeply upsetting. I wanted to shake some sense and humanity into these people. It's unfortunate that Black Lives Matter carried a certain connotation as a political movement when, really, taking the knee dates back to Martin Luther King. If players feel that passionate about it, I certainly wouldn't want to stop them. What matters is that the fight against intolerance goes on.

It's been a long road for me fighting racism in football. I was involved back in 1993 when we formed the campaigning 'Kick It Out' along with Lord Herman Ouseley and Gordon Taylor. David Davies, the broadcaster and soon to be FA official, was there too, meeting in a tiny room at the FA offices in Lancaster Gate. Thirty years later and the fight goes on. After the Euros final, I felt personally bruised by the racist abuse directed at Saka, Rashford and Sancho. Alex Scott, the wonderful football player and commentator, would come on the phone to me crying about the abuse she receives as a black woman. What could I say? 'Alex, you're going to have to grin and bear it because there will be change, and you have to show that you're better than they are.' My heart went out to her.

Of course racism is not just an evil element in England. It's often even worse elsewhere. What's more, some of the abuse I saw that had been sent to players like Saka, Sancho and Rashford was posted abroad. So, come on Instagram, Facebook and Twitter, you have to take more responsibility. You make billions out of these platforms so you should monitor better what goes out to the public. If you can't police yourselves, you should be denied a licence to operate. It seems very obvious to me that privacy is not the same as anonymity, and that anybody opening an account should be a hundred per cent traceable. Concealment in the shadows rarely elevates good behaviour over bad.

But we're all creatures of our environment and I also believe we should teach history about minorities, explaining the horrors that happen whenever one tribe likes to deceive itself of its own superiority over another, whether the result is slavery or the Holocaust or the countless cruelties in between. Barbara remembers going to school when there were separate drinking fountains for white and black people in Miami. Black kids sat at the back of the bus and white kids at the front. Racism, antisemitism, homophobia, all these evils have to be fought.

I will always remember going into a school, Ashford College, south London to give a talk. Usual routine: start at 9.30 a.m., so

I always get there at least half an hour before. As I went in, there was a policeman in the playground. I thought, A bit odd. In reception, there was another security man with a metal detector. I reached the headteacher's office.

'Is this usual, having this security?' I asked the head.

'Do you know what type of school we are?'

'No. College? Secondary school?'

'We're a PRU.'

'What's that?' I didn't know.

'Pupil referral unit,' she continued. 'We get all the students rejected from other schools or people with broken families, broken homes.' A sanctuary is what it is, right, but these kids need to be educated. I asked the head, 'What's their attention span?'

'Ten minutes.' She paused, then added, 'How long's your presentation?'

'Fifty minutes with a ten-minute Q&A.'

'No chance,' went the head.

I thought, You know what? I'm going for it and I'll see how far I get. If they all fall asleep, they all boo me, I'll take it on the chin. I got through thirty minutes without a problem, and then I saw a couple of them, their eyes were going, clearly drugs were involved, so I cut it short. Now we just had the Q&A. The first person, a black girl, put her hand up.

'Mr Dein, thank you for your presentation. Being black, will it be more difficult for me to get a job?'

Wow. What a question. When I'm so challenged, the first thing is I always try to buy time, so I said to her, 'What's your name?'

'Susie.'

'Susie, let me be personal. I'm Jewish. Don't think I haven't suffered antisemitism because I have, and heavily, when I was your age at school and it really hurt me at the time. You will suffer from racism and you have to be prepared for that. But Susie, I made it my business to make sure that I was going to be better than anybody else and climb the ladder. Nothing could stop me. Don't think you're inferior to anybody, because you're not. Go for it, because that's what I did.'

'Thanks, Mr Dein,' Susie said.

Anyway, back to the Euro 2020 final, and after the national anthems it started perfectly. When Luke Shaw scored early against Italy, it was a huge relief. It was difficult to keep the emotions suppressed at that stage. I stood up and punched the air. It's a final!

Defending that goal was always going to be dangerous. The quality of Italy's players is exceptional – as is the quality of their manager Roberto Mancini, who changed the game with some clever substitutions. England's manager Gareth Southgate must look back now and think he could have reacted more quickly to that. But Italy equalised and then we went through the torture of penalties. I've sat through a few shootouts, and when I saw Marcus Rashford and Jadon Sancho come off the bench, my honest reaction was, 'Risky'. Marcus missed. I felt terrible for him.

'Gareth took a gamble and it didn't come off,' I said to nobody in particular. Then Jadon's shot was saved, and like thousands of English fans I wincèd. Finally watching Bukayo Saka miss was agony.

Frankly, I thought the better team won, if not by a long shot. As I say, with the benefit of hindsight, Gareth might have done things differently, making his substitutions earlier, using Grealish more, being more adventurous – and perhaps less benevolent – with his penalty-takers. But we can all be clever after the event. I have seen some of the greatest players in the world miss penalties, players including: Diego Maradona, Lionel Messi, Cristiano Ronaldo, David Beckham, Roberto Baggio. He's a good guy, the players want to play for him and the country is behind him. Give him time. I truly believe he will get the very best out of his squad.

I was moved by the support for the players. There's no more bitter rivalry than between Arsenal and Spurs, yet two months later Spurs fans were gracious enough to give a wonderful ovation to Saka when he came on the pitch at their home ground. And that banner! That was special. 'North London stands with Bukayo Saka and all players against racism and discrimination. COYS.' Now, that shows you there is hope. There are more good people – many more good people – than there are bad.

Back in the hospitality area after the final I congratulated the Italians and then went over to the FA table and joined Mark Bullingham and Mark Burrows, who looked worried.

'How's it going with the crowds?' I asked Bullingham.

'It's been difficult, David,' he replied with understatement.

It was a great shame. The police deserved to be criticised – they were hopelessly ill-prepared – and so do the stewards, some of whom were inexperienced because of lockdown and the shortage of staff. But the FA and UEFA bore the brunt of the popular and media criticism – and as joint hosts they had to take responsibility.

I stayed virtually until the end. Barbara always used to accuse me of locking up at Arsenal as I was always the last to leave. And having stayed late this night I had no problems getting home. At 11.30 p.m. the tube was half-empty. In fact I began to realise the scale of the disorder at Wembley, and especially the invasion by ticketless fans, only when I got a call from my cousin, Hilton, and messages from friends. Each had a story of their own. I was getting calls from my sons, Gavin and Darren, saying, 'Dad, do you know what's happened here? There were people getting in. They were trying to invade our seats.' Many fans, Darren told me, tried to get in through his turnstile as he was going in. Tailgating they call it. He's a big fella, Darren, and actually pulled the guy out. 'You don't do that,' Darren said. Fortunately, the fan backed off. But a couple of thousand got in without tickets. There was one block, where the gate for the disabled was forced and a crowd surged in. I got a really angry message from one of our trustees at the Twinning Project, Nigel Wray, who owned Saracens Rugby Club. Nigel actually turned back he was so disgusted by what he saw on Wembley Way.

That Monday morning, I went into my study and went into overdrive. My first call was to Mark Bullingham. 'I'm really worried about our bid for 2030,' I confessed. 'Two weeks ago we were top of the class, and all of a sudden, we've gone from hero to zero. This is a huge own goal. We've beaten ourselves. We've really got to think out of the box on how to restore our chances.'

Next, I emailed a colleague from the Twinning Project, Dr Martha Newson. Martha's a behavioural psychologist, a leading expert in fan behaviour and I trust her judgement implicitly. 'What can we do about these people?' I asked.

'The racism reflects cultural problems systemic in British

culture,' she replied. 'But the disorder we saw on Sunday are problems specifically within football culture.' In short this was our problem. We had to own it. We couldn't resolve it by seeking to pass on the blame to others. Martha talks so much sense, and is so experienced in fan culture. I immediately forwarded her email to Mark Bullingham and Mark Burrows.

Martha also addressed what we now knew was a drug issue on Wembley Way. Drugs might not be as obvious as drunkenness in fan culture, she said, but cocaine especially was now in widespread use. She had surveyed 1,500 fans earlier that year and found that cocaine use in football was higher than the national average and, importantly, cocaine-using fans reported the most violence, from shouting abuse at rivals, through throwing drinks or objects, to physical assaults. 'In some groups it's even replacing alcohol because it helps keep fans on the ball much better than a day's drinking.'

'The FA needs to promote a culture of drug awareness before the cocaine situation escalates any further.'

She also highlighted the issues of poor stewarding and security, which she regarded as fundamental to the problems at the Wembley final. 'The UK sorted its stadia out hugely in the 1990s and we've become an example of excellent stadium management – until Sunday,' she argued. 'There were clearly some kind of staff issues going on. So many young stewards who didn't have a grip on the situation – many of them young women who lacked proper training and didn't stand a chance. Fans were desperate to get in to see the final – I can't understand why this wasn't better anticipated.'

Martha has studied fan behaviour across three continents and pointed out the authorities needed to be sharper in picking up hints from fans that trouble was brewing. 'Met Police and FA intelligence was limited,' she told me. 'I'm reading reports where the Met are saying they were "surprised" that people tried to break in. I'm not and neither are my colleagues. Fans had been discussing this days in advance in person and on social media, in relation to what they perceived as weak security all around Wembley at previous matches, e.g., no cordon around the stadium. Generally, the police work collaboratively with fans in advance to get good intelligence and maintain positive relationships but this didn't seem to happen.'

Next, I contacted Peter McCormick, a lawyer and chair of the Premier League, who was also acting FA chair. 'It's hugely embarrassing to the country, Peter, and some of these scenes will undoubtedly be used by our opposition as ammunition against us. The immediate problem facing us now is whether we should bid for the World Cup 2030. My view is that by not bidding we've conceded victory to a minority unruly element before we start. The bad guys can't win!'

We must be brave enough to acknowledge that we could have done better. We need to recognise that we should have been much better prepared. We should have predicted the potential for disorder given that England were in a major final for the first time in fifty-five years; that fans had just been released from sixteen months' lockdown; that it was common knowledge that because of Covid restrictions 25,000 seats were to be kept empty; and that the evening kick-off accommodated a whole day's pent-up booze, drugs and excitement. I added, 'I'm sure you'll agree, that we were lucky enough to escape without any fatalities.'

I felt that we couldn't escape punishment. UEFA quickly launched an investigation, duly charged the FA, and announced our penalty on 18 October. One game behind closed doors with the threat of another suspended for two years 'for the lack of order and discipline inside and around the stadium'. The FA were also fined €100,000.

What a mess. I stared at my computer screen, and thought, OK, we've got ourselves into a pickle, we've taken a good kicking – but now was the time to rally people. We had to climb out of this dark place and believe in ourselves again. I sent another message to Mark Bullingham. 'It is very easy to have a knee-jerk reaction and say we don't deserve to host the World Cup or Euros. I don't agree. I recollect all too well the ugly scenes of hooliganism in the late seventies and eighties and we have, by and large, recovered from that. We can recover from this. I am convinced that we will never see those ugly scenes again at Wembley and we will have learned our lesson. Out of bad must come good.'

One of the proudest moments of my life was leaving Wembley after the 1966 World Cup final with the good old Union Jack flag hanging out of my car. England, my England, had just won, and I was there to see that little piece of history being made. I felt king of the castle – at twenty-two! At the time I had a very flash, yellow E-Type Jaguar soft top, and I drove straight to the south of France with my good friend, Alan Woolff, bursting with pride to be English. People applauded as we went past yelling 'Nobbeee Stiles', 'Bobbeee Charrrrlton!' Even if it's crazy that we've not won anything since that magical day in 1966, as football fans, we have to live in hope.

After the ugly scenes at the gates before the Men's Euros final in 2021, it was such a joy to be at Wembley, on 31 July 2022, in a carnival and familial atmosphere, to see England's women become champions of Europe. Football came home with a huge smile on its face. It was such a momentous occasion both on and off the pitch.

If somebody had said to me five years ago that there would be 87,192 at Wembley watching an England women's game, 17.4m people watching on BBC1, and a Fan Zone in Trafalgar Square, I would have said, 'fly me to the moon!'. When I was involved in starting up the Arsenal Women's team in the late '80s, together with Vic Akers the kit man, we were lucky to get fifty fans at the Britania Leisure Centre in Hoxton, or anywhere else that would have us!

It was amazing to see how the Lionesses were being supported by everyone in the country. Football had truly effected a change in society. It was strange to think that the mums of the players on the pitch would have found it difficult, only a generation before, to play or get any encouragement to pursue the game. Now these young women were role models for a new generation. Beth Mead, winner of the Golden Boot and Player of the Tournament, had to suffer disappointments and setbacks, yet came through with resilience and determination. Leah Williamson, the captain, has worked and worked on her game to become one of the best defenders in the world. England were a team in the true sense of the word.

All credit to Nadine Keßler, the Chief of Women's Football for UEFA, and her team and of course Giorgio Marchetti, the Deputy General Secretary Football at UEFA, for organising the tournament together with Mark Bullingham and Mark Burrows of the FA. Also, I'm so proud of Alex Scott for her contribution to the women's game, firstly as a player and now as a broadcaster. I always use the phrase 'people are quick to criticise and slow to praise'. The FA deserve a lot of praise. Not least for their inspired choice of Sarina Wiegman as coach of the women's team.

The fact that the win was against Germany had extra relevance as in recent years England have been on the losing side. My only one regret was that there were no black players involved in the starting line-up. Clearly, there is still a lot of work to be done for this element to be addressed.

As I watched the Lionesses dancing on the Wembley pitch and being shown only love by the euphoric crowd, I reflected on the game. This is why we love football. This is why, when things go wrong and times are tough, those who love football and work for the good of the game keep going. For inspirational moments like this.

The women's game is beautifully pure and innocent, and long may it last. It hasn't been complicated yet by vast amounts of money. When I was interviewed after the successful 2019 FIFA Women's World Cup, and asked about the state of the women's football, I said 'The train has left the station and is gathering speed'. Now it's a non-stop express.

TIME ON THEIR HANDS

'PS: leave your watch and wallet at home!' That's how Greg Dyke signed off his letter back in 1998 inviting me to prison for a lunch.

Greg's got a good sense of humour and also a great sense of giving back to society. He was on the committee for the Howard League for Penal Reform which was holding a fundraiser. 'David, I'd like to invite you and Barbara to an unusual event. It's a lunch at Wormwood Scrubs Prison with an offender . . . and it's five hundred pounds a head,' Greg wrote.

Barbara picked a Rastafarian to sit opposite at lunch at the Scrubs. I chose a guy in his twenties called Steve. 'Where are you from, Steve?' I asked.

'Winchmore Hill,' said Steve.

'Arsenal or Spurs?'

'Spurs.'

'It's not your lucky day!'

Poor Steve was inside and now talking to an Arsenal fan. No escape.

'Steve, tell me what it's like in here.'

'Boring. I'm putting labels on cans. I'm climbing up the wall.' Steve told me the one thing he could really enjoy inside was watching *Match of the Day*. He seemed an intelligent, articulate guy.

I was curious. 'Steve, what are you in for, if you don't mind me asking?'

'Glassing. I've got a bit of a short temper so I was in a pub and I'm having an argument with this bloke and I smashed the glass – in his face.'

I immediately moved my seat a little further back. We had a fascinating chat about the conditions in the prison and I quickly came to the conclusion that they made any chance of rehabilitation negligible. When the lunch came to an end, I said, 'Steve, I wish you well. I'll see what I can do about your boredom.'

When we got outside, Barbara told me about the guy she talked to. 'He said this place was home, David. "It's where I live, where my friends are, I've got a roof over my head, I get fed three times a day. I've got no mates outside any more, so if I go out I'll do another crime, I come back in again."'

While Barbara's lunch companion was a hamster on the wheel, I felt Steve was different. He was bored and he needed help with his anger. 'He must be very lonely,' I said to Barbara.

I rang Alan Sugar, the chairman of Spurs. 'I've been with one of your customers today. Can you send me a couple dozen of your programmes?'

'Pleasure.' Alan's always been a generous guy.

I packaged up the Spurs programmes and, mischievously, couldn't resist slipping in a few from Arsenal. I got a handwritten letter back, 'Thank you very much, your gesture was much appreciated'. Yes, Steve had done something terrible, it was a very ugly incident, but he regretted it. Making him bored, or even angrier, was not going to make him regret it any more.

Anyway, fast forward a few years, and I had time on my hands, which is not what I'm about. I need a project. Out of the blue, in 2014, I was approached by Robert Peston, BBC business editor at the time. I'd never met Robert before but he's a Gooner, part of the Arsenal family, and he had a proposal, so I invited him to lunch.

'David,' he said, 'I've started a charity, Speakers for Schools. Thanks to the BBC, I've got an address book of successful people. My idea is to get as many as I can going into state schools to talk to youngsters who are on the cusp of making a decision about their future plans. Do they go to university? Do they get an apprenticeship? Do they get a job? If they see a successful person, they may get some inspiration. I want to give pupils in state schools access to the networking offered in fee-paying schools. To give them more of a chance. I've watched your career. Would you be interested in coming onboard?'

'Count me in, Robert.'

'I'd only expect one or two talks a year from you,' Robert said. Since that lunch ten years ago, I've given talks in over 550 schools around the country.

During the pandemic, I continued delivering the talks virtually, but I missed interacting with the students. There is nothing like a live audience (there's my love of theatre coming out). I would take them on a journey, mainly my own, and discuss how the Premier League was formed, the explosion in television rights, the women's game, modern managers, modern players, technology coming into the game and then giving the audience a chance to be a referee and show them clips where VAR has successfully intervened. The talk is sprinkled with what I hope are inspirational messages. I want the kids to 'reach for the stars'.

I always tell them, 'Every successful person I've ever met – Bill Gates, Jeff Bezos, Alan Sugar – have all had the same three qualities. Hard work – you'll not get anywhere in life unless you're prepared to work hard. Vision – you've got to know where you want to get to in life. And courage – you have got to have the determination to get there.' I also give them tips for handling an interview: 'Be punctual, look smart, make eye contact, give a firm handshake, smile and ask questions.' Fortunately, I always seemed to have a receptive audience.

It was going really well and I was getting a lot of job satisfaction. It was tiring but worthwhile. I soon wondered if it could be expanded. I still get my best ideas shaving and was staring in the mirror one Monday and thought, Where else is there a captive audience? The word 'captive' stuck in my mind. 'Prisons.' A lightbulb moment. My mind went back to poor Steve in Wormwood Scrubs, thinking what a lonely, mind-numbing existence he had inside.

I went to see a friend at the Home Office about doing talks in prison.

'Yes, sounds good to me,' he said. 'I'll have to think of which department you should go to.' I heard nothing for two months. I rang again. He said, 'Well, go and see somebody in the Ministry of Justice.' I went to see the MoJ. They said, 'You need to see someone at NOMS.' NOMS? The National Offender Management Service, now HMPPS – Her Majesty's Prison and Probation Service. I was learning a new language fast but we were moving painfully slowly. Finally, after eight frustrating months, I met a very nice lady called Bettina Crossick at NOMS.

'Yes, well, we've never had this before, but I'll tell you what we'll do, we'll give you a trial prison,' Bettina said, 'and, if you don't mind, David, we'll send a few supervisors to see how it gets on.' Fair enough, can't be too careful. So, I rocked up at HMP Rochester in Kent.

Nothing can prepare you for your first visit to a prison: the looks and scrutiny, the locks and security. From the moment you arrive, it's check, check, clank, clank. I had to show my driving licence, and even then it took me an hour and a quarter to go through the checks. In fact when I started my first talk I began, 'I understand it's hard to get out. But I can tell you it's not bloody easy to get in!'

One of the cheekier inmates shouted back, 'You ought to try robbing a bank, mate.'

Every few yards, there was another door. Clank, clank. The smell was antiseptic and, when I managed to glance into the cells, I could see a lot of them were like something from a bygone age. As I gave my presentation to the inmates I noticed three people in front of me with clipboards. I realised they were marking my homework! I'd given talks all over the world for FIFA, UEFA, the FA, spoken on World Cup bids, addressed players and staff at Arsenal and England. Now here's the highlight of my speaking career! Being assessed at a young offender institution just off the M2 in Kent. I thought, I just hope I passed!

At the end one of those markers came up. 'Mr Dein, we really like what you did. We've got 117 prisons. Would you like to roll it out?'

'Yes! I'll do what I can.' My homework had gone down well.

I left Rochester (check, check, clank, clank) and got home, where I talked it out with Barbara. 'I'm going around the country, in any case, to schools,' I said. 'If I'm travelling two hours to Leeds to a school, why don't I go into Leeds prison too? I might as well do a double-header.' Barbara approved. NOMS approved. I started in London, and I did more and more.

'Aren't you scared when you go into a prison?' people often ask. I've not had one problem in any of the prisons I've visited. If anything, it's the opposite; it seems the offenders, men, women, young and old, can't thank me enough. It's as though I'm a breath of fresh air to them. OK, not quite Michael McIntyre but, nevertheless, I'm trying to raise their spirits, I'm hoping to give them motivation, I'm certainly giving them a link with the outside world. They are lonely. They've hit rock bottom. Somebody cares.

I've now given talks at all 117 prisons in England and Wales, and met some extraordinary people. When I spoke at HMP Kirklevington Grange, in Teesside, one of the offenders came up and mentioned he had an unusual association with the Premier League. I messaged Richard Scudamore, who was executive chairman at the time. 'Google John Dodds, jail!'

'No need to Google!' Richard texted back. 'We know who John Dodds is. One of our more famous pirates and a lesson to the rest! Hope he showed remorse!'

Dodds had been jailed for four and a half years in April 2018 for selling illegal streaming devices to at least 270 pubs and clubs in the northeast. I explained to him why pirated games had a damaging impact on clubs. I honestly don't think he'd even considered the effects of his crimes on the game he loved.

I went to the high security prison Belmarsh. You get all the heavy boys in there. I gave my talk to about sixty or seventy people. A big guy came up afterwards and shook my hand. 'Mr Dein,' he said, 'I really enjoyed your talk today. Are you any relation to Jeremy Dein?'

Now, Jeremy's my first cousin who's a criminal barrister and does a lot of legal aid work. 'Yes! Why do you ask?'

'He represented me.'

You know how sometimes you say something you immediately regret? 'Well . . .' I said, 'how did he do?'

'I'm fucking in here, aren't I?'

That night, I rang Jeremy. 'I've been with one of your customers today.' I mentioned the name.

'Oh, yes, a naughty boy.' Jeremy explained that his client got twenty years for a gang murder. But for a gangster he couldn't have been more polite – knew football, had all the facts.

When I gave a presentation at HMP Parc in Bridgend, the laptop was playing up, and one of the offenders offered to help out. He seemed very computer literate, got it working and went on to work all the slides for me. 'What's your name?' I asked.

'Majid Tahar.'

'Thank you very much, Majid, you've done very well. How do you know about this?'

'Well, you know, I've studied . . .'

It's wrong to assume every prisoner is uneducated. I knew not to ask them directly what they're in for. 'How long have you got to go?'

'Oh, twelve years,' Majid replied.

'Do you want to talk about it?'

'It was a VAT problem.' Then there was a pause and Majid went, 'Well, it was two hundred million pounds.' Then, after another silence he added, 'Well, it was against HMRC.' OK!

I came across a former vice-chairman of Leyton Orient, Nicholas Levene, whom I had met in the boardroom of Brisbane Road. He was known as 'Beano' because he loved the old children's comic. Beano was a former stockbroker who ran a Ponzi scheme and swindled people out of thirty-two million pounds. Here was a highly intelligent lad, with a very quick brain. But I've since met Mr Levene many times and, all credit to him, he is now a reformed character. You get all sorts in prison.

In Newcastle, as the residents were filing in, this guy said, 'Mr Dein, I know you. I'm a football agent. I've offered you players in the past.'

'Oh, really? How long are you in here for?'

'Eight years.'

Now, I've always felt some of the agents should be inside but there was a story here. 'Do you want to talk to me about it?'

'It was very unfortunate. I was driving my car on the M6 near Cumbria and it was a rainy day. Unfortunately, I was breaking the speed limit and had a bad accident. My car flipped over the other side of the dual carriageway and I killed a Highways England traffic officer.' I learned later that he also maimed the officer's partner. 'As you can imagine, I'm in shock.' I could see he was in a bad way.

Afterwards, I said to one of the guards, 'Do you think you could have a look at this guy because I can see he's a bit unstable? Watch out for him.' What the prisoner didn't tell me at the time was that he was on his mobile phone for the thirty seconds before the accident. He was messaging one of his football clients, Zach Clough at Nottingham Forest.

I later read the BBC story: 'A football agent who killed a traffic officer on the M6 has been jailed for seven years. Peter Morrison, thirty-seven, had been speeding and sending phone messages before the crash in Cumbria in February 2016. Adam Gibb, fifty-one, from Penrith, died and Paul Hollywood,

fifty-three, from Kirkby was left paralysed from the chest down.'
I recognised Morrison's name. He'd been a player himself,
briefly, for Bolton Wanderers and Scunthorpe United.

When I got home, I told my kids, 'Here is a lesson for you.
When you get in the car, you lock your phone in the glove
compartment. Don't touch it.' Here was a guy who made a
terrible mistake, one that was going to haunt him for the rest of
his life. It takes a split second; you lose your concentration and
you can kill somebody.

It got me thinking about rehabilitation of offenders. Was Peter
Morrison a hardened criminal? No. Did he do something
stupid? Sure. He can never repair what he did to Adam Gibb and
Paul Hollywood. He can never end the grief and anguish of
their families. I know there was a controversy when he was let
out to work for his old agency in 2021, and I completely understand Paul Hollywood's anger and the anger of Adam Gibbs's
family. If I were the parents of the two traffic officers, I can
imagine I'd say, 'Throw away the key'. But he's thirty-seven. In
the cold light of day, you've got to say, 'He's serving his punishment. Do we really want to lock him away for ever, or does he
deserve the chance to start afresh and give back to society?'
What you can try and do is make him a better person when he
leaves prison, and that he contributes to society.

As I went around these prisons, I was doing my market
research and thinking, What is football doing in prisons? Virtually
nothing. I knew at Arsenal we used to do a little bit with
Pentonville. Why don't we match professional football clubs
with their local prisons? So the Twinning Project was born. Get
the clubs to coach some of the offenders inside the prison. Give
the guys a bit of discipline and a sense of self-respect.

I had the idea and the name and now I needed support. I've always believed in going to the top and I chased a 2015 meeting with the Secretary of State for Justice, Michael Gove. Dame Sally Coates, the distinguished educationalist I'd met through my friend Greg Dyke, secured an introduction. She used to turn schools around and knew Gove from his time as education secretary.

'Look, I'm doing these talks in prisons,' I told Gove. 'I think they're going very well, but I want to take it further. I want to twin a football club with its local prison.' Gove made polite noises and said he'd think about it. By July 2016, he was gone. They never last long in justice. I finally secured an interview with Gove's successor, Liz Truss, on 14 December of the year following my first meeting.

I knew I had to get my pitch to Truss spot on. I made notes on everything I'd seen behind bars. I'd met murderers, fraudsters – even that football agent. I heard their experiences of incarceration, I listened to prison governors and had come to understand that what was happening in our prisons was a national scandal. Victorian institutions, especially inner-London ones like Brixton, Pentonville, Wandsworth and Wormwood Scrubs, shame us as a civilised society. Conditions can be dreadful for prison officers as well as inmates, made worse by terrible short-staffing. I learned that during the austerity era of David Cameron more than a quarter of frontline officers left the service. Assaults and bullying are at shocking levels; and tellingly there has been an epidemic of self-harm. Perhaps most astonishing for what are supposed to be secure facilities is the prevalence of drugs. Perhaps a third of inmates were on drugs before they came inside; and in prison many others join them. They need some focus, something to relieve the monotony; and certainly they need hope for when they step back into society.

Before I went to see Liz Truss I especially wanted to hear from one of the prisoners I'd met inside. He'd served five years and really knew the system, but was also unusually outspoken and articulate. He wanted to vent his anger about the state of prisons, so I asked him to list what he thought wrong about his experience in prison.

His points were damning.

1 In cell for eighteen, nineteen hours per day on average. Reason – prison was short staffed!
2 Given menial jobs; e.g. putting stickers on salad bowls!
3 Educational courses very limited. Only occasionally allowed to go on a PowerPoint course which was some-times cancelled.
4 Prison shut down once a week because of security alert.
5 Exercise was walking around in circles. Could never get into the gym.
6 Took two weeks to get into the library.
7 No attempt made to mentally stimulate the prisoners. No educational challenge channels on TV.
8 Synthetic drugs brought in.

I thought I would do the same exercise quite independently with a prison physical education instructor . . .

1 Lack of educational courses to suit needs of prison popula-tion. Employ tutors who can deliver vocational education that will offer realistic employability upon release.

2 Reduce the accountable workload managers are required to complete by upskilling others to allow managers time to manage and be seen around the establishment.

3 Retention of staff is extremely poor mainly due to the reduction in starting salary. It is no longer seen as a career. The reduction in staffing has seen a major increase in assaults and many staff feel undervalued as the risks are too high.

4 Drug use in prison is rife. Only appropriate funding to test, punish and deter smuggling will reverse the trend.

5 Provide individual establishments the power to run their regime within a given timescale and budget rather than the national policy. A new longer core day has been introduced at a time when staff cuts are at an all-time high. This provides insecurity for both staff and prisoners.

6 Prisons are bound by national contracts for suppliers of goods, often at greater expense than could be purchased elsewhere. This results in an overspend.

7 Constantly cutting budgets and increasing expected outcome is not sustainable. We are dealing with human life and some of the disturbed and irrational behaviour comes from distorted thinking.

8 Although there are good offending programmes in some establishments, the demand is high, resulting in prisoners not being able to access courses.

9 Prisoners need to be moved quicker to the right establishment.

The two reports were remarkably similar, and equally damning.

I hoped Liz Truss would share my sense that something must be done. She was very enthusiastic and understanding. But she was off in a ministerial reshuffle. Her successor was David Lidington, before he was off, followed by David Gauke, then Robert Buckland and Dominic Raab. Six secretaries of state for justice in six years. That's almost Watford manager turnover levels.

If I couldn't rely on secretaries of state, I needed somebody to work with at HMPPS. I had to make sure everyone was ready when the clubs came in. Jason Swettenham proved my man. Jason was the key. He was in charge of physical training and industries and catering for prisons, and he was doing a remarkable job in remarkably difficult circumstances. I was amazed when he told me his budget for a prisoner's three meals a day is £2.10; he was used to producing miracles. Jason worked with the physical education instructors and we needed them to assist the club coaches. His immediate advice was to get in front of the politician who was one layer beneath the secretary of state, the Minister of State for Prisons and Probation. I told him that was also a carousel, going from Andrew Selous to Sam Gyimah to Rory Stewart. But Jason's view was that Rory was different. And he was right. I went to his office in April 2018 and thought Rory was impressive: Oxford and Harvard, army, explorer, writer – but above all he really cared about the job he had been given. Of course he didn't last long, but I got lucky that he was in charge at just the right time for me.

'Nice to meet you, Mr Stewart.'

'Call me Rory,' came the response.

'Fine, Rory, I'm sitting in the same chair that I've sat in several times before talking to your predecessors. I'm one of the few people coming to your office that's not going to ask for money.'

'Oh, that's good,' Rory replied. He sat forward. Great, I knew I had his attention.

'Here's my idea. The Twinning Project. I want to twin a professional football club with the local prison because I've seen what happens inside. You've only got 17 per cent of offenders that can get a job when they come out. The re-offending stats are enormous: 64 per cent come back into prison a year after being released. It's far too high and I believe football can help.'

'Exactly how?'

'We'll get clubs and referees to run coaching and refereeing courses. That match fee of twenty or thirty pounds as a coach or ref in a Sunday league game might just keep them out of trouble. It gives them a feeling of doing something positive. We'll get clubs running courses to give prisoners other skills to help them find jobs. We'll teach them to become a match-day steward, how to write a CV and cope with a job interview.' I paused. I wanted to stress to the minister that the Twinning Project was serious and would change lives. 'This will be a professional partnership.'

'Sounds very interesting. How do you intend to do it?'

'I'll deliver football if you deliver me the prisons, Rory. I just need three things from you. Firstly, if I'm going to put Manchester United into HMP Styal, make sure their people are safe. I'm not having any ugly incidents. They have to be supervised. And United's coaches have to be welcomed at the gate, otherwise you can waste an hour trying to get in. "Who are you?" "Why are you here?" "I need to check." All that stuff.

'Secondly, if I'm going to have twenty people on a course, I want twenty people to stay on the course. I don't want only twelve showing up one day. That has to be your responsibility.

'Thirdly, anybody on the course has to stay the length of time. It's a three-month course and people get transferred. You have to make sure these prisoners are in this prison for the three months. I know some prisons are transit centres before they go for sentencing. So, if you can guarantee those three conditions, I believe we can guarantee to help rehabilitate them. We need them to realise there is a future. We can give them that lightbulb moment.'

'Well, I'll switch the lights on for you,' Rory said. I really liked him. Turning to Jason, he said, 'We need the secretary of state to hear this but, before we do, can I trust you to deliver it?'

Jason's response was an unequivocal, 'Yes minister,' and the rest is history.

Before the meeting ended, I had one final request. 'I'd like you to write to each governor, giving them the authority to link up with the Twinning Project, to be formally twinned with their local professional football club.'

'When do you want your letter by?' Rory replied. I liked him even more. He understood and acted quickly.

I explained to Rory that I had to pitch the Twinning Project to the Premier League at its summer meeting on 7 June and to the EFL, the English Football League, which represents the three leagues below the Premier League, on 11 June. 'I'd need the letter, if I can, in the next three, four weeks.'

'You'll get it next week,' Rory replied. 'Now let's go and see the secretary of state.' To my surprise, there and then Rory led me into the office of David Gauke, Secretary of State for Justice, effectively Rory's boss. David's a huge Ipswich Town supporter so that broke the ice. David also loved the idea of the Twinning Project.

'This is brilliant. It's never been done before. We're all for it, tell us what you need. I know you asked for one letter from Rory, I'll give you a letter as well.' I had a double-whammy, and, true to their word, they both wrote to the governors to give them the authority to engage with us.

The Twinning Project was beginning to take shape.

I'd got one party to the altar. I now had to shepherd the clubs up the aisle. I learned from forming the Premier League that you've got to have the governing body onside. If the FA said, 'No, we're not crazy on clubs going into prisons,' then I wasn't going to get anywhere. I went to see Martin Glenn, the FA chief executive, and strategy director Robert Sullivan. 'Look, I'm not asking you for any money,' I said. I find that's always the best way to pitch an idea, especially to the FA. 'I'd just like your official endorsement. It'll be the Premier League and the EFL clubs delivering the courses, but I need your blessing.'

'Go ahead,' Glenn said immediately. I dashed to the Premier League and presented my case to Richard Scudamore, the executive chairman.

'Crime wrecks the lives of both victim and perpetrator,' I told Richard. 'All, barring a small number of offenders, will return to live among us. Our society is morally obliged to prepare prisoners for release. This is how we can prevent future victims. We also know the odds are stacked against the children of offenders. The chances of an offender's offspring going to prison is 80 per cent. If we, as the football family, can help the "prisoner parent" get a job, their children will have a much more stable home.'

'Go ahead,' said Richard. 'I'll arrange for you to talk to our clubs.'

I gave the same speech to Andy Williamson at the English Football League, and he also backed the Twinning Project. So did Gordon Taylor at the Professional Footballers' Association and Richard Bevan at the League Managers Association. Next I went to see Mike Riley at Professional Game Match Officials Limited to get the refs onside. Mike agreed.

Finally, I'd got all of the football authorities; that was quite a coup in itself. Added to that, with Rory's blessing, the prison service had come to the party. Now we had to get the clubs there.

Freddie Hudson at Arsenal in the Community was my first port of call. I knew Freddie from when he started at Arsenal and he marked my card.

'It's not the football club you need, it's really their foundations – their charitable arms, the community departments – they are the organisations that deal with soccer schools, hospital visits and all community work.' Freddie was right. The club won't get involved, so now we're dealing with a different animal, because many of the foundations don't have the funds. They have to raise money themselves and some of the lower division ones get only maybe £300,000 a year. They'll receive grants, money from national programmes and EFL core funding of thirty-five thousand pounds, and they'll supplement that with bingo evenings and sponsored bicycle rides. It's not a huge revenue stream.

'You may get away with it with the Premier League clubs because they've got bigger foundations,' Freddie said. 'But going down the league, you're going to have to finance them. They just don't have the resources.'

Straight away, we made a decision that the Twinning Project would assist the EFL clubs with the cost of the courses. With the

Premier League clubs' foundations, we'd help them with kit. And what a kit it was! We had a beauty parade from the various suppliers and wanted to differentiate ourselves from clubs. In the end, Barbara had the casting vote and chose green. The green looked good and bonded the prisoners – they were in a team.

'Anybody who completes the course can keep the kit,' I told the offenders.

Now, we were working on the finer details. 'We need this to be an FA-approved coaching course,' I told the FA.

'Ninety-five per cent of courses are IT nowadays,' they replied. This would be a huge problem as prisons do not have access to IT equipment.

Well, hold on, I thought. I bet Arsène Wenger, Alex Ferguson and José Mourinho didn't do an IT course, I can tell you that for nothing! 'Can't we turn the clock back?' I said.

'Very difficult.'

Sorry, I wouldn't give up. My research took me to a guy called Les Howie, the FA's head of grassroots coaching. Les, very kindly, designed a bespoke course for offenders, virtually a Level 1 course, which was remarkable; we had a major breakthrough.

In the summer, I flew back from the World Cup in Russia and attended the Premier League's community meeting in Wetherby. Nick Perchard, head of communities at the Premier League, could not have been more helpful. He organised the clubs and gave Jason and me an hour to present the case for the Twinning Project. I used my time to tell them about life inside.

'Prison life is not pleasant. I know it's not meant to be the Four Seasons hotel but offering hope is the first step to re-engaging the disengaged. The Premier League clubs can lift them.'

Some clearly liked the Twinning Project, some were a bit

unsure, but they all backed us. Now for the other leagues. My last hurdle in football's hierarchy was the EFL Trust.

Their summer meeting was four days later, but it could have been a different century – the nineteenth century. We were not allowed to have all seventy-two clubs in one room and instead had to make several presentations to splinter groups. In the end we had to do it the hard way.

I knew that to get the Twinning Project motoring I would have to establish it as a charity. We needed a good chief executive, and I found one in Hilton Freund, my second cousin who was running a marketing consultancy and wanted a new challenge. He was a skilled operator at comms as well as marketing and financing. With Hilton joining Jason, I felt confident I was building a strong operational team.

We organised a big launch of the Twinning Project at Wembley on 31 October 2018. I rang Rory.

'Will you open the meeting? It will mean so much.'

Rory addressed an audience of around four hundred at Wembley, many from clubs and prisons, alongside friends like Arsène and Gérard Houllier. 'We should embrace sport,' he said, 'as a way of giving offenders worthwhile skills and qualifications and I'm confident this project will have a real impact on the lives of offenders – and ultimately help to reduce reoffending.'

Ian Wright hosted the event. He understood what the Twinning Project could do. Don't forget, Ian spent two weeks in HMP Chelmsford at nineteen for failing to pay driving fines. 'It was petrifying in there,' Ian told the audience. 'I was crying almost every night as I'd lost total control over my liberty; basic things like turning off the light. I discovered claustrophobic feelings I never thought I had.'

Former offender John McAvoy then told his story. He'd been sentenced to ten years for armed robbery and been shunted from prison to prison. I met John during his last few months inside. During his time in HMP Lowdham Grange, Nottinghamshire, he used to keep fit by going to the gym as often as he could. Whilst he was on the rowing machine, the PE officer, Darren Davis, noticed that he had tremendous upper body strength and started to clock his time. Remarkably, whilst in prison, he broke the world record for indoor rowing. He was soon picked up by Nike and is now a role model for the power of rehabilitation. He competes in Iron Man events.

'Football can give prisoners some purpose, get them physically active, provide them with an education and coaching qualifications,' John said. 'Like me, it can plant that seed in their head where they have the potential that they can do something else other than just spending their life sitting in their prison cell.'

Baroness Karren Brady, West Ham's vice-chair, spoke too. She was wonderful. 'My grandmother taught me that you must never look down on people unless you are helping them up. I believe this project goes to the heart of that sentiment.'

West Ham were the first club to sign up, and Hilton, Jason and I privately set ourselves the target of getting twenty clubs to sign within the first twelve months. In fact we achieved that number in twelve weeks.

We also achieved charitable status to help fund the kit and clubs outside the Premier League.

Now I needed trustees.

One of the first on my trustee team sheet was Karren. She's a personality, she believed in the Twinning Project and she makes things happen! Somebody after my own heart. I remember when she was at Birmingham, I loaned her players like Jermaine Pennant in 2005 and Nicklas Bendtner in 2006 to make sure Birmingham did OK.

Then, I thought, Well, we've got to get somebody, perhaps who's been inside, but who has also a bit of stardust. On my own doorstep: Ian Wright. This was after he did so well for me at the launch. I asked him if he'd like to be a trustee.

'Yes, Mr Dein, of course I will.'

Going inside changed Ian. He came from such a difficult background, he was almost certainly going to go wrong at some stage. I always regarded Ian as my son from the day he signed.

Robert Sullivan was head of strategy at the Football Association, and I wanted the governing body of football to be involved. I also wanted somebody from a legal background, so I recruited Mark Phillips QC, who worked with Arsenal and helped form the Premier League. I asked Rick Parry to join too. I liked Rick's level-headedness when he had helped us to form the Premier League. I wanted somebody from PR and got another fantastic guy who had worked with me on the launch, Rollo Head from the Finsbury media agency. I recruited a neighbour of mine in Totteridge, Nigel Wray, whom I like very much. Nigel owned Saracens and was already doing impressive work with his rugby club at HMP Feltham. I thought I also needed someone from TV, someone always ready for a challenge, and I knew there was no one better than Greg Dyke. I love him dearly. After all, it was Greg's letter that led me to prisons in the first place. I'd almost got my dream team of trustees. But I still wanted somebody from education. The ideal candidate was Dame Sally Coates, who had built a reputation for turning difficult schools around. And I wanted someone from banking and compliance, so I approached Jonathan Norbury who is head of wealth at Lloyds Bank. All the trustees work pro bono. Their only condition was that there are certain offenders we should not work with – those with sex convictions or serious terrorists.

A month later, on 27 November, I visited HMP Nottingham to give a talk and saw how urgently the Twinning Project was needed. Peter Clarke, the chief inspector of prisons, called Nottingham 'dangerous, disrespectful and drug-ridden . . . some could face it no longer and took their own lives'.

About a hundred prisoners came to my talk. I always use the technique of saying 'ding-a-ling', as if I'm ringing a bell, to emphasise an important point. We played a film of players diving and the prisoners booed. 'It's wrong to cheat. Ding-a-ling. Big message. And another: keep your body fit. Not only will you live longer, but your mind will be stronger.' It was all about trying to get messages through to them. I had another – 'ding-a-ling' – big message for them. Attitude. I spoke about Arsenal's Invincibles.

'Technique's important but it's about desire, to want to win,' I told them. 'Those at the top of the tree have the right behaviour and attitude. Those that don't have the right attitude will feign injury, turn up late, and let down their team. Teamwork's vital. Thierry Henry owed a lot of his goals to Dennis Bergkamp and Robert Pires. You're in a team, stick together.'

Respect was vital. Ding-a-ling. I told them a story about our keeper Wojciech Szczęsny from 2015. 'Arsenal lost to Southampton, and one of our players was smoking a cigarette in the dressing room, Arsène dropped him and he's not at the club any more.' They couldn't believe that somebody could get fined for smoking but I wanted to make them understand it was about respect. 'Whatever you're doing – ding-a-ling, big message – have pride in your work. Any day of the week, Thierry and Dennis were working on shooting and free kicks when everyone else had gone home. To be successful takes hard work, vision and courage.'

The Nottingham inmates enjoyed watching the goals section. The highlights reel showed Wayne Rooney's overhead kick for Manchester United against Manchester City in 2011. We played Steven Gerrard scoring for Liverpool at Manchester United in 2009 and then kissing the camera lens. They really loved that. I left HMP Nottingham believing that we could bring them hope through the power of football.

By 23 January 2019, we had thirty-two clubs on board: Arsenal, Aston Villa, Bournemouth, Brentford, Brighton & Hove Albion, Bristol Rovers, Bury, Cardiff City, Charlton Athletic, Chelsea, Doncaster Rovers, Everton, Exeter City, Fulham, Leeds United, Leicester City, Lincoln City, Liverpool, Manchester City, Millwall, Newcastle United, Notts County, Oldham Athletic, Plymouth Argyle, QPR, Rochdale, Rotherham United, Southampton, Stoke City, Tottenham Hotspur, Tranmere Rovers and West Ham.

It wasn't all plain sailing. Manchester United were at first reluctant to come on board. However, after months of persuasion, John Shiels, the head of their foundation, a really nice guy, was fully engaged with the Twinning Project. United are twinned with HMP Styal. They couldn't be left behind.

The real stampede to get involved with the Twinning Project came from university criminology departments. 'This is a fantastic study for our students,' one professor told me. 'Can we do some research with you? At no cost to you.' I learned that universities have a lot of money. We staged a beauty parade of eight universities and picked Loughborough University because they've got the best sports facilities and a world-leading criminology department. Then Oxford piped up. 'You can't leave us out. We have to be involved in it, it's very important.' I realised even more how impactful the Twinning Project could be if a place like Oxford was pleading to be involved. Dr Chris Kay and Carolynne Mason of Loughborough and Dr Martha Newson and Professor Harvey Whitehouse of Oxford agreed to split their research on behaviour inside and outside prison.

Within two months of launching, we had two keen and prestigious universities signed up for five years, at their cost, analysing behavioural changes in inmates! This was really important research into how society keeps people out of prison. Actually, when you think about it, government should really be doing this research. Why aren't they? Money.

Oxford soon delivered a report about the importance of the coaching, asking, 'Can the Twinning Project provide kinship and this emotional engagement of the prisoners?' They found it could; it was about creating unity, a sense of belonging. The courses made prisoners feel they were part of a team. Martha and Harvey also stressed the need for aftercare by clubs, staying in touch with prisoners when they went out into society.

I was doing my own research and discovered there were a few prisons out in the wild — in other words, situated where there were no local professional football clubs. Believe it or not, the ninety-two clubs don't cover the whole country. This was where we could send the refs to do their courses, I felt. The football course was already up and running. I had to sort the refereeing. I rang Mike Riley and he put me in touch with the FA's head of technical and referee development, Dan Meeson, a big Stoke supporter, really nice guy.

'I'll do it personally,' Dan said. 'I'd love to.'

Dan proved to be a real star and, with the FA's blessing, headed up the referees delivering in prisons. He ran the course at HMP Lancaster Farms, where we had our first graduation in 2019 from a cohort of sixteen offenders. Dan brought in Anthony Taylor, the FIFA and Premier League referee, to present certificates. Anthony was also a prison officer and enjoyed the ceremony immensely. He could see the benefits.

'There are three guys here who can actually referee on a Sunday morning, straight away,' Dan said. That was brilliant to hear. Just those two words – 'straight away' – meant so much. These offenders could find some legitimate income immediately.

Our numbers of 'twins' kept rising, soon reaching more than sixty. Good old Arsenal were involved from the start – they have a fantastic foundation and community department – going into HMP Pentonville and Alex Scott came with me to Downview women's prison on 11 April 2019. She did some coaching, and I'll never forget one of the inmates saying to me as we left, 'It's the first time in months that I've smiled.'

Elsewhere, Everton have the best community scheme. Denise Barrett-Baxendale made such a success of Everton in the Community that Bill Kenwright asked her to become CEO of the club. Sue Gregory, their director of youth engagement, has proven a great ally. Liverpool were quickly involved. We had Ian

Rush at HMP Altcourse, where their foundation ran a ten-week programme for twelve inmates. We always like a bit of stardust, so whenever we go and see a course or a graduation, I like to take a player of his stature. West Ham legends like Michail Antonio and Tony Cottee presented certificates at HMP Chelmsford.

We were beginning to see some incredible results. Burton Albion went into HMP Sudbury, where the best student in the class was so good he was given a job at the club. Wow! This was the impact we were waiting for!

Gillingham are twinned with HMP Rochester. They were struggling for coaches, so I asked Paul Peschisolido, Karren Brady's husband, to help out. 'Of course,' Paul replied. Paul was a brilliant football player and has always been a team player. He ran a three-day course called 'Developing Leadership Through Football'. Paul and David Streetley, an FA coach developer now working for the Twinning Project, talked to the prisoners about how they would benefit from coaching, first-aid and safeguarding. They organised coaching, focusing on decision-making and 'creating a safe, respectful and learning environment'. At the end of the course, Paul gave out FA certificates. That meant so much, having that FA logo, and the inmates were smiling. For some this was the first time they had ever achieved anything notable, let alone got a certificate presented by a celebrity. I have a picture of the presentations and often look at it. It reminds me of what we're trying to do. Give them hope. Look how proud they are.

The Twinning Project picked up such momentum that the UN asked us to make a presentation to countries around the world. Hilton, Jason and I, all spoke on a videocall during lockdown. Japan and Scotland immediately came on to us, saying, 'Fantastic idea. Can you tell us how to do it?'

I honestly think that the Twinning Project will become a franchise like McDonald's. We'll tell other countries how to do it, set it up for them and then perhaps get a contribution for our charity. Once we start to roll out the programme globally we will have a stronger case for funding from international organisations' own foundation. Cutting to the chase, they have got two hundred million dollars in there.

We had to raise more money. The Twinning Project was going to cost us the best part of two million pounds a year. Whenever I talk to people about our revenue compared to other charities, I always ask them, 'How much do you think the Dogs Trust generates a year?' They guess ten or twenty million pounds. The true figure is ninety million pounds from bequests. That's how much people leave to dogs in their will. Well, we're not that lucky, people are not going to leave the Twinning Project money in their will, so we've got to go out and get it.

I had a lightbulb moment when Arsène invited me to a charity fundraiser at a nice theatre called Olympia near the Madeleine church in Paris on 1 April 2019. Arsène was interviewed on stage by a close friend of his, French commentator Christian Jeanpierre, who has his own charity. There were 1,400 people in the audience listening to Arsène and Christian and it set my mind racing. What about an audience with Arsène and me? I thought. That would raise a lot of money. Arsène had written his book but he'd not been seen much in public.

I started one of my favourite activities – putting a team together. Arsène agreed – fortunately – then I asked a good friend of mine, Graham Fry who runs IMG television. He said, 'I'll do the TV production gladly but you need an events producer.' So I asked Tom Toumazis, who puts on big events for the NSPCC.

'We've got to find a venue,' Tom said. I asked Bill Kenwright.

'You have to go for the Palladium. Don't mess around, David, forget the others,' Bill said. The Palladium! Flashback, I was thinking to myself, I'd been to the Palladium, and seen Shirley Bassey, Tom Jones, Frank Sinatra, Tony Bennett, Liza Minnelli and Judy Garland, famous stars! Now I could be on that stage. I thought again of my mum's motto, 'Shoot for the moon. Even if you miss, you'll land amongst the stars.' The Palladium agreed a date.

I assembled another team to host the show. Ian Wright and Alex Scott were the first two names on the sheet. They both agreed immediately and did it for nothing. Such great people. We needed an interviewer, someone who wasn't the usual sports TV reporter and was a personality in their own right.

'You know Dermot O'Leary of *X Factor* fame is a big Arsenal fan,' my son Darren said. I tracked him down, we had a cup of tea, and he was the next name to confirm. I always feel good with an O'Leary on the sheet.

I knew that we were going to have an auction and I thought, Who better than Clive Anderson, the TV host, with a wonderful sense of humour to do the job? I had seen him before in the role of auctioneer and felt he would be ideal. He also agreed immediately.

I then started to think about the guest list and immediately thought about the Invincibles and other players who worked under Arsène. I managed to get hold of Glenn Hoddle, Arsène's old Monaco player. Glenn had played a part in Arsène arriving at Arsenal. I'd contacted him for background and he was extremely complimentary. Glenn's a Spurs legend, but I really wanted him at the Palladium to pay tribute.

Arsenal gave us space in the programme to promote the event. What gave me comfort and encouragement was the fact that, within the first ten days, we sold 1,500 tickets. 'An Audience with Arsène Wenger & David Dein' at the Palladium, London, 8 November 2021, was already in clear water financially.

On the eve of the big night, Arsène and I had dinner with Graham Fry at our local Italian restaurant, San Giorgio in Whetstone.

'Do you feel worried about tomorrow?' Arsène asked. He was almost questioning whether we could pull it off, I felt. And, OK, it seemed daunting. After all, it was a packed audience of two thousand VIPs with a show streamed live to 189 territories.

'Arsène, when I'm next to you I'm always OK,' I replied. 'It'll be fine.'

By that point Arsène had been out of Arsenal for three years, but had still not got over it. He'd not been back to the Emirates since. He felt disappointed by a section of the fans, particularly those at the Stoke away game on 13 May 2017, with the plane trailing a 'Wenger – out means out!' banner over the bet365 Stadium. The Palladium was going to be a huge event for him emotionally as he knew it would be filled with Arsenal people, and more fans outside. I sensed that hurt again over dinner.

Arsène got an idea of how he'd be received when we went into the nightclub Inca next to the Palladium before the show. He spent an hour posing for pictures with guests who paid five hundred pounds for the VIP experience. They were all over-joyed to see Arsène and told him how much he meant to them.

Shortly before curtain up, I looked out from the wings at the Palladium, and thought, If only my mum could see me now. That gave me inner strength. 'I'll give it my best shot, Mum,' I said to myself. I didn't have any nerves after that and especially after Wrighty took one look at the audience, and announced, 'It's a home crowd!' Patrick Vieira and Martin Keown were walking to their seats, getting a huge reception. We could hear it backstage. 'Vi-eir-a'. It was the North Bank on tour. 'Ke-own'. When Arsène strode on stage, he brought the house down. I looked at Arsène standing there smiling and knew this was cathartic for him.

I followed him, and he whispered, 'I love this! It's wonderful! It's fantastic!' He looked out and saw so many players with whom he had shared so many special memories at Arsenal: Patrick, Martin, Kolo Touré, Jens Lehmann, Cesc Fàbregas and Robert Pires. Wrighty picked them all out and then said, 'And here's one of my mates, Glenn Hoddle.' Fair play to Glenn, he was walking into the lion's den, but he got a good reception and I was delighted. We also had people from the Twinning Project, the prisons and the MoJ. The Twinning Project came of age that night.

I felt so proud of how Ian and Alex hosted. Ian was word perfect. Such a pro. They're really important to me, these two, as I've always felt both of them have been searching for a father figure. I've always tried to be there for them and seeing them looking so smart and confident and lighting up the Palladium was wonderful. Alex was magnificent and I knew how much the night meant to her. I knew she had been down after some unfair comments about her pronunciation from Lord Digby-Jones, the former head of the CBI. Alex grew up in east London and has always been proud of her accent and, as she says, 'proud of the young girl who overcame obstacles' to become a famous footballer and presenter. She really is a star.

As he walked on stage, Clive Anderson soon had the audience in the palm of his hand. Charity auctions can be hard-going, Most people aren't going to bid and here many were meeting old friends and were happy to chat. But Clive held everyone's attention and raised a lot of money. In fact he managed to sell a golf day with Ian Wright twice and a dinner with Arsène at Annabel's twice.

Dermot hosted a brilliant interview. He asked me how I felt when Arsène left.

'Without being too critical of anybody, I think the club made a huge mistake,' I replied. 'As the song goes, there's only one Arsène Wenger.' That got a lot of applause. 'They should have found a place for him within the organisation, make him chairman, make him whatever.' That got even more applause. I'd been waiting a long time to say this publicly. 'And I think what rankles is the fact that personally, and I will say this openly, whoever made the decision did not think he was good enough for Arsenal, but yet he is good enough to be head of global football development for the world. Frankly, I don't understand it.'

'Why did you leave?' Dermot asked Arsène.

'Well, it wasn't my decision,' Arsène replied. Arsène revealed he had intended to quit when I was ousted in 2007, but that I had advised him to stay. 'I thought it's the right thing for the club,' I added. 'Also I happened to be a major shareholder!'

We raised £275,000 on the night, which one kind guest then

topped up to £300,000, and it rose higher afterwards. A day later, an investment banker from Basle in Switzerland rang up the Twinning Project and said, 'If I offered £30,000 could I have dinner with Arsène and David Dein?'

I said to Arsène, 'The guy's in Basle, why don't we have it in Zurich near FIFA?' Arsène agreed.

So did the banker. 'Perfect for me, I'm only an hour away, and I'll pay for dinner as well. I'm so excited I'm going to propose to my girlfriend tonight!'

The money raised at the Palladium was vital and, by the start of 2022, we had sixty-six clubs twinned. But the longer I spent in prisons, the more I realised how much needed to be done. The average literacy level is equivalent to a reading age of twelve or thirteen. And if life has failed these inmates, prisons are failing them miserably. I suggested to the MoJ that we add education to the football offer. They immediately saw the benefits and as a result, a teacher – in a West Ham tracksuit – will soon be working with sixteen inmates at Chelmsford, doing maths and English in the morning before they do the football course in the afternoon.

An important development for us was receiving government backing. I went to see Antonia Romeo, permanent secretary at the MoJ, and an Arsenal season-ticket holder. She was very impressed with the project and asked me what could stand in the way of success.

'Money,' I replied. 'Around twenty of the EFL clubs simply haven't got the money to run Twinning Project courses.'

Within a week, I received a letter from Antonia saying, 'The government will fund the balance of your clubs which haven't got the money.'

This was the first time in the history of the Twinning Project that the government was putting its money behind us. A real breakthrough!

The Twinning Project has been a phenomenal success and much of that is due to the commitment to it by Hilton Freund, the chief executive of the charity and Jason Swettenham of HMPPS (who have done a sensational job in getting the project to where it is today). I am no stranger to assembling a team and I know that I've got a match-winning one here!

The Twinning Project is one of the most rewarding things I've ever done in my life.

I really believe we're giving hope to those like Steve, the guy I met in Wormwood Scrubs all those years ago.

MY FRIEND GÉRARD

'Please don't sit there.' This was my one request to guests joining me on my plane to the long-postponed Euro 2020 games. 'That's Gérard's seat.'

Flying to Seville in June 2021 for Spain against Sweden was my first trip without my wingman, Gérard Houllier. I strapped in opposite that empty seat, reflecting on what a special man Gérard was, and how he brought such joy into my life.

Gérard had passed away on 14 December 2020 and that date is seared into my mind. For the past seven or eight years we'd so often travelled around to tournaments together. Sometimes it was a challenge to sort out the logistics, but Gérard would select the games and I would have to create an intricate itinerary, joining all his dots. Together we handled it like a military manoeuvre. Then we'd contact Arsène and plumb him in somewhere, depending on what TV commitments he had. We were known on the tournament circuit as the Three Musketeers.

When I joined the board of Arsenal in 1983, Pat Rice said something that's since become a bit hackneyed but I hadn't heard before: 'Fail to prepare, prepare to fail'. Gérard and I certainly prepared!

Gérard and Arsène were my closest friends in football. In

recent years, Gérard was head of global football for Red Bull, and also helped out his good friend Jean-Michel Aulas, the owner of Olympique Lyonnais. Gérard was still working hard, giving all the expertise he acquired as manager of Paris Saint-Germain, Liverpool, Aston Villa and France. Like Arsène, Gérard sat on technical committees and gave his wisdom to UEFA and FIFA. Like me and Arsène he was reaching his early seventies but shrugged it off. 'We're in the years of significance,' Gérard used to say – meaning we weren't old, just experienced, and we still had so much to offer.

I loved the competitive edge between Arsène and Gérard, and also their enormous mutual respect. Their close friendship went back a long way. They had gone through their coaching badges together, virtually in the same class, were both football purists and I loved listening to them exchanging ideas on the game. They were my sounding boards and would be my first two calls if I wanted to bounce an idea around. They understood the game far better, technically, than I ever could. And what a privilege! Flying to a match, I would be seated between two of the world's best football pundits. I was in heaven – well, at 35,000 feet actually- and it couldn't get better for a football lover. I didn't need the newspapers to give me background and tell me the expected line-ups for the game we were flying to. Gérard and Arsène knew who'd start, who'd be on the bench, and who'd employ which tactics.

Anyway, as I sat on that flight to Seville, I couldn't help but reminisce on the first time we really spent time together. Two decades earlier Barbara and I were in Cuba. The day before New Year's Eve we decided to spend the day at the Club Med near Havana. (As we were checking in, the receptionist said, 'Oh, Mr Dein, we have someone else here from football.'

'Who's that?'

'Gérard Houllier.' He was there with his wife Isabelle.

'Oh, can I speak to him?'

'Yes, I'll ring his room, sir.'

'Gérard, it's David Dein.'

Gérard came down immediately. We chatted and he asked, 'What are you doing tomorrow night, New Year's Eve? You have to join Isabelle and me.' As I was to discover, Gérard was one of life's givers.

We frequently stayed with Gérard and Isabelle at their apartment near the Eiffel Tower and at their second home in Corsica; and when they were in London, they always stayed with us. It may sound oversentimental, but for me an hour, even just a minute, spent with Gérard was somehow magical. He always gave advice, guidance and opinion in the most polite way you could imagine, and whether talking to the club tea-lady or the president of France, he treated them the same. I'd like to think I live my life to Gérard's standards.

I hope Gérard knew how deeply loved he was. I've often seen the outpouring of affection for him. In fact on one occasion it almost got out of hand. On 19 April 2015, two of Gérard's old clubs, Liverpool and Villa, met in the semi-final of the FA Cup at Wembley. Gérard was with me as I was driving down Wembley Way, when a group of fans spotted him in the car. They rushed around, peering in the window, waving and shouting. Villa fans applauded while all I could hear from Liverpool fans was 'Hou let the Reds out? Hou, Hou Houllier!' (Liverpool hero-worshipped him for the treble in 2001.) They surged and crowded round the car, thumbs up, grinning, and banging on the bonnet. I did get a bit twitchy. The last few hundred yards took us half an hour.

When we finally parked, I looked at my car, and said, 'Thanks a million, Gérard! My bonnet's full of dents!' We both burst out laughing. He was worth it.

Gérard became an extension of my family. We spoke every night, midnight Paris time. Gérard was a late bird and we'd shoot the breeze and put the world to rights. For the last couple of years those midnight calls were supplemented by weekly daytime ones. Religiously each Sunday at midday, Gérard, Arsène and I would have a three-way call to go through the week's events and talk about the games. I used to call it 'That was the week that was', after the British sixties' comedy show. I so miss those calls and Gérard's warm, friendly voice.

I knew my friend had heart problems. He told me about that night at Anfield on 12 October 2001 when Liverpool played Leeds United, and how he suffered chest pains and had to be rushed to A&E. He had an eleven-hour operation, carried out by his wonderful surgeon, Abbas Rashid, to save his life.

But Gérard couldn't stay away from football. It was his first love. 'I'm missing it so much,' he told me, 'I simply have to manage a team.' Eventually he did go back, joining Aston Villa in 2010, but soon he suffered more chest pains, and he had to leave after only a single season. He knew his heart had only been patched up and that he was still very much at risk. He had to have a scan every three to four months. Unfortunately, in 2020 an extended tear was found in his lower aorta. Gérard decided to have surgery and asked Abbas to attend.

A few days after his operation, the doctors decided to discharge him. On 13 December, when Arsène and I called our old friend as usual, he said 'I'm very weak, and you'll have to forgive me if we can't speak much.'

He woke early the next day and went into his study to work. Typical Gérard, always working. When Isabelle got up, she went into the study to find Gérard slumped over his computer. My phone rang shortly after.

'Gérard's died,' Isabelle said.

'A star has fallen out of the sky,' I told her.

Gérard was only seventy-three and had so much more to give. My own life is so much poorer without him.

AND FINALLY . . .

My book would not be complete without mention of the one thing closest to my heart . . . my family.

Barbara and I always included our three children – Darren, Gavin and Sasha – in everything we did. Our life revolved around football, and we were all part of the team. The children came to all the home matches and indeed most of the away games too, so we always travelled together. It was part of our life. At Highbury each director had six seats, five of which were already spoken for and invariably one of the kids' friends would get the spare. (They would take it in turns, very democratically!) Football was a major bonding experience for the family. To wind me up, the boys claimed that they used to 'pocket sausage' from the cocktail lounge at half time – which meant they would occasionally take a couple of small sausages each and place them into visitor's pockets without them knowing.

I was fortunate that we had some wonderful footballing occasions together. Finals, winning the league, European games. It was always an adventure. Who best to share these special occasions with than your family?

I feel very fortunate that, between Barbara and myself, we have through sheer luck or some judgement (or a happy combination of both) created a loving and considerate family of three children and eight grandchildren. We love being together; we get on well together; we have a lot of fun together. We speak pretty much every day.

I was always competitive. I used to make the kids take on each other for maths, swimming and skiing, or even a kickabout at home, and that was a mistake. 'I am better than you,' I heard them shouting at each other. I really should have stepped in and said, 'Just be the best you can be'.

I was passionate about them having a good education. I think they're pretty well-adjusted and, above all else, they get on well with their fellow human beings and that means a lot to me.

They are all wonderful parents, and I refer to our grandchildren as 'nippos' from the Italian *nipotini* (Sasha lives in Rome). To teach the grandchildren good manners, I created a make-believe character, 'The Food Patrol Man'. I wear a policeman's helmet, stick on a fake moustache and put on a jacket, displaying 'Food Patrol Man' badges. It's amazing that it has really helped the 'nippos'; and even today when they know it's me, they still ask if he will make an appearance at the dinner table.

I had a very strong upbringing with my mum and dad. They made sure they nurtured both my brother and me. And I think that's important. If you start your kids off well in life, there's a good chance you'll reap the rewards afterwards. Not always . . . but more often than not.

These are the highs of life. But love brings its own sadness.

My dear brother, Arnold, died in 2002 at just sixty-seven of lung cancer, although he hadn't smoked for forty years. It was

Arnold who set me on a business path. He was wonderfully supportive, and I couldn't have wished for a better brother. He is survived by his loving wife Leila and her adoring kids Alan and Carole.

One of the biggest regrets of my life is that my father passed away too early. I was only twenty-five when he died aged sixty-four in 1968. I never had the chance to take him to Arsenal. I loved him dearly and still miss him deeply.

My mother died while I was at the 1994 World Cup in Los Angeles. I remember on my flight home thinking, everything else in life pales into insignificance compared to this. My old friend, Bill Kenwright, sent me a poignant note of condolence: 'The trouble with mums is they only come in ones.' At least my mother saw I'd made something of myself in life, and for that I owe her so much – as well as for teaching me how to call the shots!

I always used to say to the kids when they were growing up: 'I want you to have a good time, enjoy yourself, do your best whatever you do, just try not to embarrass me along the way!' I think I've probably embarrassed them more than they've embarrassed me.

My family have been my inspiration and my source of energy. Long may it continue.

Acknowledgements

I am no stranger to assembling a team. For this book I believe I have managed to pull together a Champions League winning squad. I am particularly grateful to the following people for all their hard work and support (and talent)!

First and foremost, my family for being my inspiration; especially my wife Barbara for always supporting me, even when I'm right!

Arsène Wenger for not only his gracious foreword but also for his friendship and sharing with me so many happy and successful occasions and enriching my life.

Henry Winter and Amy Lawrence for helping convert my words into pages. You have both been a joy to work with, and the journey has been pleasurable and painless. Somehow, you've brought the best out of me.

Andreas Campomar, you have been a magnificent conductor of the orchestra and have made the book into an entertaining symphony.

A big thank you to the Little, Brown Team of Charlie King, Holly Blood, Henry Lord, Aimee Kitson, Duncan Spilling and Lucian Randall.

My PA, Natalie Feldman, for flying the plane with me and making sure we had a safe landing.

Jon Wood, Geoff Duffield, Bob Bookman, Sasha Dein Fugazzola, Nick Ross, Tom Toumazis and Marvin Berglas, thank you for painstakingly going through the manuscript and adding some salt and pepper to the soup.

Stuart MacFarlane, for patiently trawling through four decades of photographs and for making the cover shot look like one of my sons.

Graham Fry, for masterminding the production at the Cambridge Theatre and tolerating me as a frustrated producer. Paul Roberts and Fiona Pearce, for co-ordinating the launch. Sophia Mason and Victoria Calvert at LW Theatres for their assistance with the Cambridge Theatre.

Ian Wright, Alex Scott, Sven-Göran Eriksson, George Graham, Jenni Hicks, Antonia Romeo, Alistair McGowan, some of the Invincibles, for putting the icing on the cake.

And the following people for jogging my memory: Greg Dyke, Rick Parry, Baroness Karren Brady, Paul Peschisolido, Alan Dein, Tony Reiff, Mark Phillips QC, Adrian Bevington, Antony Spencer, Athole Still, Tony Green, Geoffrey Klass, Mark Bullingham, Mark Burrows, Jane Bateman, David Davies, Nick Coward, Mike Foster, Hilton Freund, Jason Swettenham, Rollo Head, Steven Katz, Fernando Martinez, David Miles, John Beattie, Freddie Hudson, Richard Coleman, Mihir Bose, DCI Cooper, Jamie Archer, Jeffrey Archer, Natasha Brookner, Roger Drew, Guy East, Adam Craig, Brian Marwood, Jerome Anderson, Darren Dein, Gavin Dein.

Bernie, my adorable and super smart dog who always believes in me.

Index